FAGIN THE JEW

BY
Will Eisner

DARK HORSE BOOKS®

Diana Schutz • *editor*
Cary Grazzini • *book design*
Chris Horn • *digital production*
Mike Richardson • *publisher*

Mike Richardson *Publisher* • Neil Hankerson *Executive Vice President*
Tom Weddle *Chief Financial Officer* • Randy Stradley *Vice President of Publishing*
Michael Martens *Vice President of Book Trade Sales* • Anita Nelson *Vice President of Business Affairs*
Scott Allie *Editor in Chief* • Matt Parkinson *Vice President of Marketing*
David Scroggy *Vice President of Product Development* • Dale LaFountain *Vice President of Information Technology*
Darlene Vogel *Senior Director of Print, Design, and Production* • Ken Lizzi *General Counsel*
Davey Estrada *Editorial Director* • Chris Warner *Senior Books Editor*
Diana Schutz *Executive Editor* • Cary Grazzini *Director of Print and Development*
Lia Ribacchi *Art Director* • Cara Niece *Director of Scheduling*
Tim Wiesch *Director of International Licensing* • Mark Bernardi *Director of Digital Publishing*

Fagin the Jew was originally published in October 2003 by Doubleday, in soft cover.
With the exception of page 122, this new hardcover edition has been entirely rescanned from
the original artwork, with only minor adjustments made to the digital files for the sake of readability.

Published by Dark Horse Books
A division of Dark Horse Comics
10956 SE Main Street
Milwaukie, Oregon 97222
United States of America

DarkHorse.com
WillEisner.com

Second edition: August 2013
ISBN 978-1-61655-126-1

1 3 5 7 9 10 8 6 4 2
Printed in China

FOREWORD

by Brian Michael Bendis

LIKE MOST OF YOU, I HAVE been reading comics ever since I could read, and I have been reading Will Eisner ever since I discovered him. Like some of you, I learned to make comics by reading *Comics & Sequential Art* by Will Eisner. And for a few years now I have been teaching a college-level graphic novel writing course in my hometown of Portland. One of the reasons I teach is because Will Eisner was a teacher.

In the class, obviously, we cover a great deal of Will Eisner's work, legacy, and teachings. So when I got the call to write the introduction to this graphic novel, I immediately said yes! A huge honor. But I was also shocked: *Fagin the Jew*?

I scrambled over to my, I must say, substantial Will Eisner shelf only to discover that *I did not own this graphic novel.*

Have I even heard of this graphic novel? Is there a Will Eisner graphic novel floating around in the world that I don't have? And I'm a Jew! How can I not have this book?? "Jew" is in the title!!

Of course the amazing Diana Schutz sent me a copy, which I immediately read and have spent a great deal of this month thinking about.

As you will soon discover, it is a fascinating work of a man using all of his abilities, but what fascinates *me* is the motivation behind this work.

As he describes in his original introduction, Will Eisner had been struggling with the fact that decades ago, he had a character in his seminal work, *The Spirit*, that was, frankly, quite a racist caricature. So much so that it flies in the face of everything else he ever created before or after. Everything about Will and his writing had been progressive and sometimes substantially ahead of its time.

This character was always a conundrum to me, as a fan. I, like many, would just wash it away in my head as a sin of the times. But I wondered how Will felt about it.

In my class, we screen the quite outstanding Will Eisner documentary, *Portrait of a Cartoonist*, in which Will frankly addressed the controversy surrounding this character and his rather pragmatic feelings about it. He said, as one would hope, that back then he just didn't know any better. As he

YASSUH, THIS IS EBONY!
WHAT !?
IS DAT WHAT IT IS? OKAY, AH'M ON MAH WAY!

Racial caricature was common in the early days of comics, and *The Spirit*'s Ebony was no exception.

PAPPA...YOU SWITCHED IT...HIS WAS A GOOD COIN...BUT YOU GAVE HIM BACK A BAD ONE?!

SO I DID !

In his later years Eisner developed a softer look to his art while nonetheless wrestling with darker themes, as in this scene from *Fagin*.

In the Will Eisner documentary, one of the interviews reflects on how interesting it is that early in his career, when Will's artwork was more of a stark black-and-white, his actual view of the world was more whimsical. As Will aged, his artwork took on a palette of grays, yet his view of the world, his writing, became black-and-white. Harsher. Darker.

By the time Will Eisner sat down to write *Fagin the Jew*, it is safe to say that Will Eisner the romantic was long gone. Will spent his time here reflecting on just how someone becomes the stereotype. His theory here is that you are not born to stereotype; you become the stereotype through circumstance and environment. That stereotype, in turn, becomes the weapon of hate that the ignorant will use to try to destroy you.

So what we have here is the work of a man, later in his years, trying desperately to understand how things get to a point where someone of his obvious intellect was able to create his own literary racial stereotype.

lived a more full life, after he had been to war, he realized that the character was a horrible, insensitive caricature and quickly altered his writing to reflect that.

Decades later, as he discussed this subject, you could see it still bothered him. You could see that maybe it even haunted him. Well, that was my theory. I had no proof. I just like to project my own neuroses on anyone or anything I can find.

But this time it looks like I was right. Someone tell my wife.

This entire book is a reaction to that character.

This entire book is Eisner's analysis of another great writer, Charles Dickens, and his misfortunes with caricature. But I would have imagined that if any author were to travel down this road, you'd think he would tit-for-tat. You'd think that Will would choose to delve into an African-American character or story or historical figure.

Instead, Will took his complicated feelings about race and caricature and applied them directly to his feelings about Judaism and how Jews have been reflected in the media for hundreds of years, by sinking his teeth directly into the classic *Oliver Twist* and one of the most famous Jewish stereotype characters in all of fiction . . . Fagin.

As I finished the graphic novel, I literally exhaled and said, "Well, I am very glad I read this." I believe you will be, too.

I guess the true mark of a master is that even a minor work is an important work.

As for Charles Dickens, he went on to do a short run on *Uncanny X-Force* before settling into a long run as the seminal writer of the *Red Sonja* comics.

Wait, that's not him? Who am I thinking of?

Bendis!
Portland, Oregon
October 2012

INTRODUCTION
TO THE FIRST EDITION
by Will Eisner

IN JUNE OF 1940, I began a syndicated newspaper comic book insert called *The Spirit*, about a masked crime fighter. It featured a young African-American boy, Ebony, as a humorous counterfoil. This was hardly innovative; Jack Benny had Rochester, the movies had Stepin Fetchit, and radio had Amos 'n' Andy. These were accepted stereotypical caricatures of the time. It was an era in our cultural history when the misuse of English based on ethnic origin was fashionable humor. Ebony spoke with the classic "Negro" dialect and delivered a gentle humor that gave warmth to balance the coldness of crime stories. In my eagerness for readership, I thought I was on to a good thing.

In 1945, after an interruption for military service, I returned to the feature. By then, I had become more aware of the social implications of racial stereotypes, and I began to treat Ebony with greater insight. As often happens with cartoonists, I became very fond of him and sought to make him as real as I imagined him. As the rising civil rights movement became more prominent, I introduced a well-spoken black detective and treated my hero's black assistant in a more sensitive manner.

One day, I received a letter from an old high school classmate who had become a civil rights activist, chiding me for abandoning the "liberal" views we shared back in school. That same day, I got a letter from the editor of a Baltimore Afro-American newspaper commending me on my "fine treatment" of Ebony in my comic strip. These letters alerted me to the reality that, while my stories were designed as entertainment, I was nonetheless feeding a racial prejudice with this stereotype image. Still looking for ethnic

HOLD STILL, EBONY!
HOW CAN I ? THIS IS THE MOST EMBARRASSIN' THING AS EVUH HAPPENED TO A CRIME FIGHTER!

Ebony was created as a "humorous counterfoil" in the context of *The Spirit*'s crime stories. From "Beagle's Second Chance," originally published November 3, 1946.

diversity, I replaced Ebony with an Eskimo boy and later with Sammy, a white boy. The series ended in 1952, and as I continued my career in instructional comics, I never recognized that my rendering of Ebony, when viewed historically, was in conflict with the rage I felt when I saw anti-Semitism in art and literature.

While I didn't experience any guilt over my creation of Ebony, I became conscious of the problem over the years while teaching sequential art, as my lectures invariably had to confront the issue of stereotype. I concluded that there was "bad" stereotype and "good" stereotype; intention was the key. Since stereotype is an essential tool in the language of graphic storytelling, it is incumbent on cartoonists to recognize its impact on social judgment. In twenty-first century America, we struggle with "racial profiling." We are in an era that requires graphic portrayers to be sensitive to unfair stereotypes.

Eisner's good-hearted caricatures were democratic in their scope. From the March 23, 1947, *Spirit* strip.

So it was with this background and an awareness of the influence of imagery on the popular culture that I began to produce graphic novels with themes of Jewish ethnicity and the prejudice Jews still face. A few years ago, as I was examining folktales and literary classics for possible graphic adaptation, I became aware of the origins of the ethnic stereotypes we accept without question. Upon examining the illustrations of the original editions of *Oliver Twist*, I found unquestionable examples of visual defamation in classic literature. The memory of their awful use by the Nazis in World War II, one hundred years later, added evidence to the persistence of evil stereotypes. Combating that became an obsessive pursuit, and I realized that I had no choice but to undertake a truer portrait of Fagin by telling his life story in the only way I could.

This book, therefore, is not an adaptation of *Oliver Twist*! It is the story of Fagin the Jew.

Monks and the Jew

One of the original illustrations by George Cruikshank for Dickens's *Oliver Twist*. Even the title of the piece subsumes Fagin's character to his ethnicity.

Will Eisner
Florida, 2003

I AM FAGIN THE JEW OF OLIVER TWIST

THIS IS MY STORY, ONE THAT HAS REMAINED UNTOLD AND OVERLOOKED IN THE BOOK BY CHARLES DICKENS.

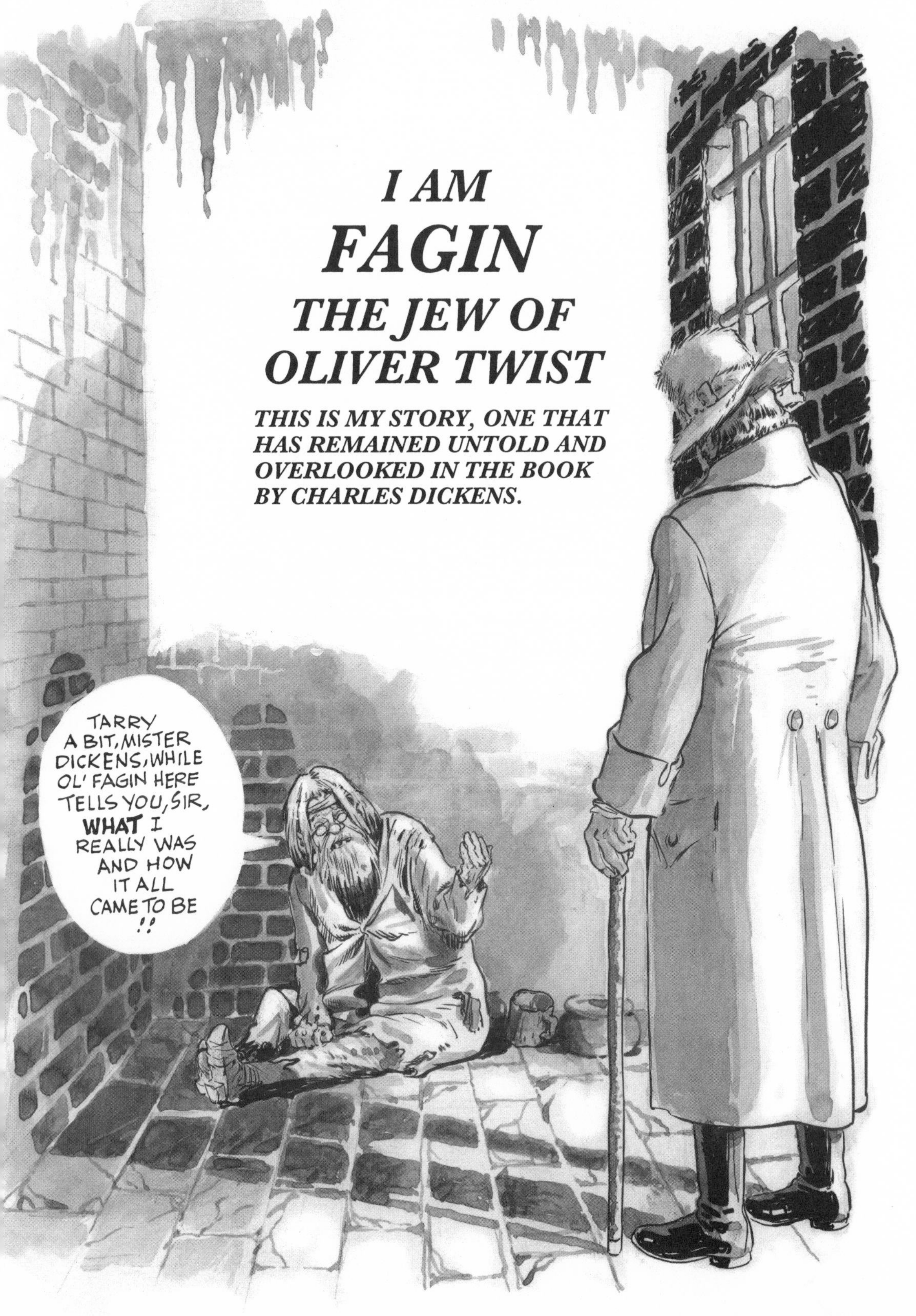

TARRY A BIT, MISTER DICKENS, WHILE OL' FAGIN HERE TELLS YOU, SIR, WHAT I REALLY WAS AND HOW IT ALL CAME TO BE !!

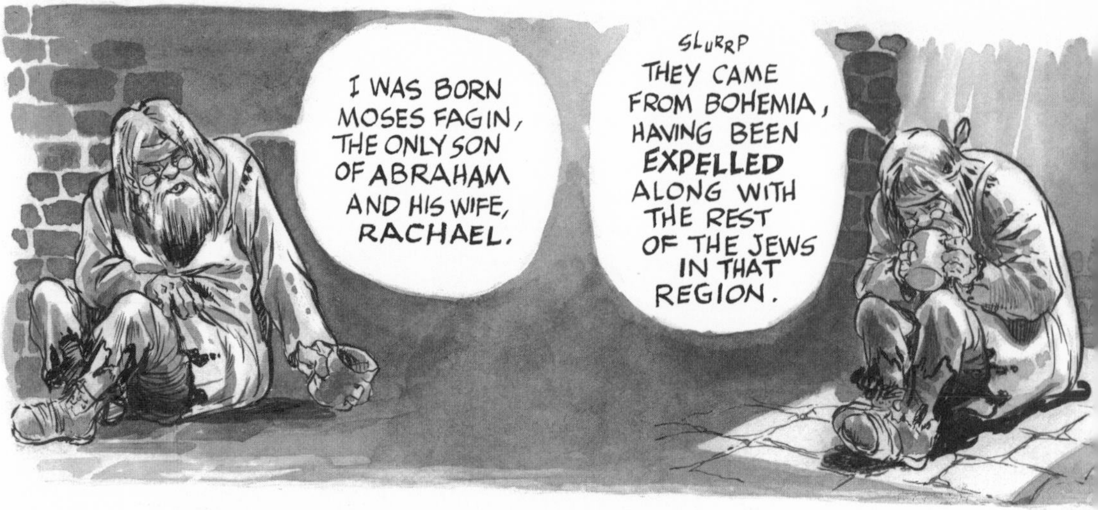
I WAS BORN MOSES FAGIN, THE ONLY SON OF ABRAHAM AND HIS WIFE, RACHAEL.
SLURRP
THEY CAME FROM BOHEMIA, HAVING BEEN **EXPELLED** ALONG WITH THE REST OF THE JEWS IN THAT REGION.

My parents arrived in London along with other Jews fleeing Middle Europe. How they managed the journey, God only knows.

Here they found a better community, where Jews were not subject to special laws or legal pogroms. England was a country that had long been a refuge for Spanish and Portuguese Jews known as Sephardim. They were the earliest to arrive and had become well established, whereas the newly arriving Middle Europeans were regarded as lower class. Germans, Poles, and the like were called Ashkenazim.

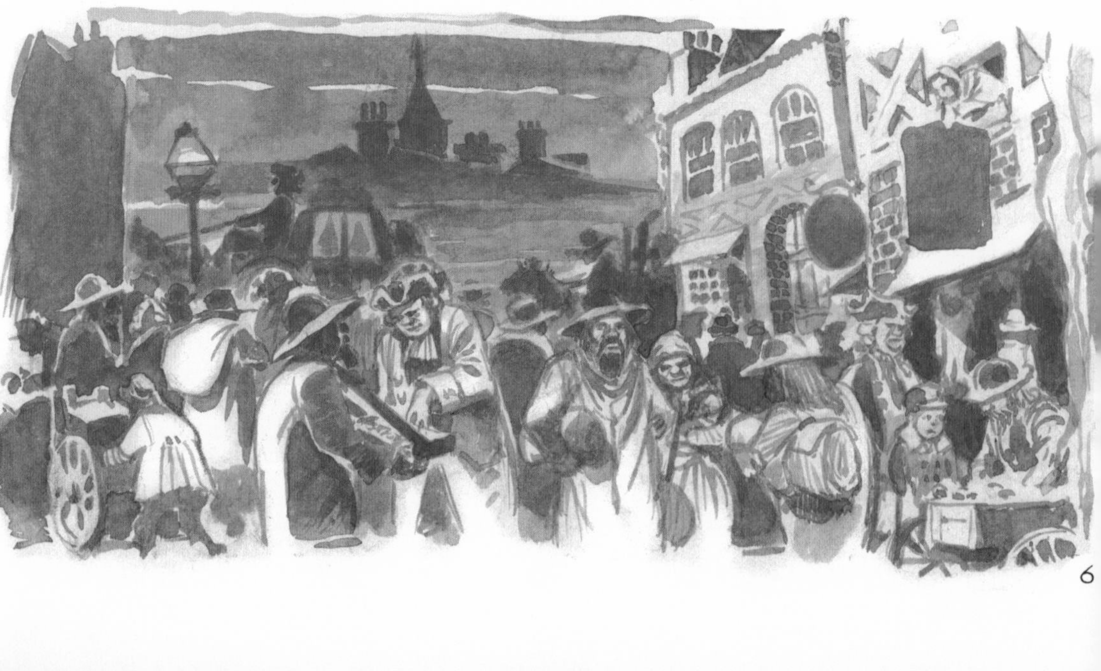

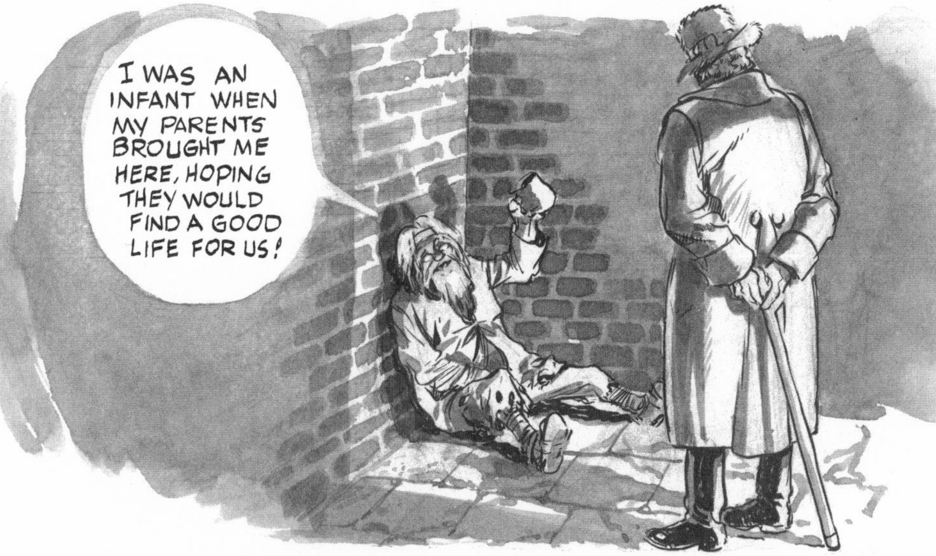
I WAS AN INFANT WHEN MY PARENTS BROUGHT ME HERE, HOPING THEY WOULD FIND A GOOD LIFE FOR US!

But for us, even London life was not so simple. These were grim times, and yet the best of times for us newcomers. We were uneducated, and endured a pauperdom perfumed by the promise of opportunity.

Aye, 'twas, not to put too fine a point on it, a time when opportunity bloomed in the dirty streets of London. It was where, when I was still a mere tyke, my parents put me out to peddle needles and buttons.

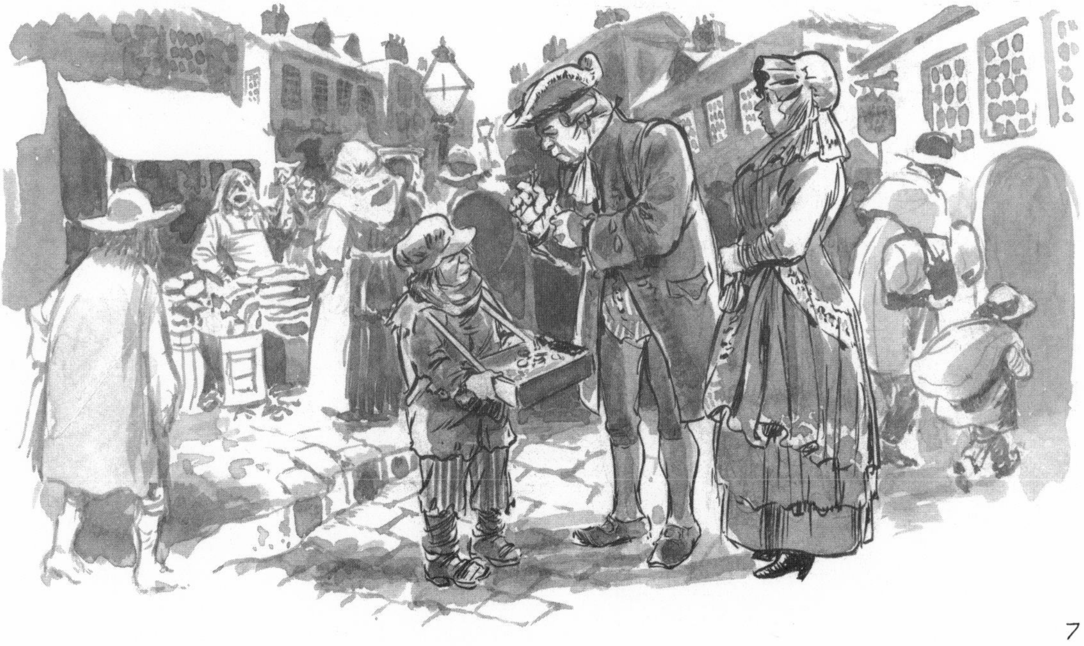

I was "educated" by my father, who, having learned by emulating other Jews, had become skilled in the trades of the street.

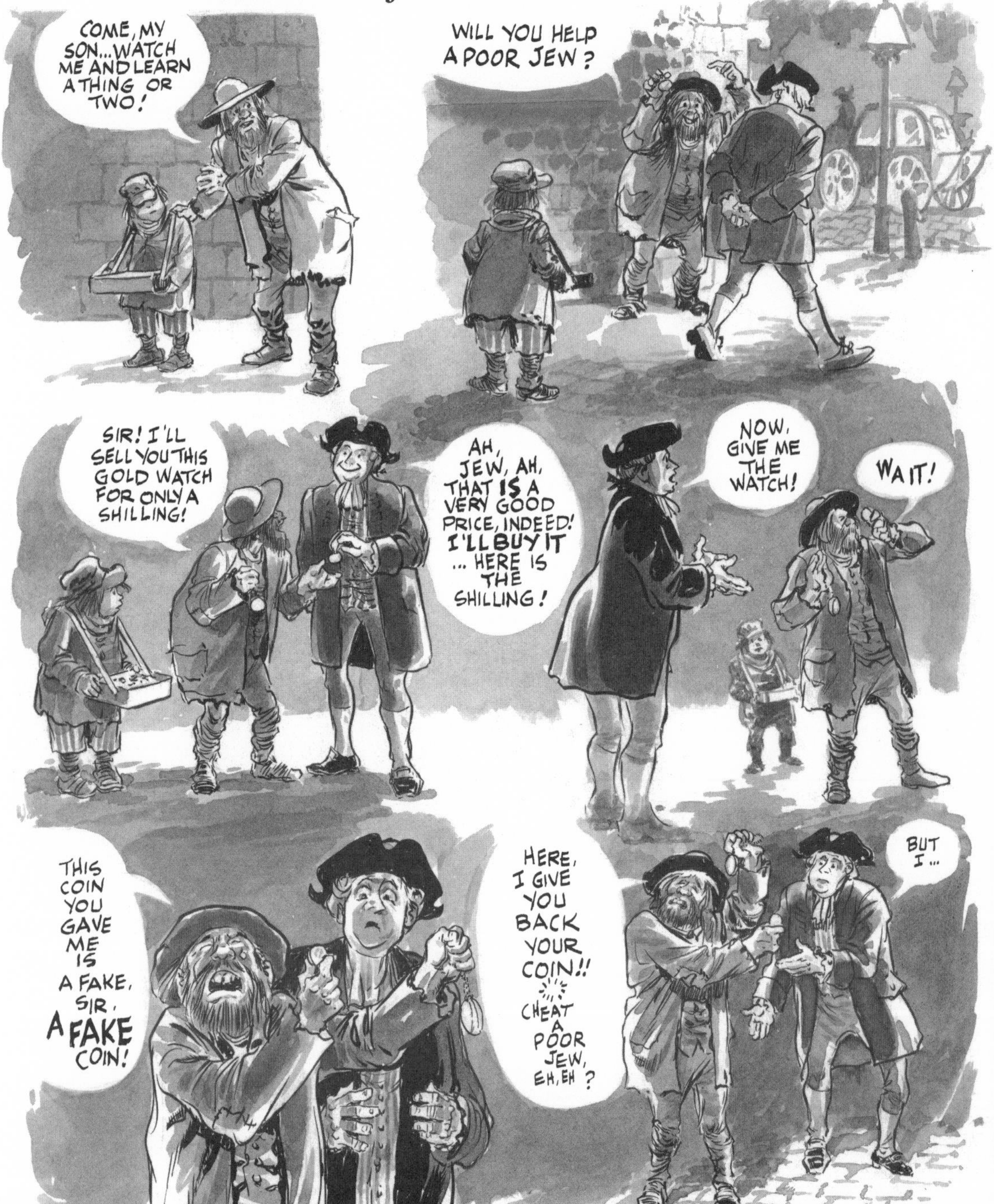
COME, MY SON...WATCH ME AND LEARN A THING OR TWO!
WILL YOU HELP A POOR JEW?
SIR! I'LL SELL YOU THIS GOLD WATCH FOR ONLY A SHILLING!
AH, JEW, AH, THAT IS A VERY GOOD PRICE, INDEED! I'LL BUY IT ... HERE IS THE SHILLING!
NOW, GIVE ME THE WATCH!
WAIT!
THIS COIN YOU GAVE ME IS A FAKE, SIR. A FAKE COIN!
HERE, I GIVE YOU BACK YOUR COIN!! CHEAT A POOR JEW, EH, EH?
BUT I...

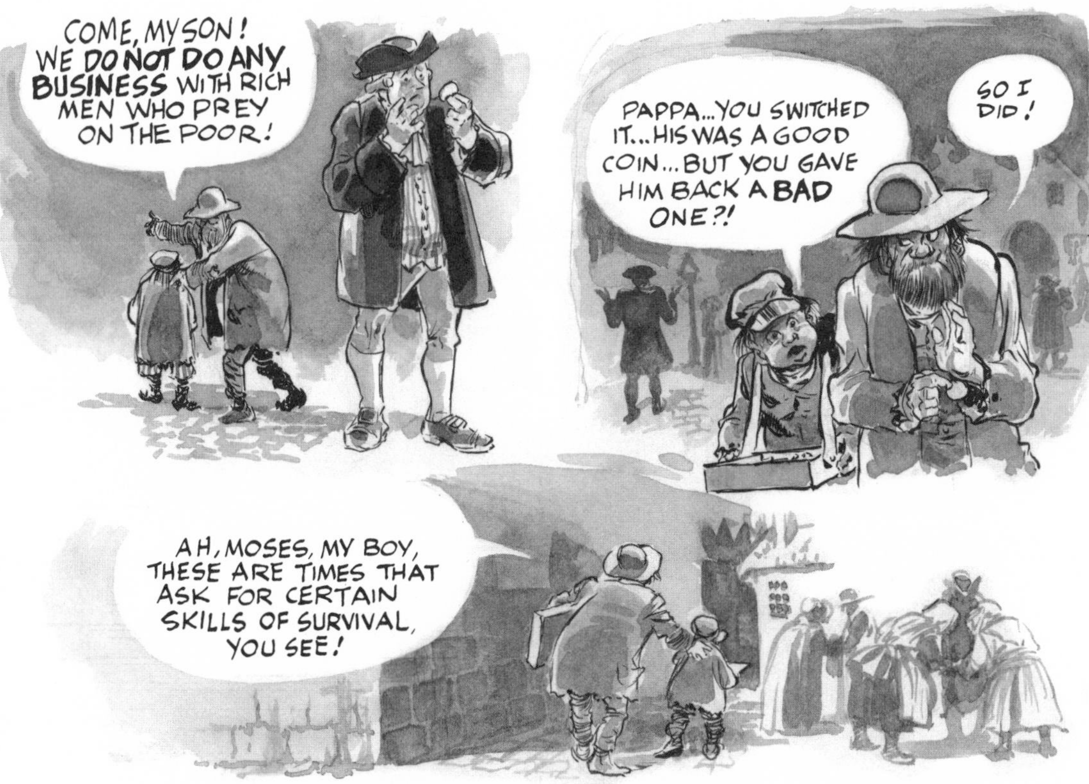
COME, MY SON! WE DO NOT DO ANY BUSINESS WITH RICH MEN WHO PREY ON THE POOR!
PAPPA...YOU SWITCHED IT...HIS WAS A GOOD COIN...BUT YOU GAVE HIM BACK A BAD ONE?!
SO I DID!
AH, MOSES, MY BOY, THESE ARE TIMES THAT ASK FOR CERTAIN SKILLS OF SURVIVAL, YOU SEE!

This was the nature of my formative years... until I neared my thirteenth birthday.

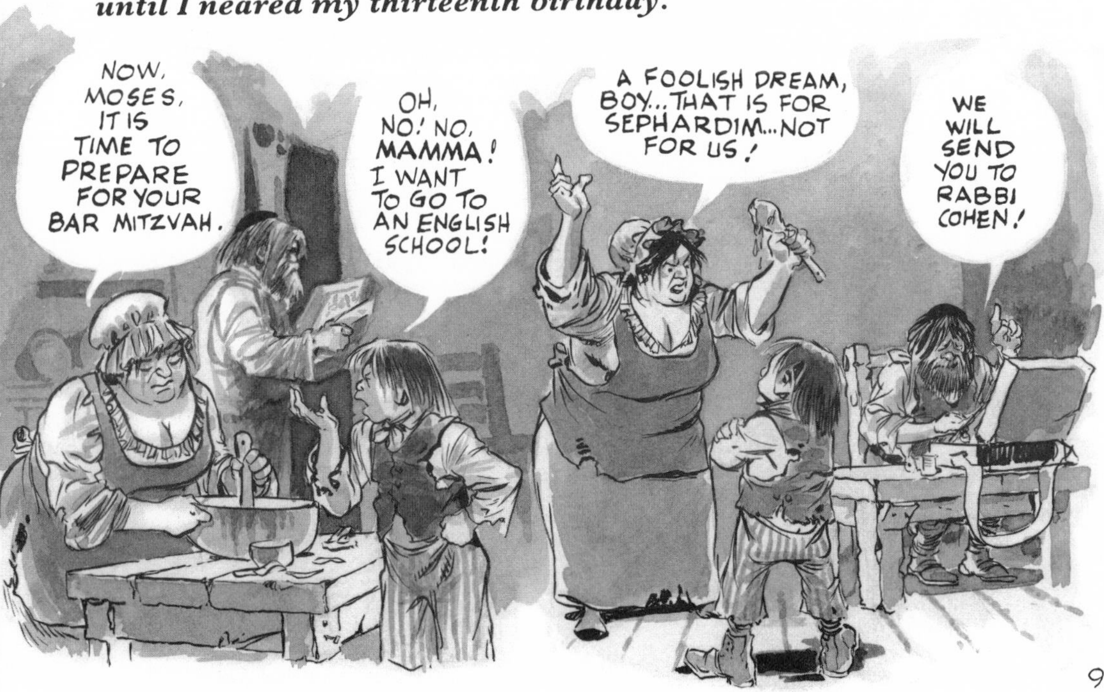
NOW, MOSES, IT IS TIME TO PREPARE FOR YOUR BAR MITZVAH.
OH, NO! NO, MAMMA! I WANT TO GO TO AN ENGLISH SCHOOL!
A FOOLISH DREAM, BOY...THAT IS FOR SEPHARDIM...NOT FOR US!
WE WILL SEND YOU TO RABBI COHEN!

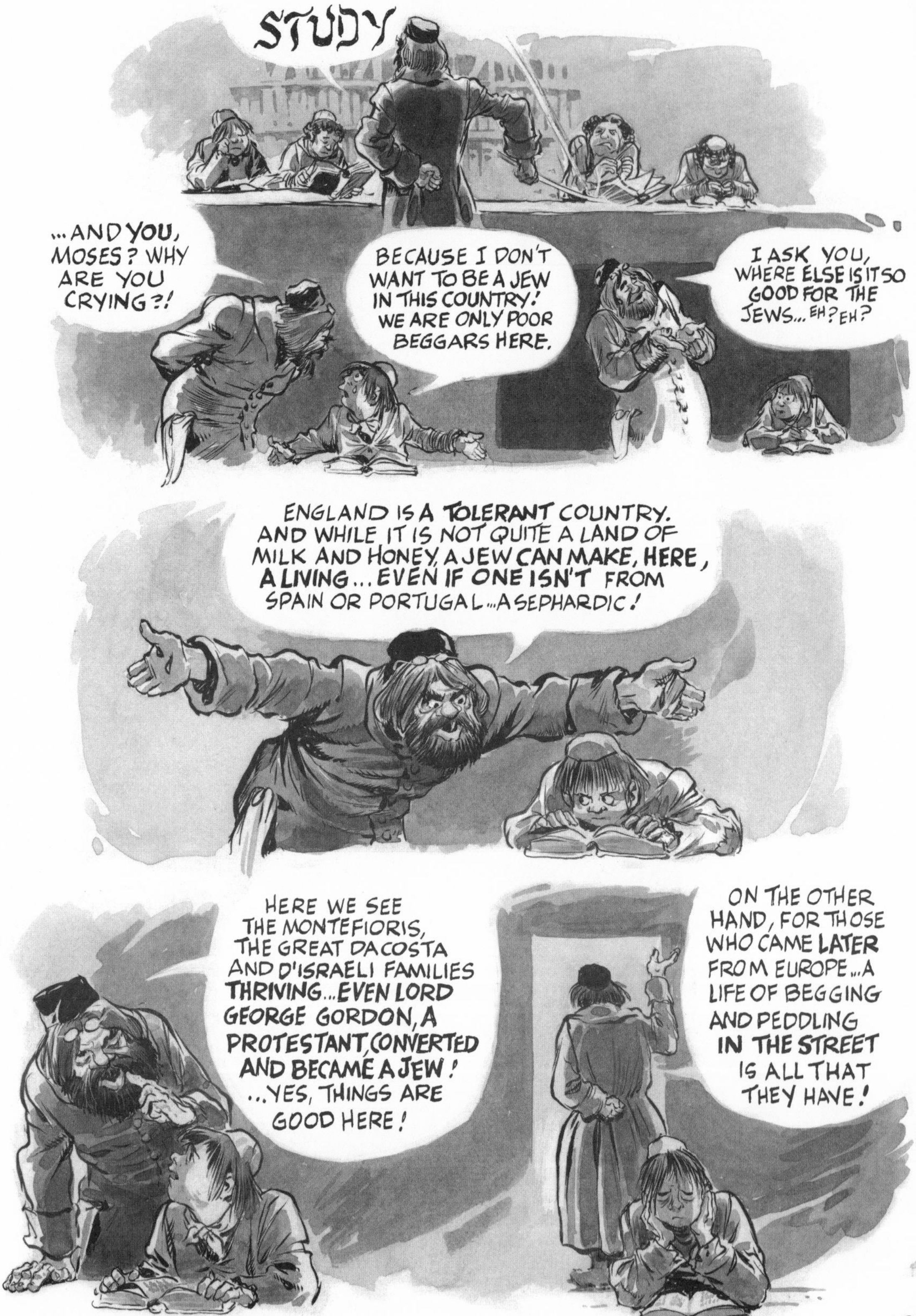
STUDY
...AND YOU, MOSES? WHY ARE YOU CRYING?!
BECAUSE I DON'T WANT TO BE A JEW IN THIS COUNTRY! WE ARE ONLY POOR BEGGARS HERE.
I ASK YOU, WHERE ELSE IS IT SO GOOD FOR THE JEWS... EH? EH?
ENGLAND IS A TOLERANT COUNTRY. AND WHILE IT IS NOT QUITE A LAND OF MILK AND HONEY, A JEW CAN MAKE, HERE, A LIVING... EVEN IF ONE ISN'T FROM SPAIN OR PORTUGAL...A SEPHARDIC!
HERE WE SEE THE MONTEFIORIS, THE GREAT DACOSTA AND D'ISRAELI FAMILIES THRIVING...EVEN LORD GEORGE GORDON, A PROTESTANT, CONVERTED AND BECAME A JEW! ...YES, THINGS ARE GOOD HERE!
ON THE OTHER HAND, FOR THOSE WHO CAME LATER FROM EUROPE...A LIFE OF BEGGING AND PEDDLING IN THE STREET IS ALL THAT THEY HAVE!

Meanwhile, even as I began my young manhood, I remained in the streets with my father.

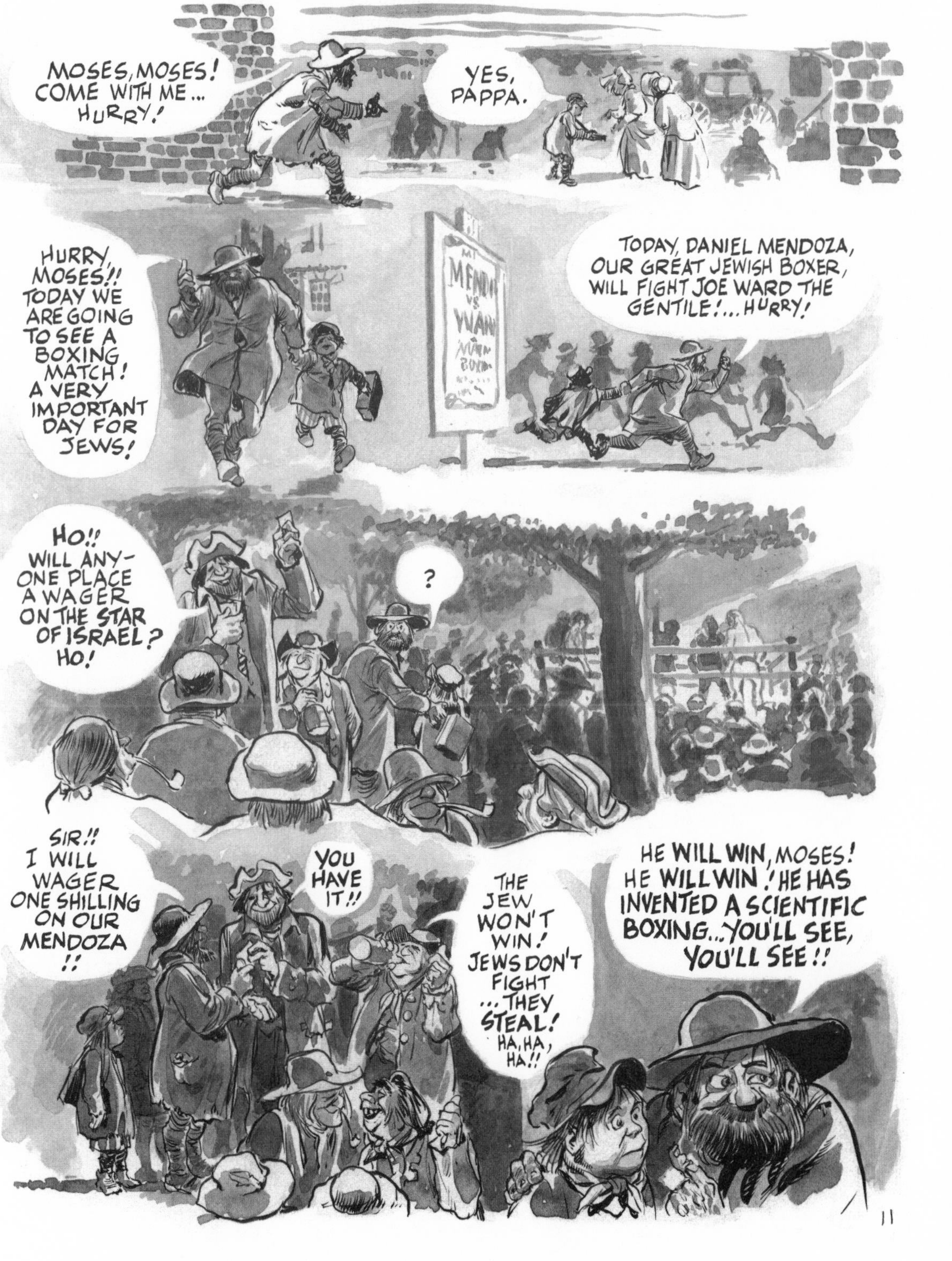

MOSES, MOSES! COME WITH ME... HURRY!
YES, PAPPA.
HURRY, MOSES!! TODAY WE ARE GOING TO SEE A BOXING MATCH! A VERY IMPORTANT DAY FOR JEWS!
TODAY, DANIEL MENDOZA, OUR GREAT JEWISH BOXER, WILL FIGHT JOE WARD THE GENTILE!... HURRY!
HO!! WILL ANY-ONE PLACE A WAGER ON THE STAR OF ISRAEL? HO!
?
SIR!! I WILL WAGER ONE SHILLING ON OUR MENDOZA !!
YOU HAVE IT!!
THE JEW WON'T WIN! JEWS DON'T FIGHT ...THEY STEAL! HA, HA, HA!!
HE WILL WIN, MOSES! HE WILL WIN! HE HAS INVENTED A SCIENTIFIC BOXING... YOU'LL SEE, YOU'LL SEE!!

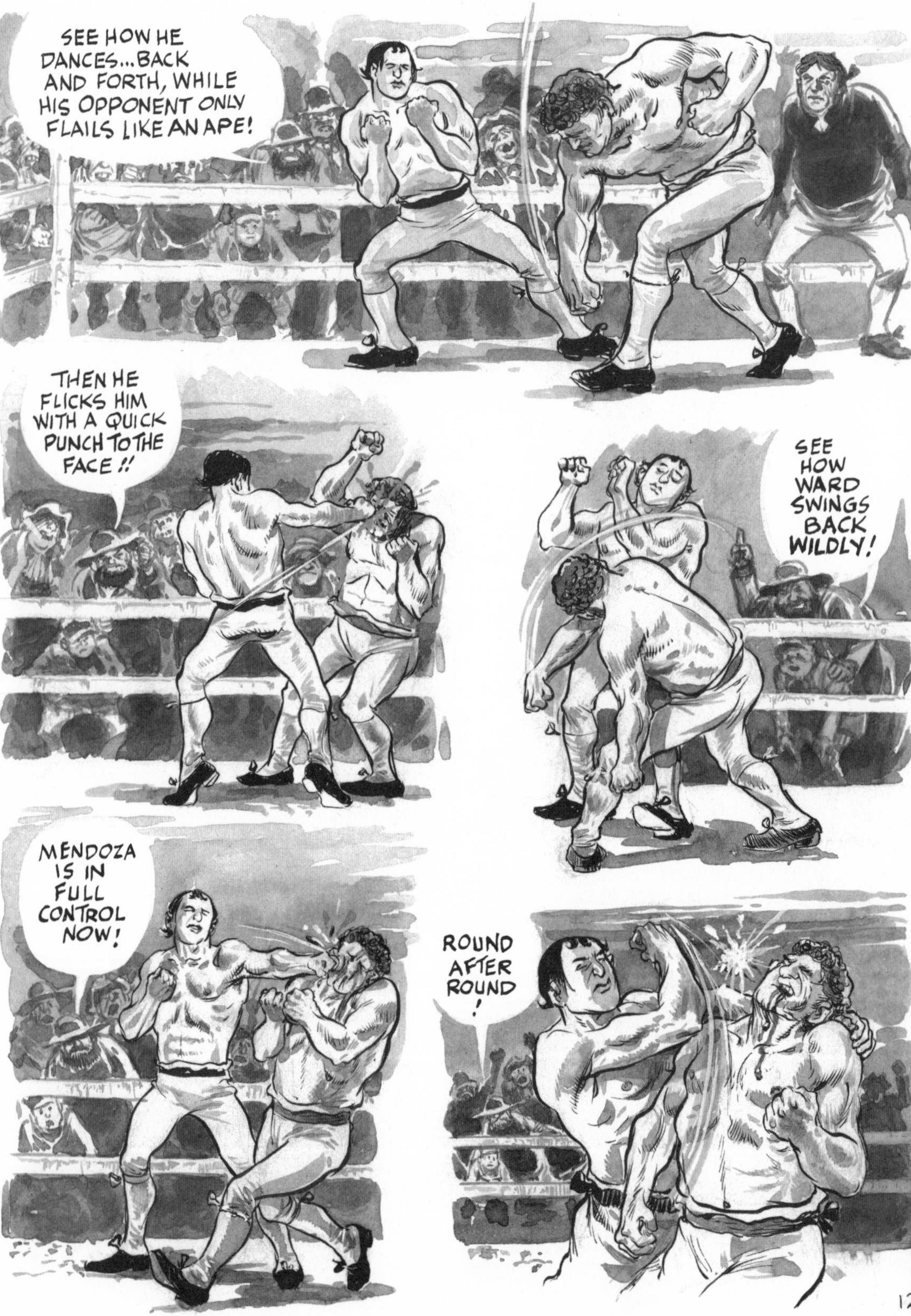
SEE HOW HE DANCES...BACK AND FORTH, WHILE HIS OPPONENT ONLY FLAILS LIKE AN APE!
THEN HE FLICKS HIM WITH A QUICK PUNCH TO THE FACE !!
SEE HOW WARD SWINGS BACK WILDLY!
MENDOZA IS IN FULL CONTROL NOW!
ROUND AFTER ROUND!

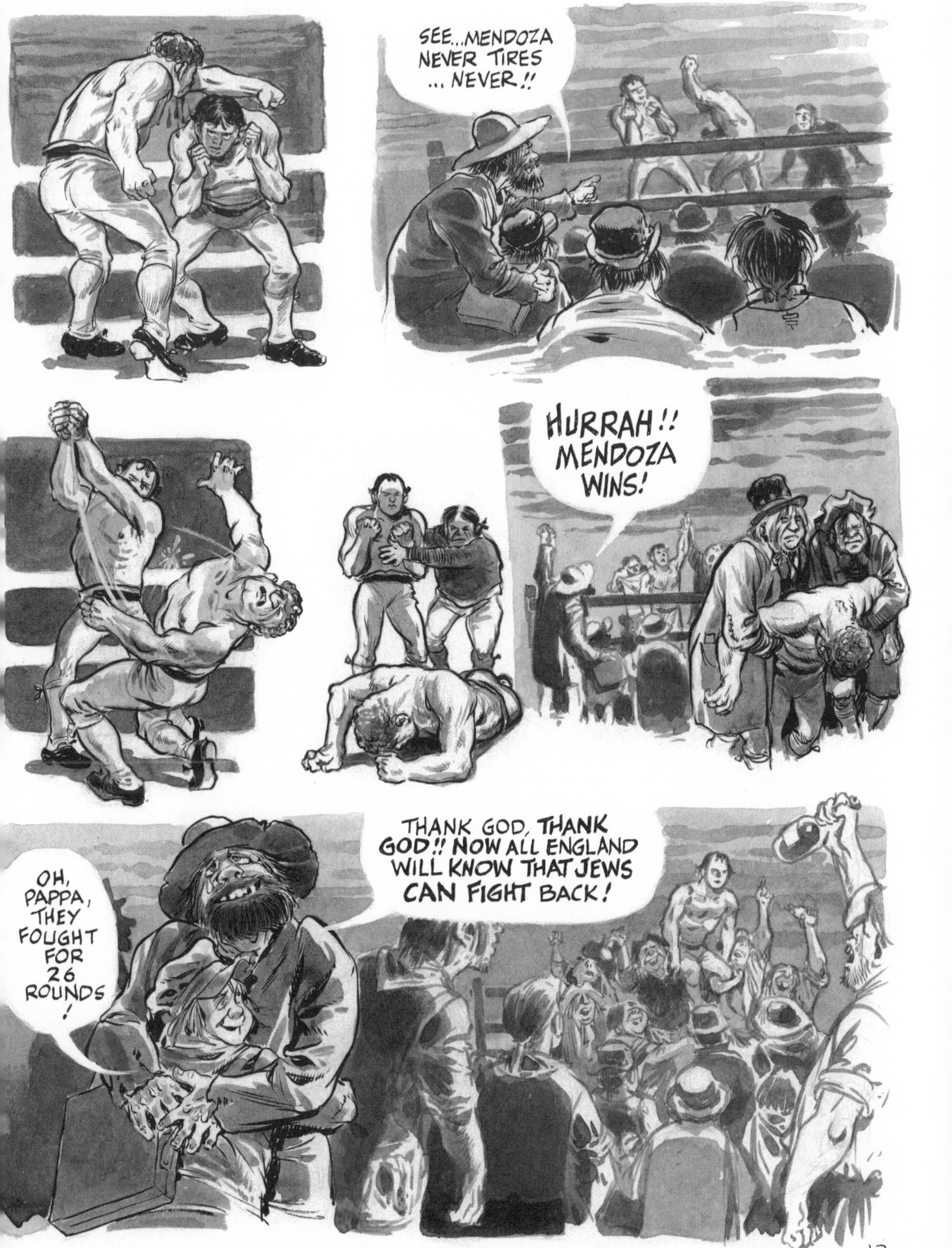
SEE...MENDOZA NEVER TIRES ...NEVER!!
HURRAH!! MENDOZA WINS!
OH, PAPPA, THEY FOUGHT FOR 26 ROUNDS!
THANK GOD, THANK GOD!! NOW ALL ENGLAND WILL KNOW THAT JEWS CAN FIGHT BACK!

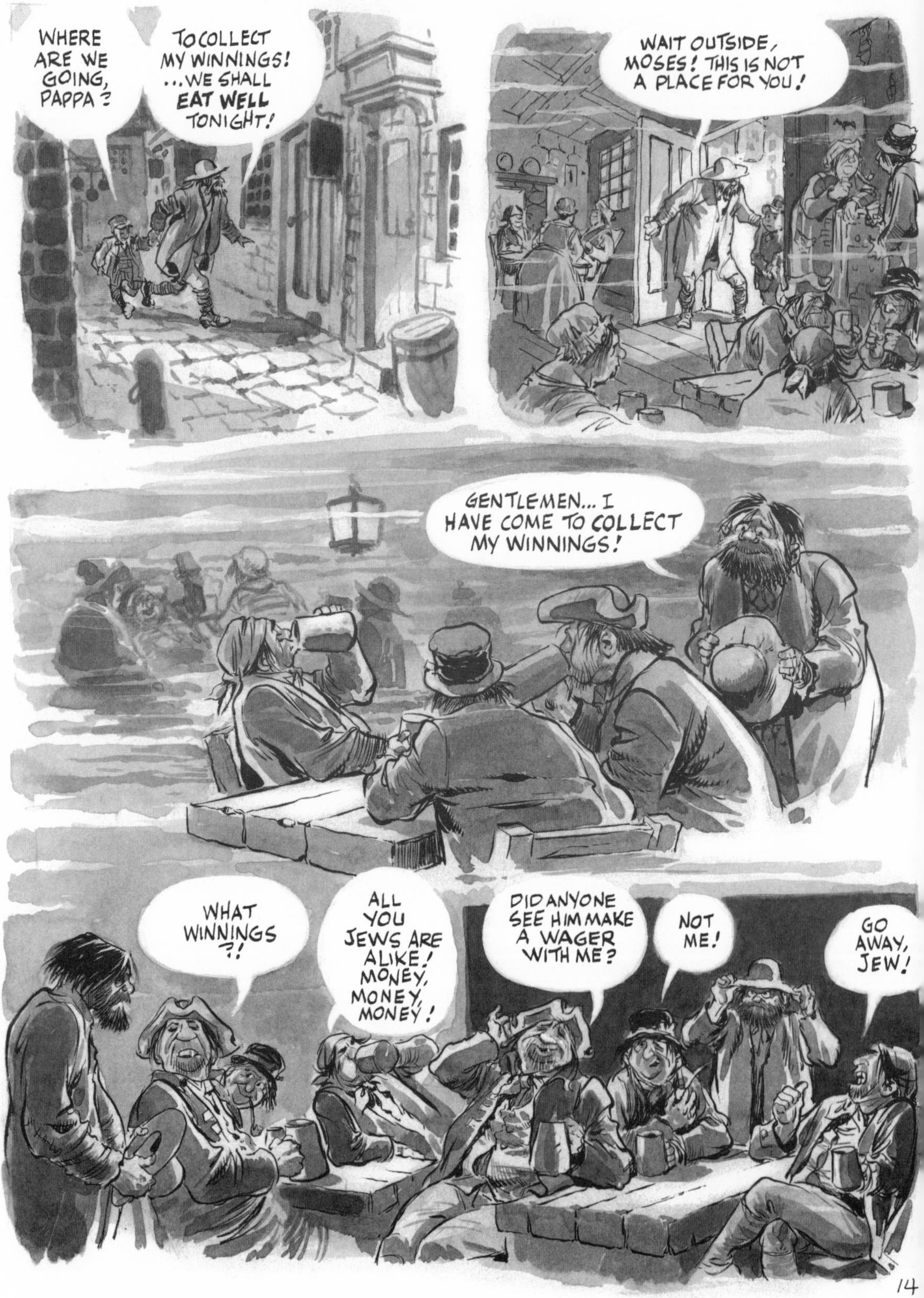
WHERE ARE WE GOING, PAPPA?
TO COLLECT MY WINNINGS! ...WE SHALL **EAT WELL** TONIGHT!
WAIT OUTSIDE, MOSES! THIS IS NOT A PLACE FOR YOU!
GENTLEMEN... I HAVE COME TO COLLECT MY WINNINGS!
WHAT WINNINGS ?!
ALL YOU JEWS ARE ALIKE! MONEY, MONEY, MONEY!
DID ANYONE SEE HIM MAKE A WAGER WITH ME?
NOT ME!
GO AWAY, JEW!

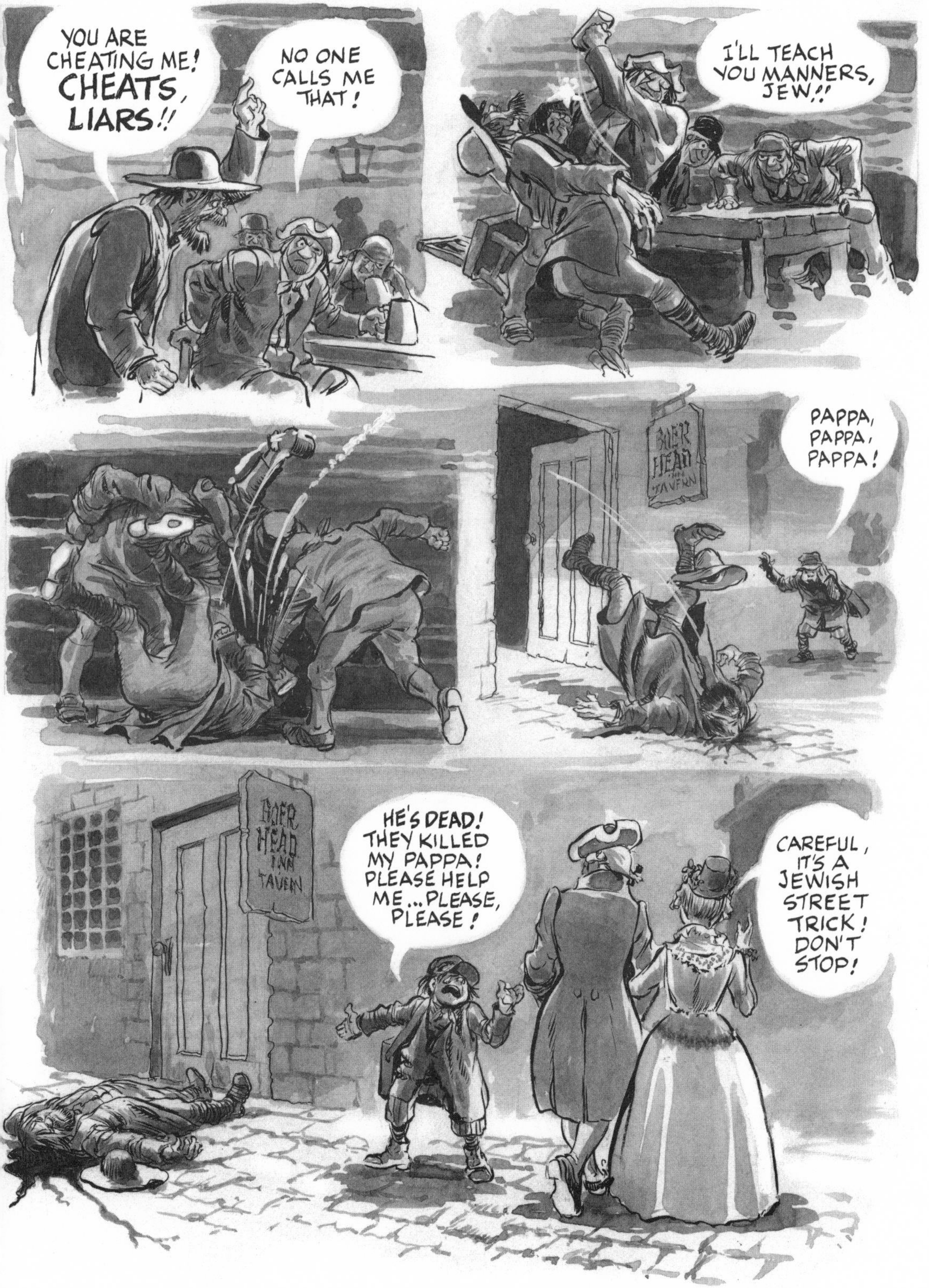
YOU ARE CHEATING ME! CHEATS, LIARS!!
NO ONE CALLS ME THAT!
I'LL TEACH YOU MANNERS, JEW!!
BOER HEAD TAVERN
PAPPA, PAPPA, PAPPA!
BOER HEAD INN TAVERN
HE'S DEAD! THEY KILLED MY PAPPA! PLEASE HELP ME... PLEASE, PLEASE!
CAREFUL, IT'S A JEWISH STREET TRICK! DON'T STOP!

My father's death left me the sole support of my mother. One day...

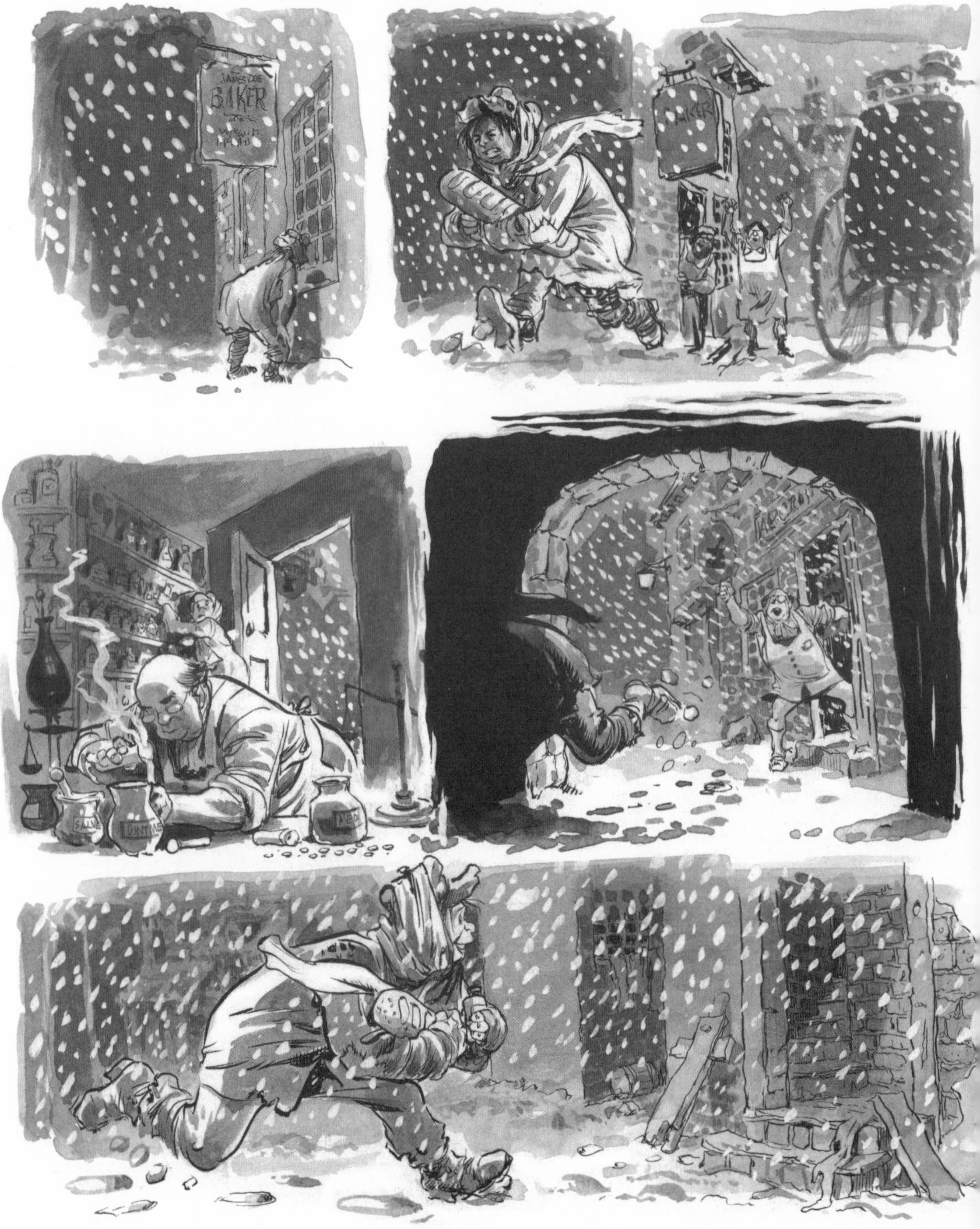

BAKER

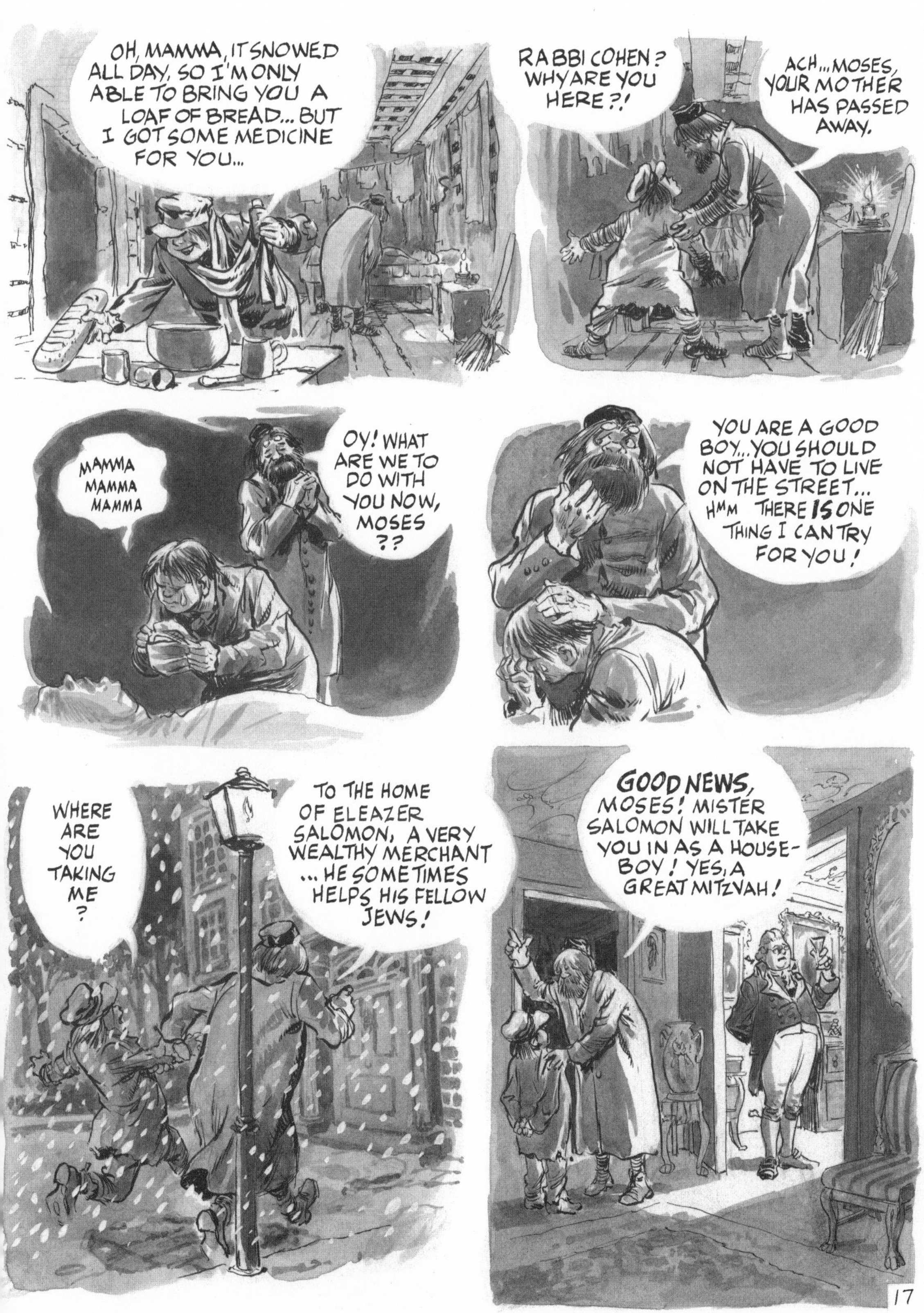
OH, MAMMA, IT SNOWED ALL DAY, SO I'M ONLY ABLE TO BRING YOU A LOAF OF BREAD... BUT I GOT SOME MEDICINE FOR YOU...
RABBI COHEN? WHY ARE YOU HERE?!
ACH... MOSES, YOUR MOTHER HAS PASSED AWAY.
MAMMA MAMMA MAMMA
OY! WHAT ARE WE TO DO WITH YOU NOW, MOSES ??
YOU ARE A GOOD BOY... YOU SHOULD NOT HAVE TO LIVE ON THE STREET... HMM THERE IS ONE THING I CAN TRY FOR YOU!
WHERE ARE YOU TAKING ME ?
TO THE HOME OF ELEAZER SALOMON, A VERY WEALTHY MERCHANT ... HE SOMETIMES HELPS HIS FELLOW JEWS!
GOOD NEWS, MOSES! MISTER SALOMON WILL TAKE YOU IN AS A HOUSE-BOY! YES, A GREAT MITZVAH!

As a houseboy in the Salomon household, I could accompany the master and see a very different side of Jewish life.

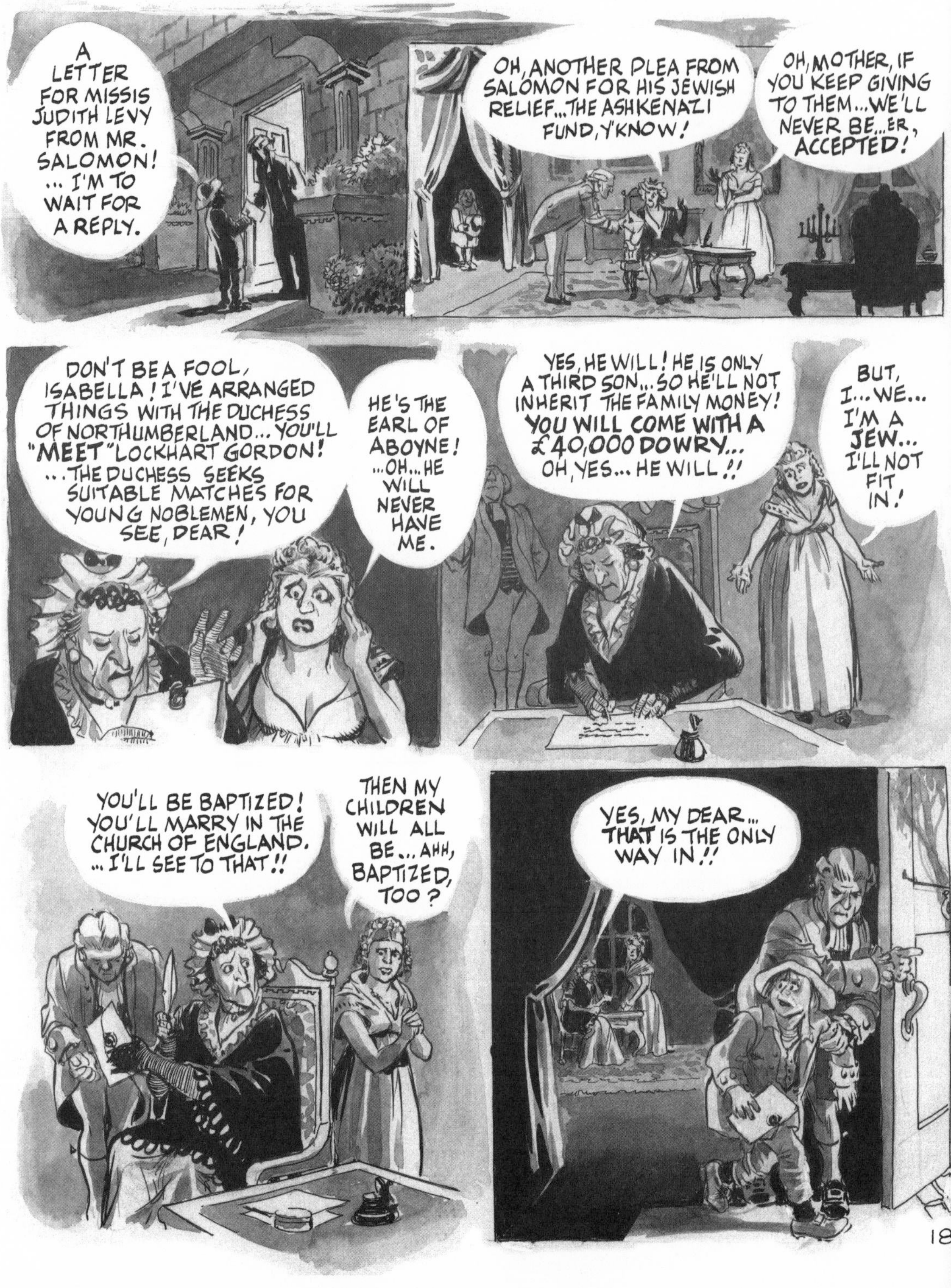
A LETTER FOR MISSIS JUDITH LEVY FROM MR. SALOMON! ... I'M TO WAIT FOR A REPLY.
OH, ANOTHER PLEA FROM SALOMON FOR HIS JEWISH RELIEF... THE ASHKENAZI FUND, Y'KNOW!
OH, MOTHER, IF YOU KEEP GIVING TO THEM... WE'LL NEVER BE... ER, ACCEPTED!
DON'T BE A FOOL, ISABELLA! I'VE ARRANGED THINGS WITH THE DUCHESS OF NORTHUMBERLAND... YOU'LL "MEET" LOCKHART GORDON! ... THE DUCHESS SEEKS SUITABLE MATCHES FOR YOUNG NOBLEMEN, YOU SEE, DEAR!
HE'S THE EARL OF ABOYNE! ...OH... HE WILL NEVER HAVE ME.
YES, HE WILL! HE IS ONLY A THIRD SON... SO HE'LL NOT INHERIT THE FAMILY MONEY! YOU WILL COME WITH A £40,000 DOWRY... OH, YES... HE WILL!!
BUT, I... WE... I'M A JEW... I'LL NOT FIT IN!
YOU'LL BE BAPTIZED! YOU'LL MARRY IN THE CHURCH OF ENGLAND. ... I'LL SEE TO THAT!!
THEN MY CHILDREN WILL ALL BE... AHH, BAPTIZED, TOO?
YES, MY DEAR... THAT IS THE ONLY WAY IN!!

The reputation of the Jews in the London slums continued to soil the status of their betters. This only prodded Mr. Salomon and his colleagues into stronger efforts to build a fund for the school. Mr. Salomon, at last undeterred by Jewish class prejudices, called on Mr. Isaac D'Israeli, a leader in the Sephardic community.

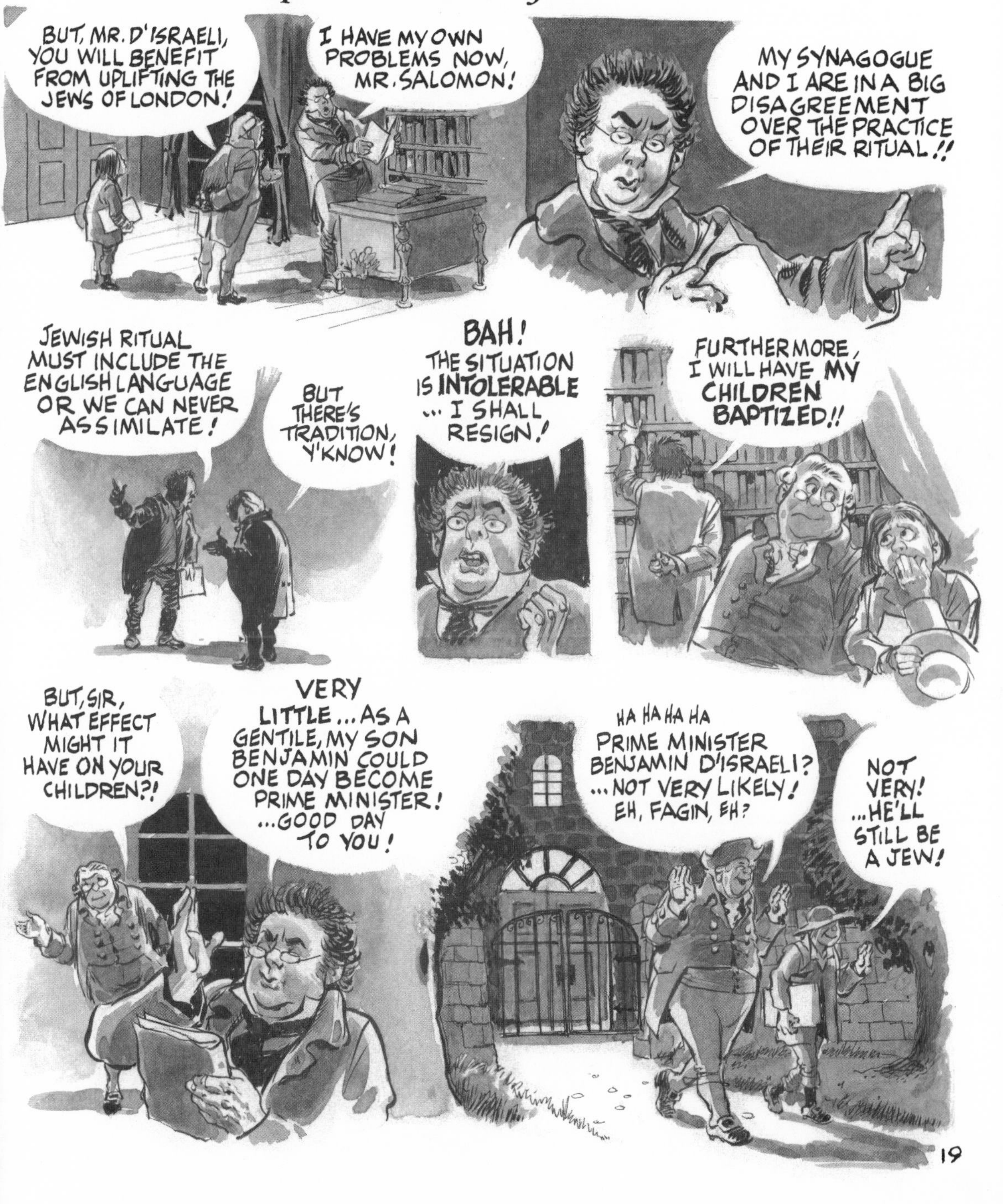

BUT, MR. D'ISRAELI, YOU WILL BENEFIT FROM UPLIFTING THE JEWS OF LONDON!
I HAVE MY OWN PROBLEMS NOW, MR. SALOMON!
MY SYNAGOGUE AND I ARE IN A BIG DISAGREEMENT OVER THE PRACTICE OF THEIR RITUAL!!
JEWISH RITUAL MUST INCLUDE THE ENGLISH LANGUAGE OR WE CAN NEVER ASSIMILATE!
BUT THERE'S TRADITION, Y'KNOW!
BAH! THE SITUATION IS INTOLERABLE ... I SHALL RESIGN!
FURTHERMORE, I WILL HAVE MY CHILDREN BAPTIZED!!
BUT, SIR, WHAT EFFECT MIGHT IT HAVE ON YOUR CHILDREN?!
VERY LITTLE ... AS A GENTILE, MY SON BENJAMIN COULD ONE DAY BECOME PRIME MINISTER! ...GOOD DAY TO YOU!
HA HA HA HA PRIME MINISTER BENJAMIN D'ISRAELI? ...NOT VERY LIKELY! EH, FAGIN, EH?
NOT VERY! ...HE'LL STILL BE A JEW!

During the time I spent observing life in the Salomon household, I learned how Jews succeeded in rising in this world.

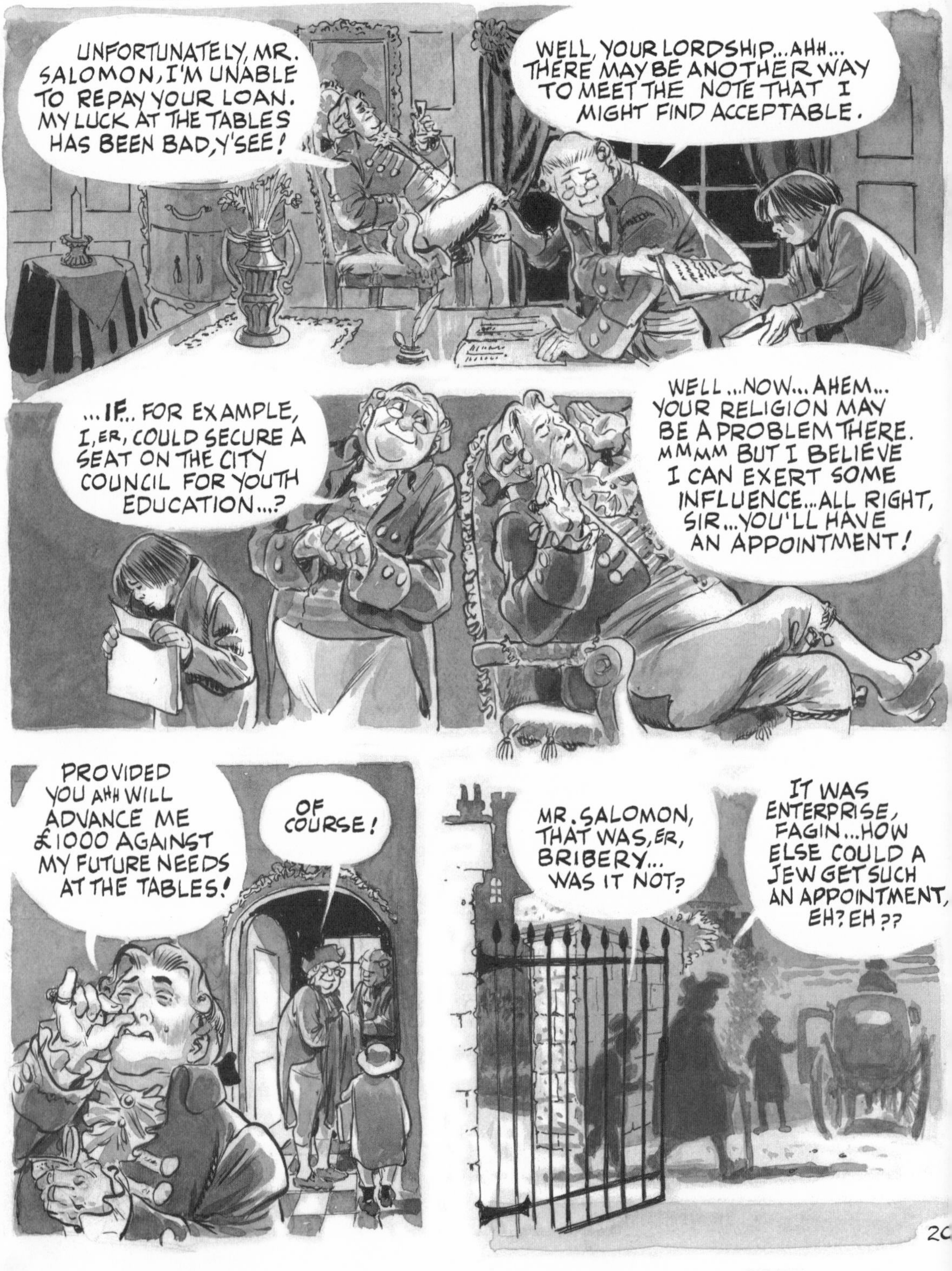

UNFORTUNATELY, MR. SALOMON, I'M UNABLE TO REPAY YOUR LOAN. MY LUCK AT THE TABLES HAS BEEN BAD, Y'SEE!
WELL, YOUR LORDSHIP... AHH... THERE MAY BE ANOTHER WAY TO MEET THE NOTE THAT I MIGHT FIND ACCEPTABLE.
...IF... FOR EXAMPLE, I, ER, COULD SECURE A SEAT ON THE CITY COUNCIL FOR YOUTH EDUCATION...?
WELL ...NOW... AHEM... YOUR RELIGION MAY BE A PROBLEM THERE. MMMM BUT I BELIEVE I CAN EXERT SOME INFLUENCE... ALL RIGHT, SIR... YOU'LL HAVE AN APPOINTMENT!
PROVIDED YOU AHH WILL ADVANCE ME £1000 AGAINST MY FUTURE NEEDS AT THE TABLES!
OF COURSE!
MR. SALOMON, THAT WAS, ER, BRIBERY... WAS IT NOT?
IT WAS ENTERPRISE, FAGIN... HOW ELSE COULD A JEW GET SUCH AN APPOINTMENT, EH? EH??

Mr. Salomon still pursued his search for funds to uplift the lower-class Jews of London by establishing a school to educate young Ashkenazim and help them advance by ways other than crime.

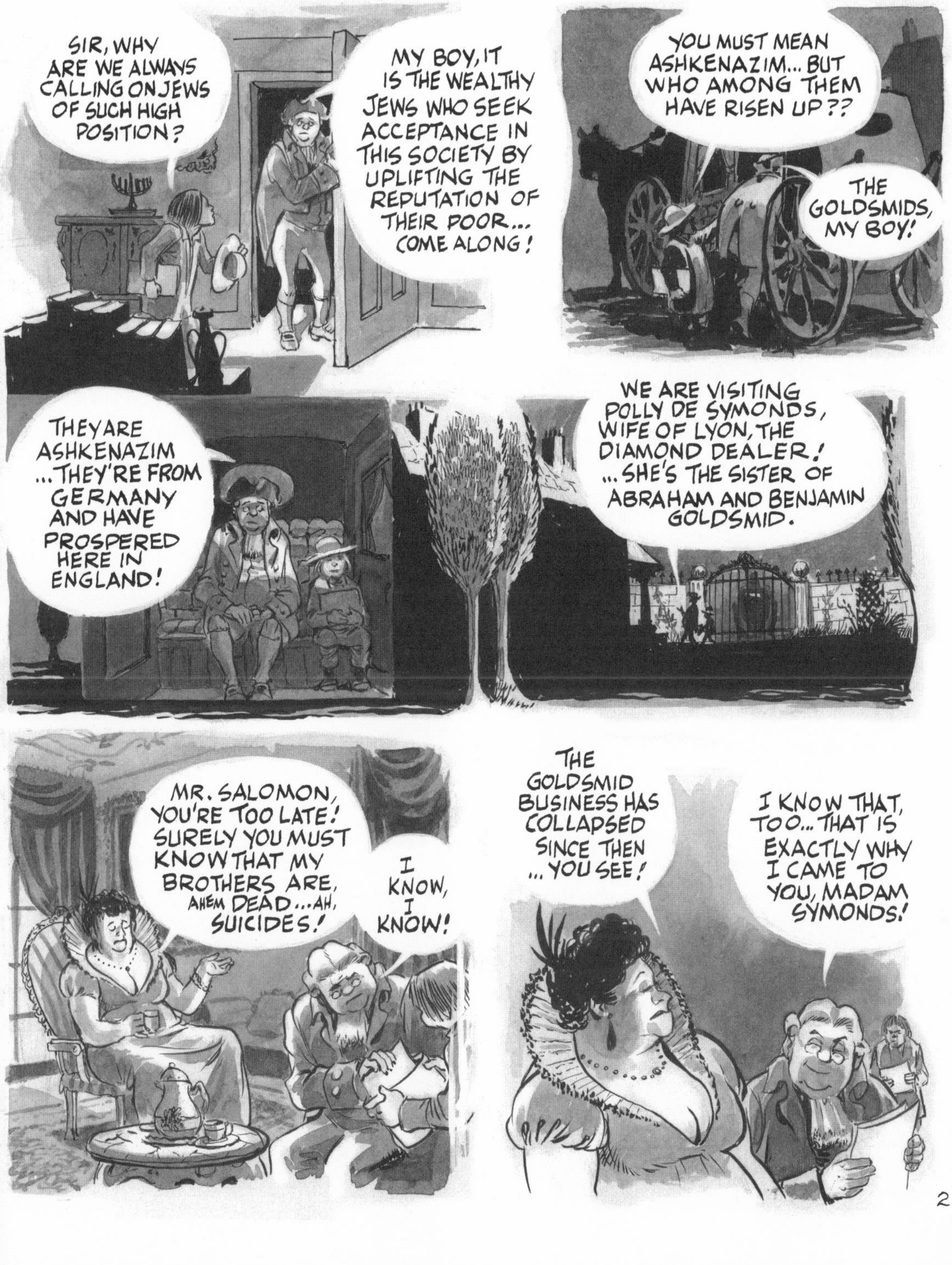

SIR, WHY ARE WE ALWAYS CALLING ON JEWS OF SUCH HIGH POSITION?
MY BOY, IT IS THE WEALTHY JEWS WHO SEEK ACCEPTANCE IN THIS SOCIETY BY UPLIFTING THE REPUTATION OF THEIR POOR... COME ALONG!
YOU MUST MEAN ASHKENAZIM... BUT WHO AMONG THEM HAVE RISEN UP??
THE GOLDSMIDS, MY BOY!
THEY ARE ASHKENAZIM ...THEY'RE FROM GERMANY AND HAVE PROSPERED HERE IN ENGLAND!
WE ARE VISITING POLLY DE SYMONDS, WIFE OF LYON, THE DIAMOND DEALER! ...SHE'S THE SISTER OF ABRAHAM AND BENJAMIN GOLDSMID.
MR. SALOMON, YOU'RE TOO LATE! SURELY YOU MUST KNOW THAT MY BROTHERS ARE, AHEM DEAD...AH, SUICIDES!
I KNOW, I KNOW!
THE GOLDSMID BUSINESS HAS COLLAPSED SINCE THEN ...YOU SEE!
I KNOW THAT, TOO... THAT IS EXACTLY WHY I CAME TO YOU, MADAM SYMONDS!

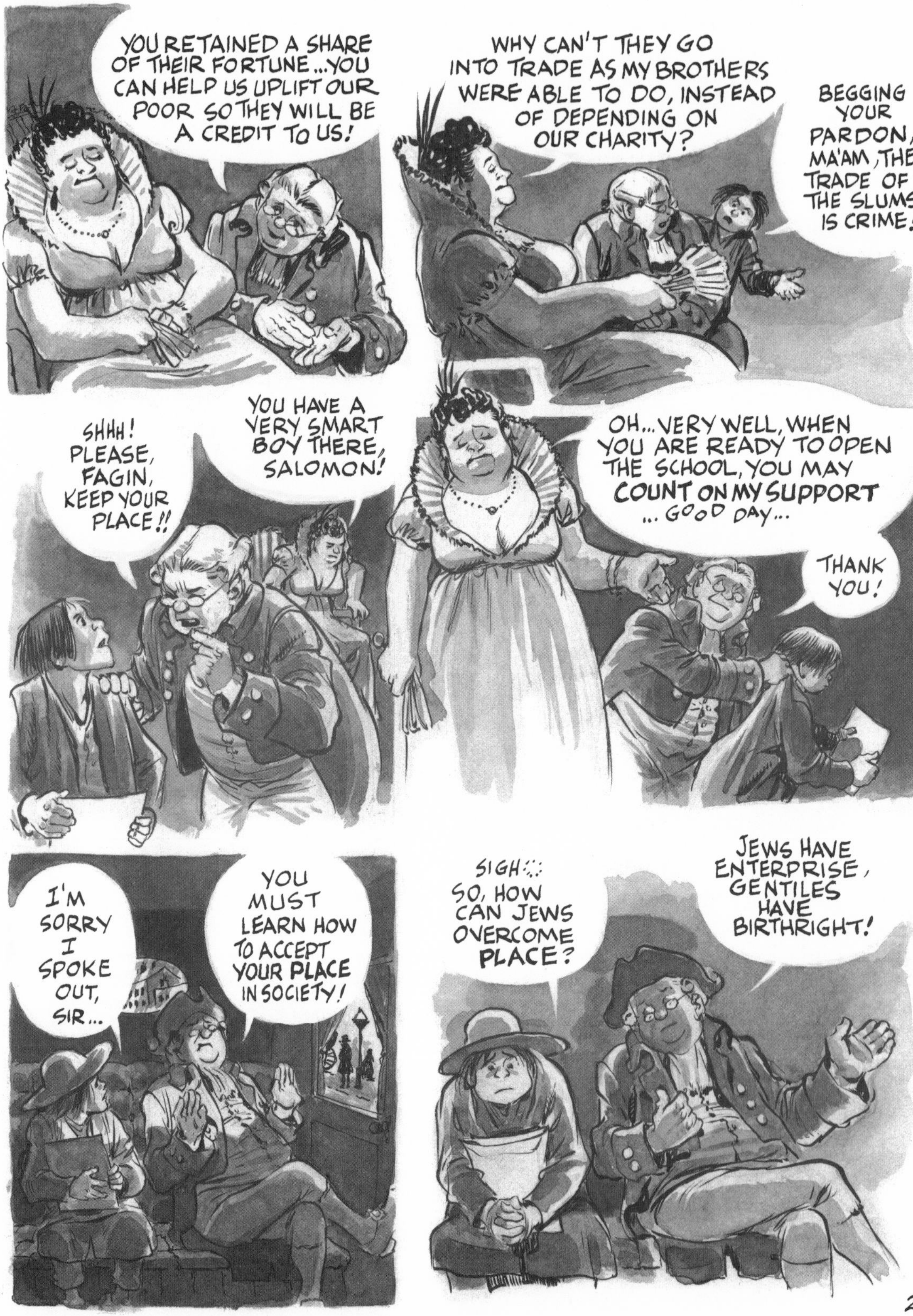
YOU RETAINED A SHARE OF THEIR FORTUNE...YOU CAN HELP US UPLIFT OUR POOR SO THEY WILL BE A CREDIT TO US!
WHY CAN'T THEY GO INTO TRADE AS MY BROTHERS WERE ABLE TO DO, INSTEAD OF DEPENDING ON OUR CHARITY?
BEGGING YOUR PARDON, MA'AM, THE TRADE OF THE SLUMS IS CRIME!
SHHH! PLEASE, FAGIN, KEEP YOUR PLACE!!
YOU HAVE A VERY SMART BOY THERE, SALOMON!
OH... VERY WELL, WHEN YOU ARE READY TO OPEN THE SCHOOL, YOU MAY COUNT ON MY SUPPORT ... GOOD DAY...
THANK YOU!
I'M SORRY I SPOKE OUT, SIR...
YOU MUST LEARN HOW TO ACCEPT YOUR PLACE IN SOCIETY!
SIGH... SO, HOW CAN JEWS OVERCOME PLACE?
JEWS HAVE ENTERPRISE, GENTILES HAVE BIRTHRIGHT!

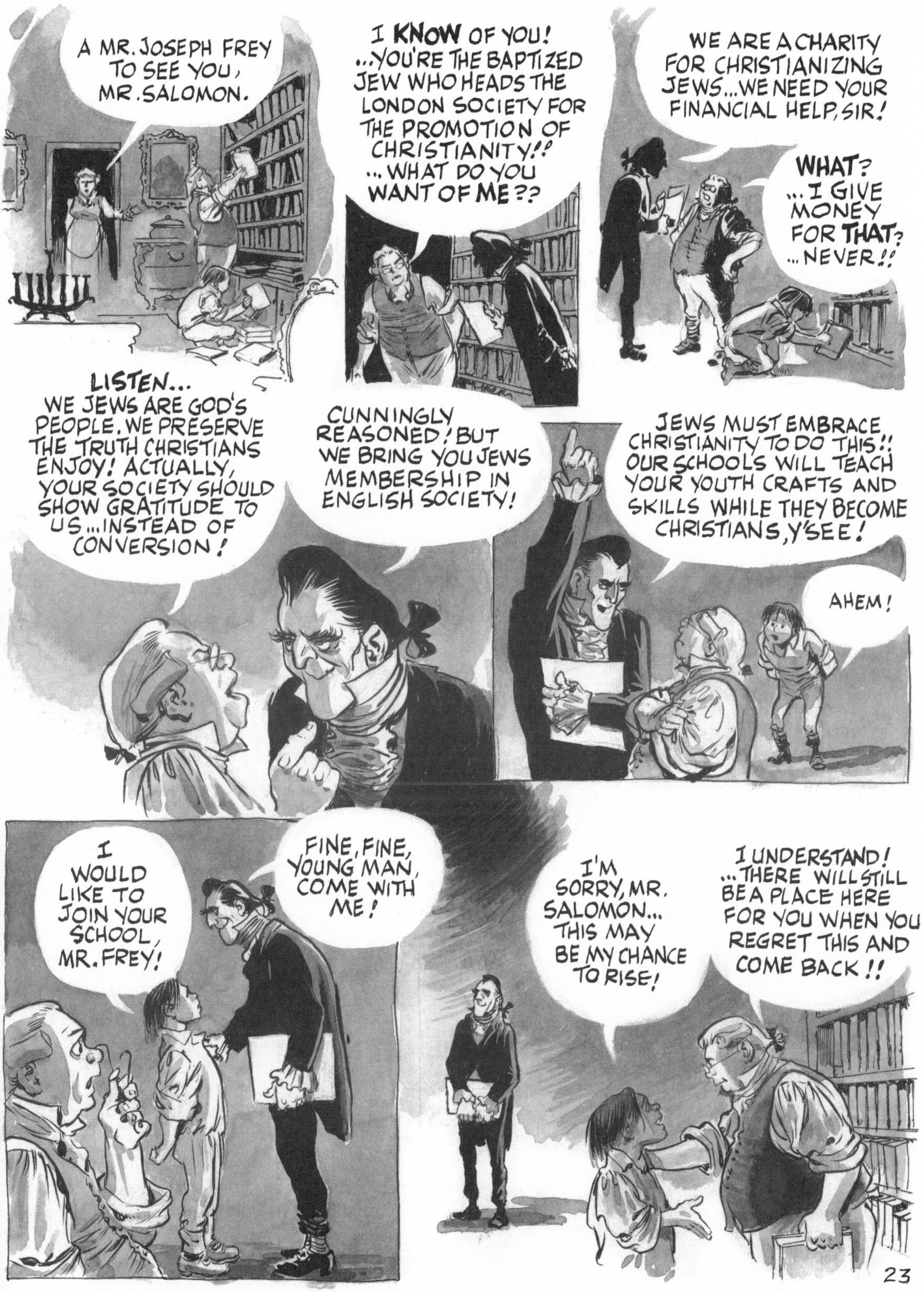
A MR. JOSEPH FREY TO SEE YOU, MR. SALOMON.
I KNOW OF YOU! ..YOU'RE THE BAPTIZED JEW WHO HEADS THE LONDON SOCIETY FOR THE PROMOTION OF CHRISTIANITY!! ... WHAT DO YOU WANT OF ME??
WE ARE A CHARITY FOR CHRISTIANIZING JEWS... WE NEED YOUR FINANCIAL HELP, SIR!
WHAT? ... I GIVE MONEY FOR THAT? ... NEVER!!
LISTEN... WE JEWS ARE GOD'S PEOPLE. WE PRESERVE THE TRUTH CHRISTIANS ENJOY! ACTUALLY, YOUR SOCIETY SHOULD SHOW GRATITUDE TO US... INSTEAD OF CONVERSION!
CUNNINGLY REASONED! BUT WE BRING YOU JEWS MEMBERSHIP IN ENGLISH SOCIETY!
JEWS MUST EMBRACE CHRISTIANITY TO DO THIS!! OUR SCHOOLS WILL TEACH YOUR YOUTH CRAFTS AND SKILLS WHILE THEY BECOME CHRISTIANS, Y'SEE!
AHEM!
I WOULD LIKE TO JOIN YOUR SCHOOL, MR. FREY!
FINE, FINE, YOUNG MAN, COME WITH ME!
I'M SORRY, MR. SALOMON... THIS MAY BE MY CHANCE TO RISE!
I UNDERSTAND! ... THERE WILL STILL BE A PLACE HERE FOR YOU WHEN YOU REGRET THIS AND COME BACK!!

One year later, Joseph Frey's school for the Christianizing of young Jews lay in failure. Mr. Frey was reprimanded and reassigned by his backers for an indiscreet affair with a Mrs. Josephson. All I had accumulated in my time there was some skill at sewing, basket weaving, and repair, which would be of use to me later in life. But Christianizing me had failed.

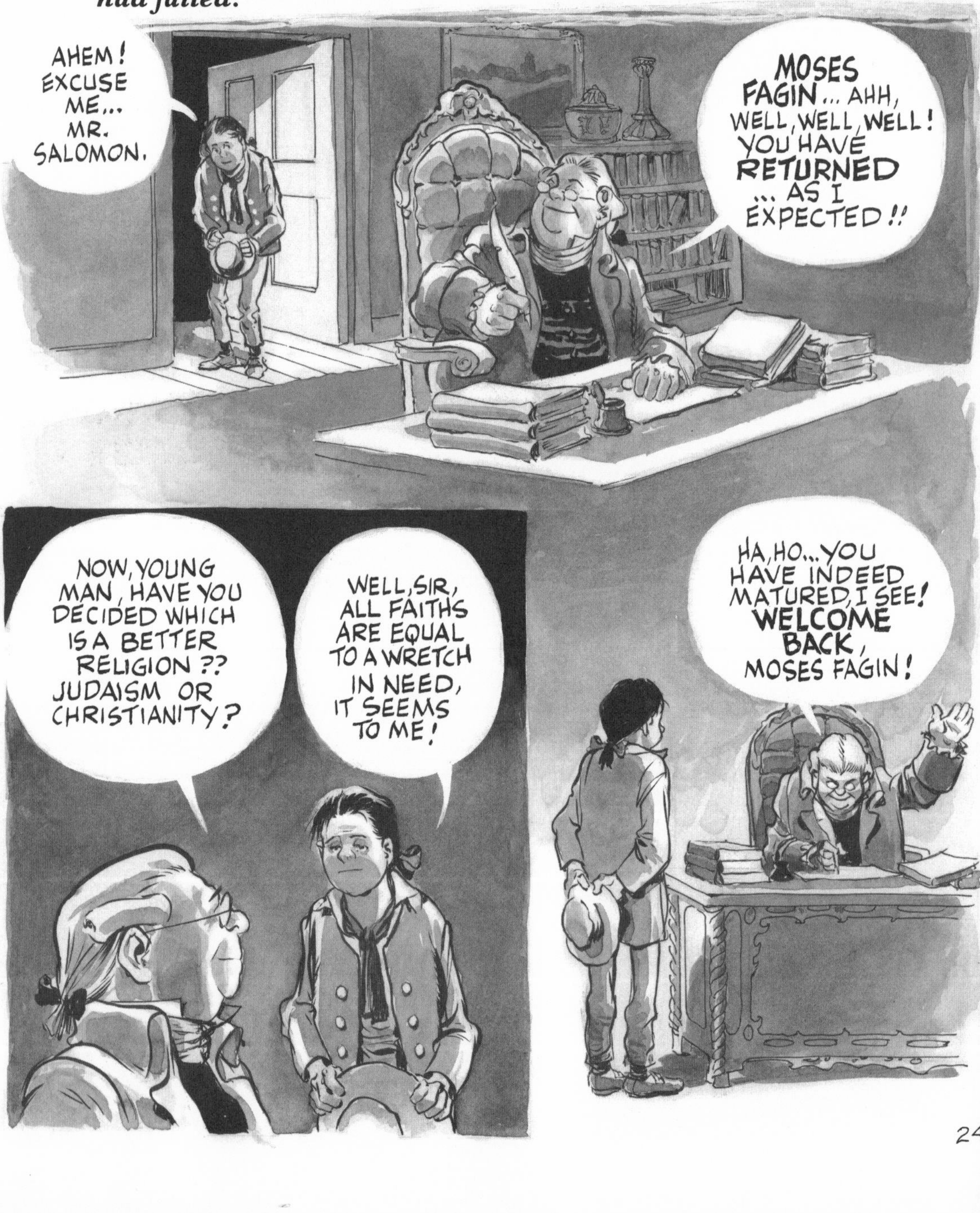
AHEM! EXCUSE ME... MR. SALOMON.
MOSES FAGIN... AHH, WELL, WELL, WELL! YOU HAVE RETURNED ... AS I EXPECTED!!
NOW, YOUNG MAN, HAVE YOU DECIDED WHICH IS A BETTER RELIGION?? JUDAISM OR CHRISTIANITY?
WELL, SIR, ALL FAITHS ARE EQUAL TO A WRETCH IN NEED, IT SEEMS TO ME!
HA, HO... YOU HAVE INDEED MATURED, I SEE! WELCOME BACK, MOSES FAGIN!

Well… a few years passed and I was in my seventeenth year, still a servant in the Salomon house. Then one day…

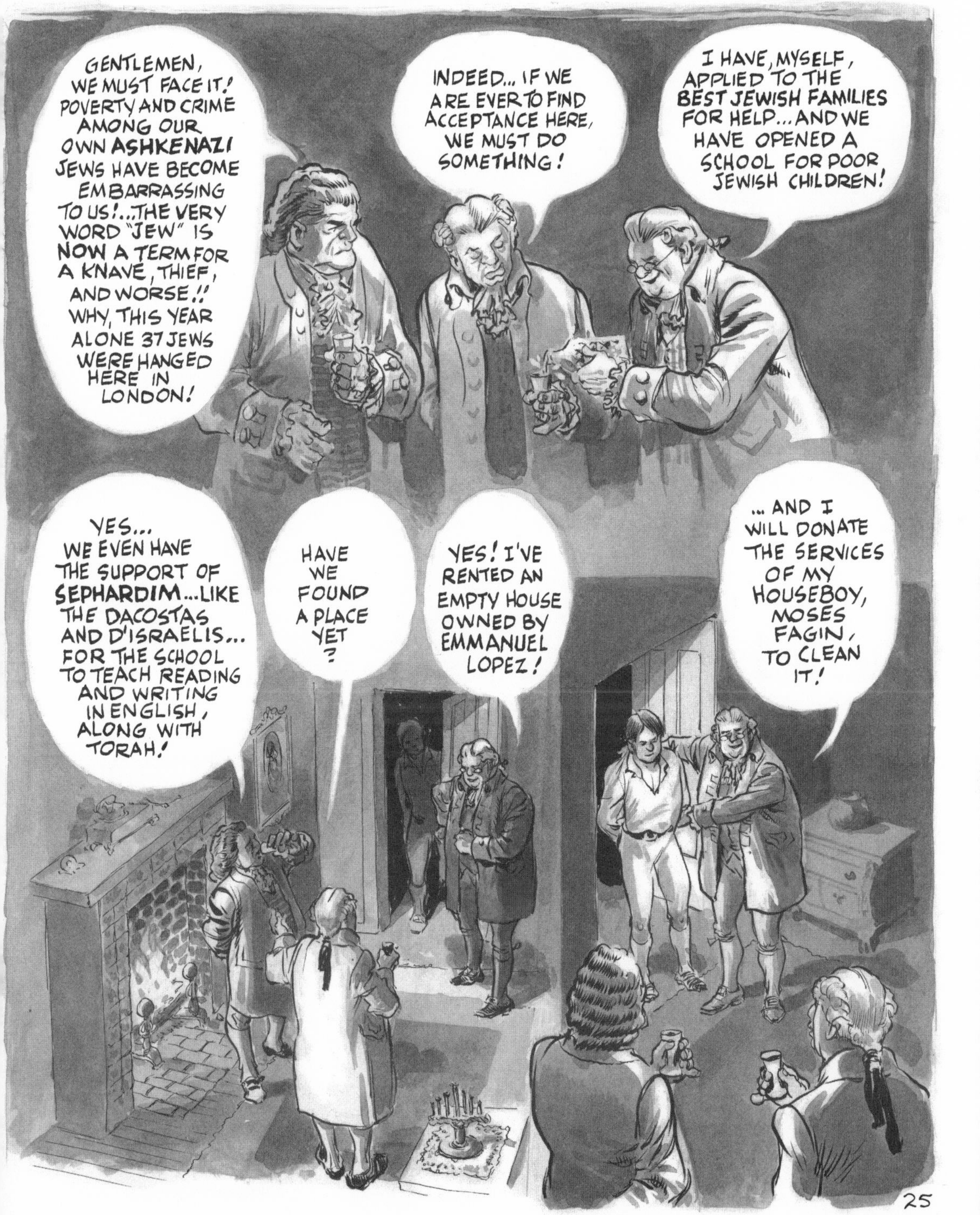
GENTLEMEN, WE MUST FACE IT! POVERTY AND CRIME AMONG OUR OWN ASHKENAZI JEWS HAVE BECOME EMBARRASSING TO US!...THE VERY WORD "JEW" IS NOW A TERM FOR A KNAVE, THIEF, AND WORSE!! WHY, THIS YEAR ALONE 37 JEWS WERE HANGED HERE IN LONDON!
INDEED... IF WE ARE EVER TO FIND ACCEPTANCE HERE, WE MUST DO SOMETHING!
I HAVE, MYSELF, APPLIED TO THE BEST JEWISH FAMILIES FOR HELP... AND WE HAVE OPENED A SCHOOL FOR POOR JEWISH CHILDREN!
YES... WE EVEN HAVE THE SUPPORT OF SEPHARDIM...LIKE THE DACOSTAS AND D'ISRAELIS... FOR THE SCHOOL TO TEACH READING AND WRITING IN ENGLISH, ALONG WITH TORAH!
HAVE WE FOUND A PLACE YET?
YES! I'VE RENTED AN EMPTY HOUSE OWNED BY EMMANUEL LOPEZ!
... AND I WILL DONATE THE SERVICES OF MY HOUSEBOY, MOSES FAGIN, TO CLEAN IT!

And so I went to work at the school...

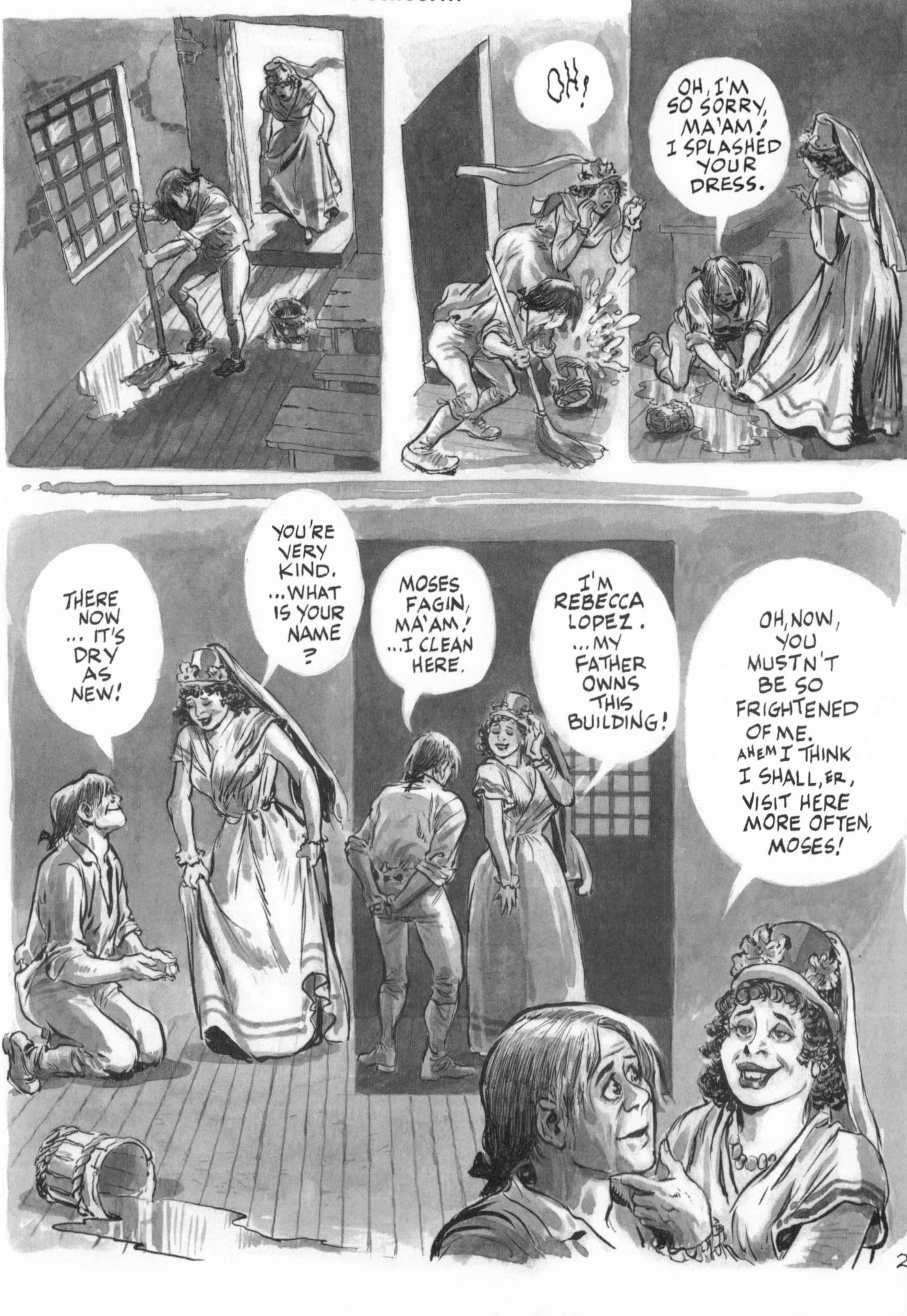

OH!
OH, I'M SO SORRY, MA'AM! I SPLASHED YOUR DRESS.
THERE NOW ... IT'S DRY AS NEW!
YOU'RE VERY KIND. ...WHAT IS YOUR NAME?
MOSES FAGIN, MA'AM! ...I CLEAN HERE.
I'M REBECCA LOPEZ. ...MY FATHER OWNS THIS BUILDING!
OH, NOW, YOU MUSTN'T BE SO FRIGHTENED OF ME. AHEM I THINK I SHALL, ER, VISIT HERE MORE OFTEN, MOSES!

So began my short romance with Rebecca Lopez.

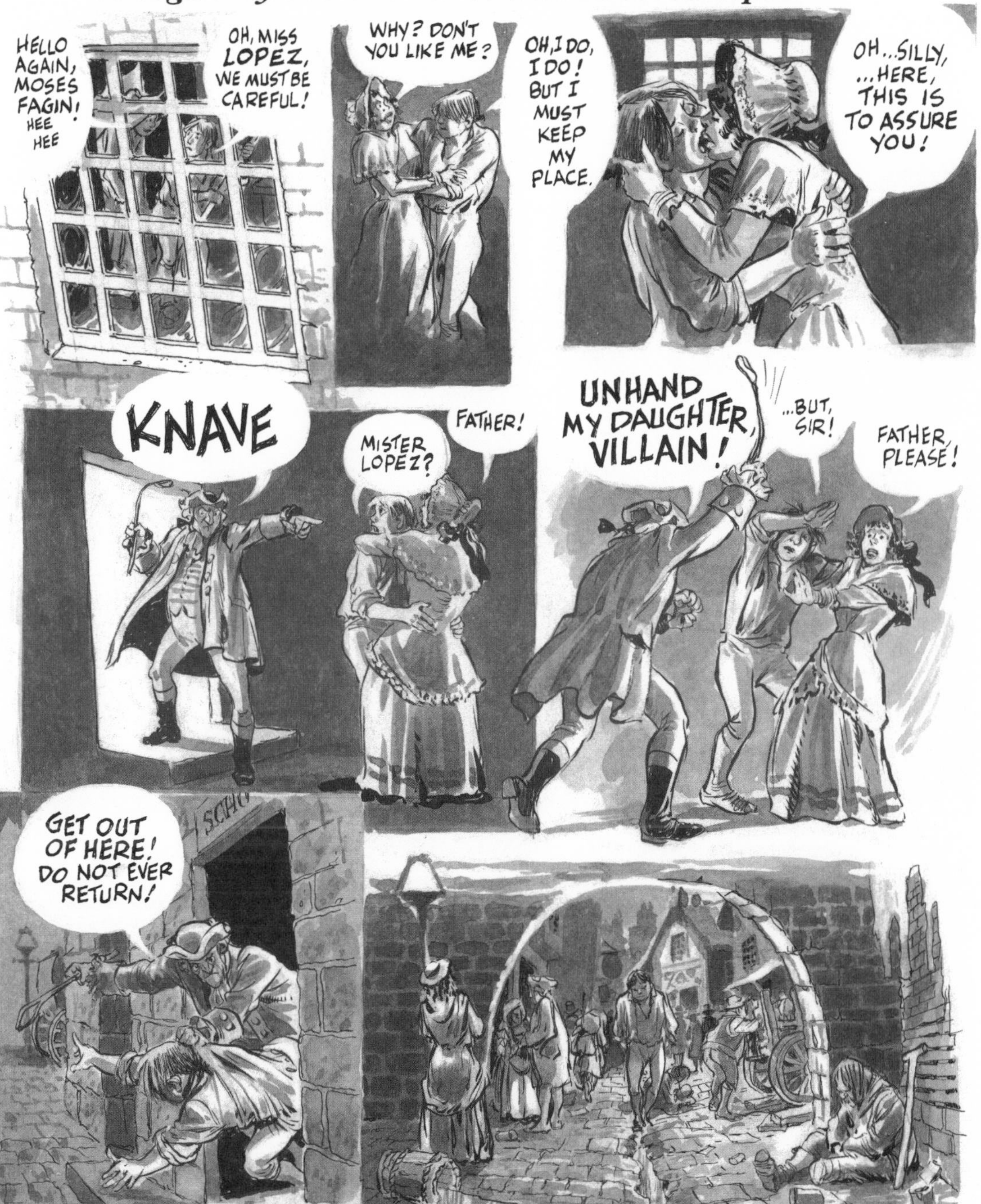
HELLO AGAIN, MOSES FAGIN! HEE HEE
OH, MISS LOPEZ, WE MUST BE CAREFUL!
WHY? DON'T YOU LIKE ME?
OH, I DO, I DO! BUT I MUST KEEP MY PLACE.
OH...SILLY, ...HERE, THIS IS TO ASSURE YOU!
KNAVE
MISTER LOPEZ?
FATHER!
UNHAND MY DAUGHTER, VILLAIN!
...BUT, SIR!
FATHER, PLEASE!
GET OUT OF HERE! DO NOT EVER RETURN!

So it ended... as did my place in the school, and with it, all hope for improvement in my station. With this turn of events began my return to the dregs of the streets of London.

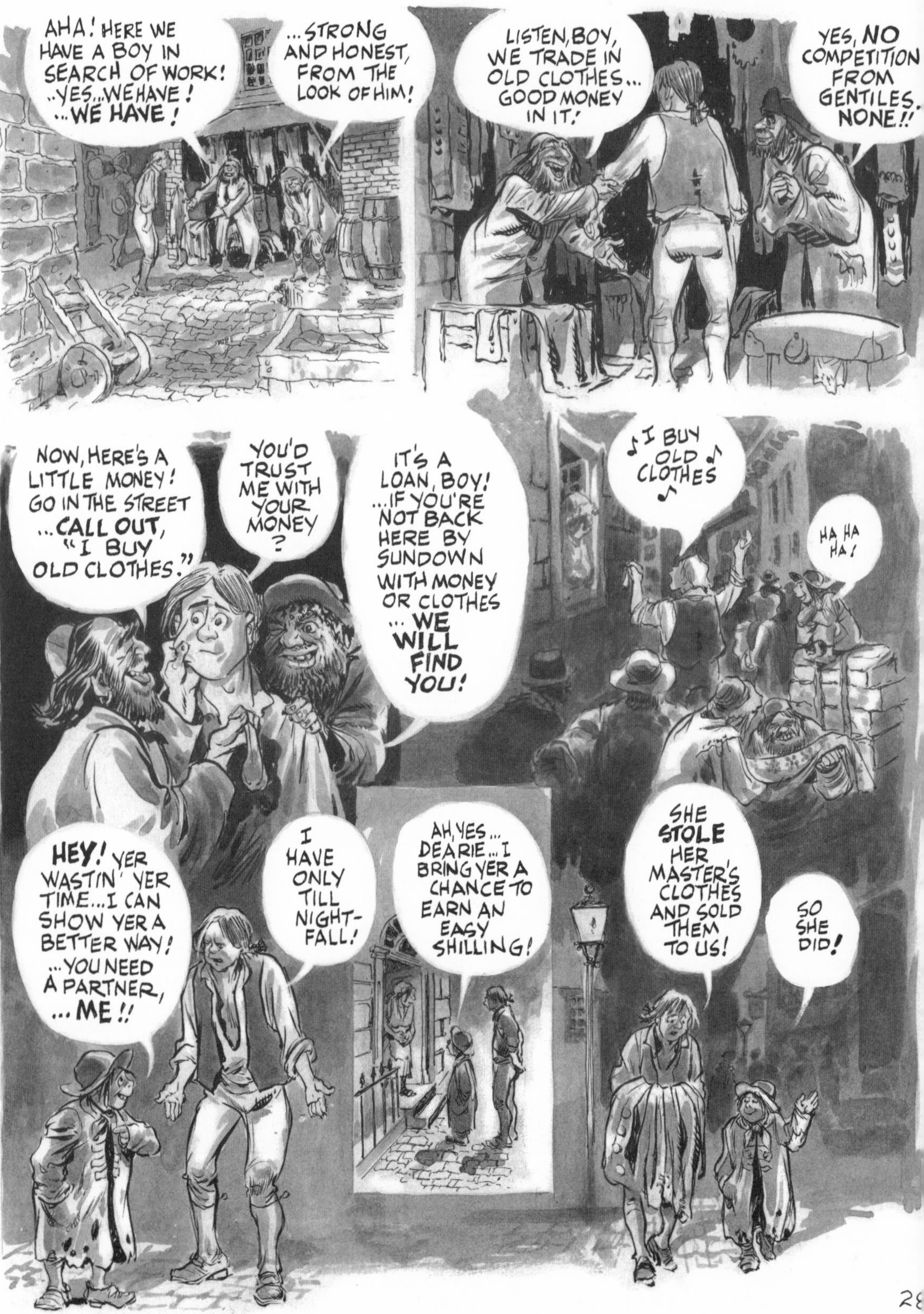
AHA! HERE WE HAVE A BOY IN SEARCH OF WORK! ..YES..WE HAVE! ...WE HAVE!
...STRONG AND HONEST, FROM THE LOOK OF HIM!
LISTEN, BOY, WE TRADE IN OLD CLOTHES... GOOD MONEY IN IT!
YES, NO COMPETITION FROM GENTILES. NONE!!
NOW, HERE'S A LITTLE MONEY! GO IN THE STREET ...CALL OUT, "I BUY OLD CLOTHES."
YOU'D TRUST ME WITH YOUR MONEY?
IT'S A LOAN, BOY! ...IF YOU'RE NOT BACK HERE BY SUNDOWN WITH MONEY OR CLOTHES ...WE WILL FIND YOU!
♪ I BUY OLD CLOTHES ♪
HA HA HA!
HEY! YER WASTIN' YER TIME...I CAN SHOW YER A BETTER WAY! ...YOU NEED A PARTNER, ...ME!!
I HAVE ONLY TILL NIGHT-FALL!
AH, YES... DEARIE... I BRING YER A CHANCE TO EARN AN EASY SHILLING!
SHE STOLE HER MASTER'S CLOTHES AND SOLD THEM TO US!
SO SHE DID!

Ah, how the business of survival does take perilous turns. Before long, I was more deeply involved in the trade of the streets than ever.

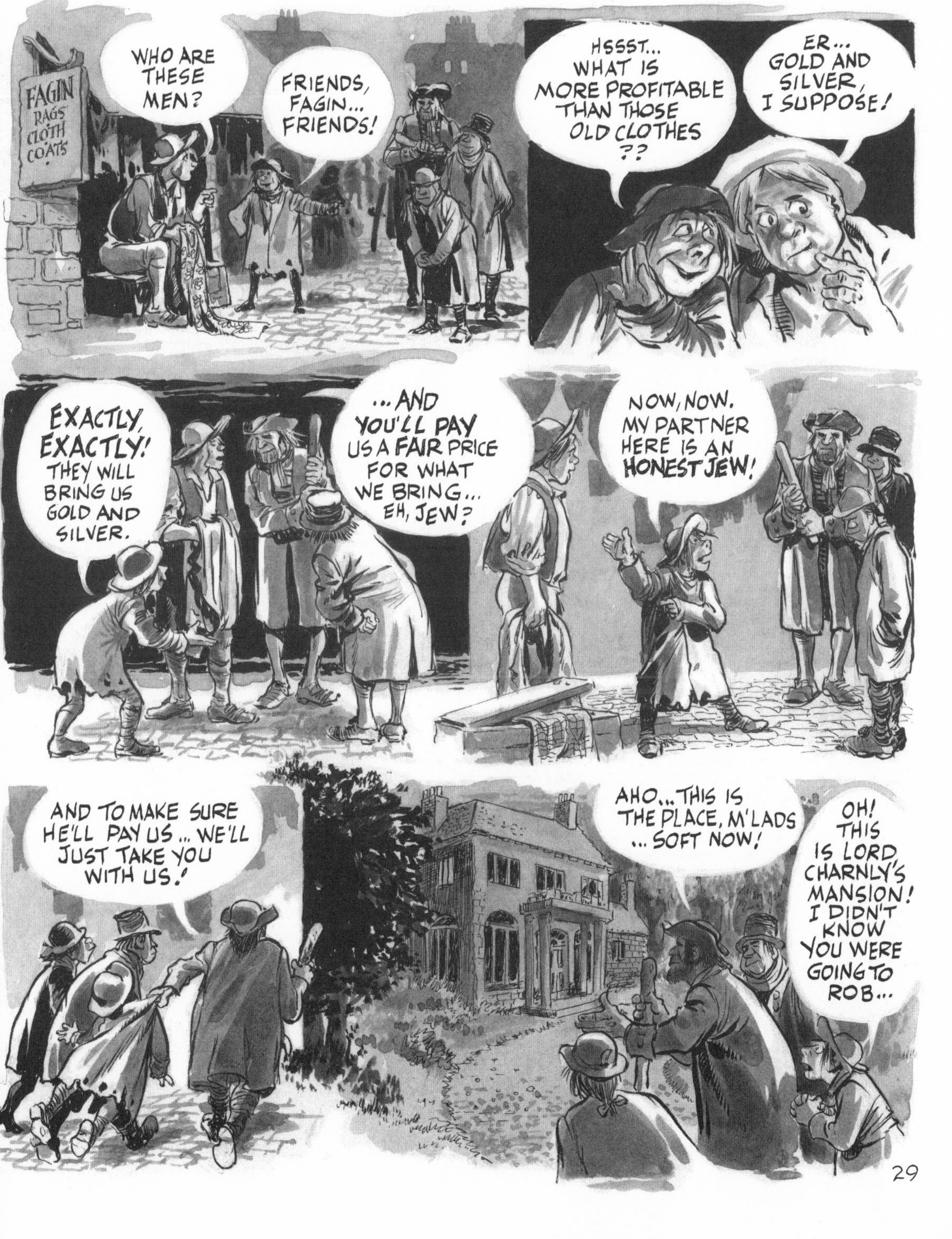
FAGIN RAGS CLOTH COATS
WHO ARE THESE MEN?
FRIENDS, FAGIN... FRIENDS!
HSSST... WHAT IS MORE PROFITABLE THAN THOSE OLD CLOTHES ??
ER... GOLD AND SILVER, I SUPPOSE!
EXACTLY, EXACTLY! THEY WILL BRING US GOLD AND SILVER.
...AND YOU'LL PAY US A FAIR PRICE FOR WHAT WE BRING... EH, JEW?
NOW, NOW. MY PARTNER HERE IS AN HONEST JEW!
AND TO MAKE SURE HE'LL PAY US... WE'LL JUST TAKE YOU WITH US.!
AHO... THIS IS THE PLACE, M'LADS ... SOFT NOW!
OH! THIS IS LORD CHARNLY'S MANSION! I DIDN'T KNOW YOU WERE GOING TO ROB...

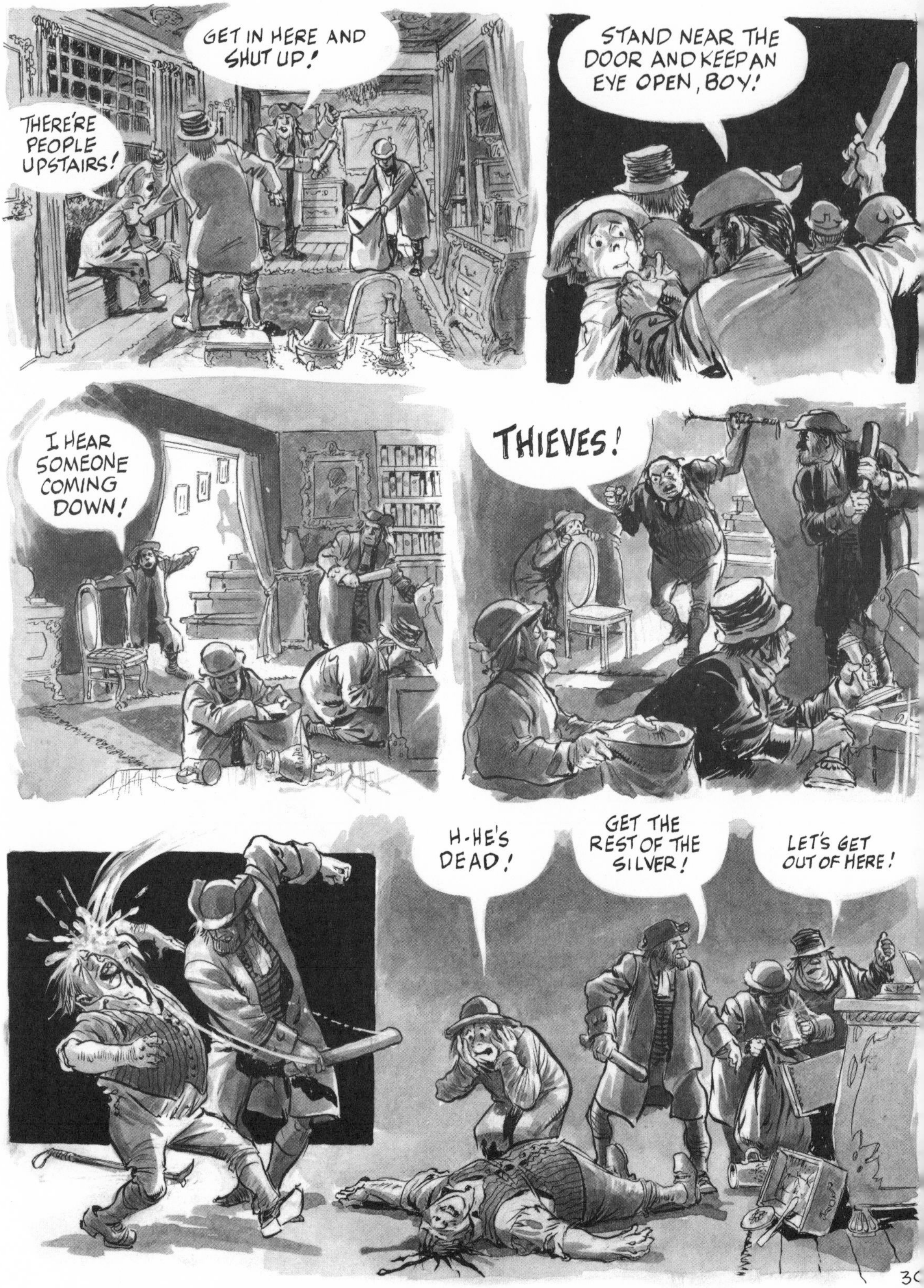
THERE'RE PEOPLE UPSTAIRS!
GET IN HERE AND SHUT UP!
STAND NEAR THE DOOR AND KEEP AN EYE OPEN, BOY!
I HEAR SOMEONE COMING DOWN!
THIEVES!
H-HE'S DEAD!
GET THE REST OF THE SILVER!
LET'S GET OUT OF HERE!

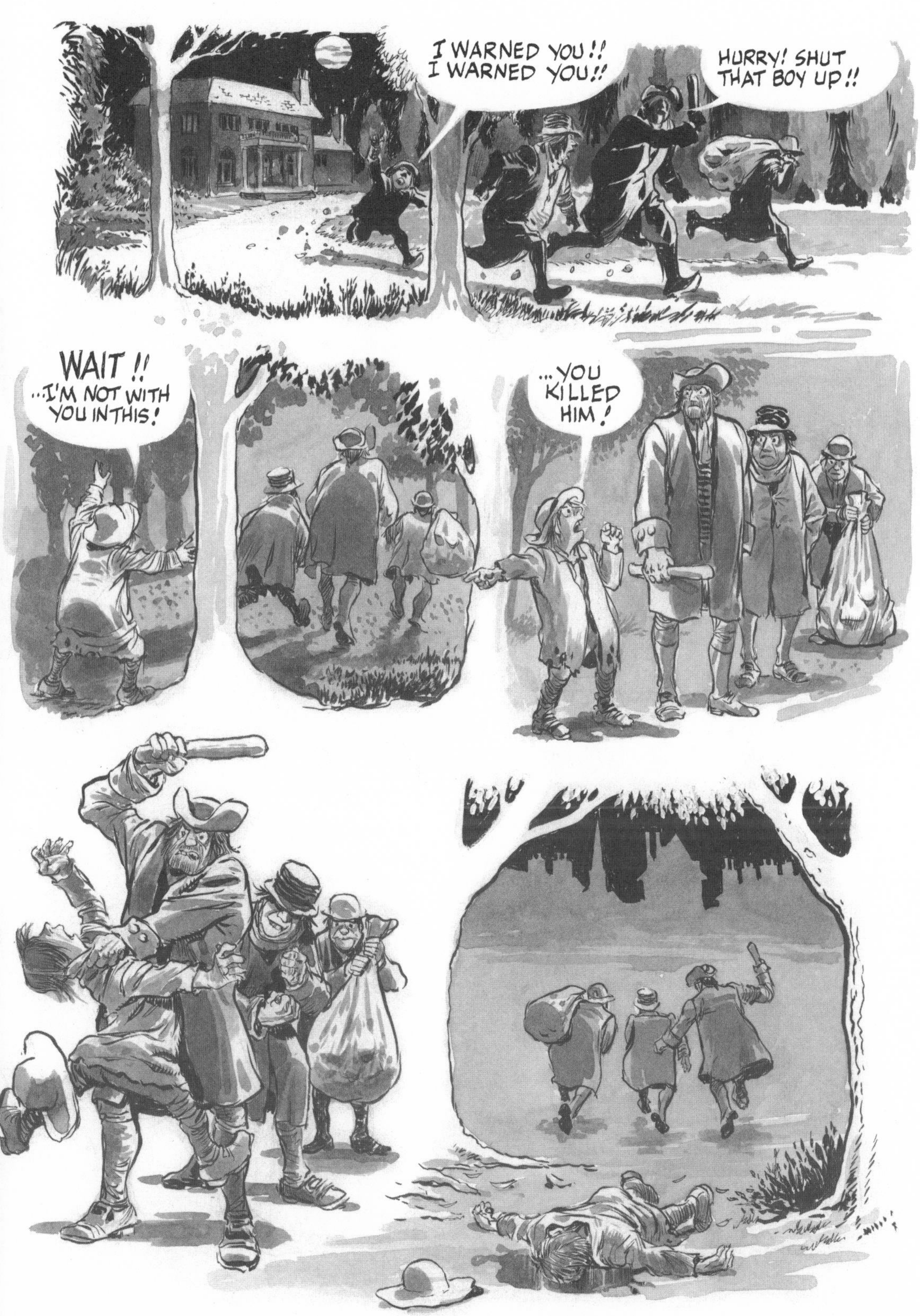
I WARNED YOU!! I WARNED YOU!!
HURRY! SHUT THAT BOY UP!!
WAIT!! ...I'M NOT WITH YOU IN THIS!
...YOU KILLED HIM!

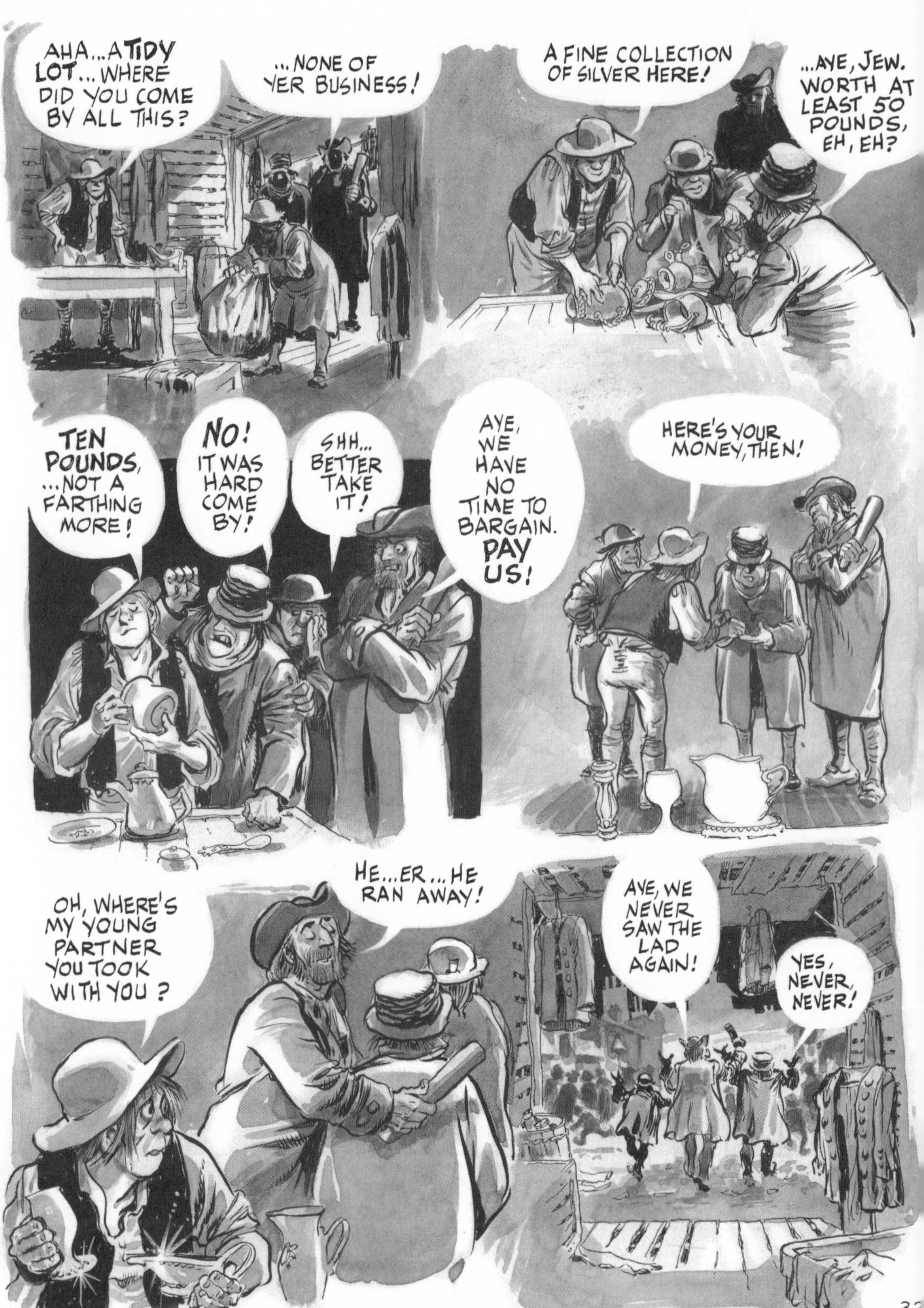
AHA...A TIDY LOT...WHERE DID YOU COME BY ALL THIS?
...NONE OF YER BUSINESS!
A FINE COLLECTION OF SILVER HERE!
...AYE, JEW. WORTH AT LEAST 50 POUNDS, EH, EH?
TEN POUNDS, ...NOT A FARTHING MORE!
NO! IT WAS HARD COME BY!
SHH... BETTER TAKE IT!
AYE, WE HAVE NO TIME TO BARGAIN. PAY US!
HERE'S YOUR MONEY, THEN!
OH, WHERE'S MY YOUNG PARTNER YOU TOOK WITH YOU?
HE...ER...HE RAN AWAY!
AYE, WE NEVER SAW THE LAD AGAIN!
YES, NEVER, NEVER!

By now I had learned that in this trade, it was best not to ask questions. So I stored my newly purchased treasures in a safe place. They would bring me a tidy profit. I could sleep well…

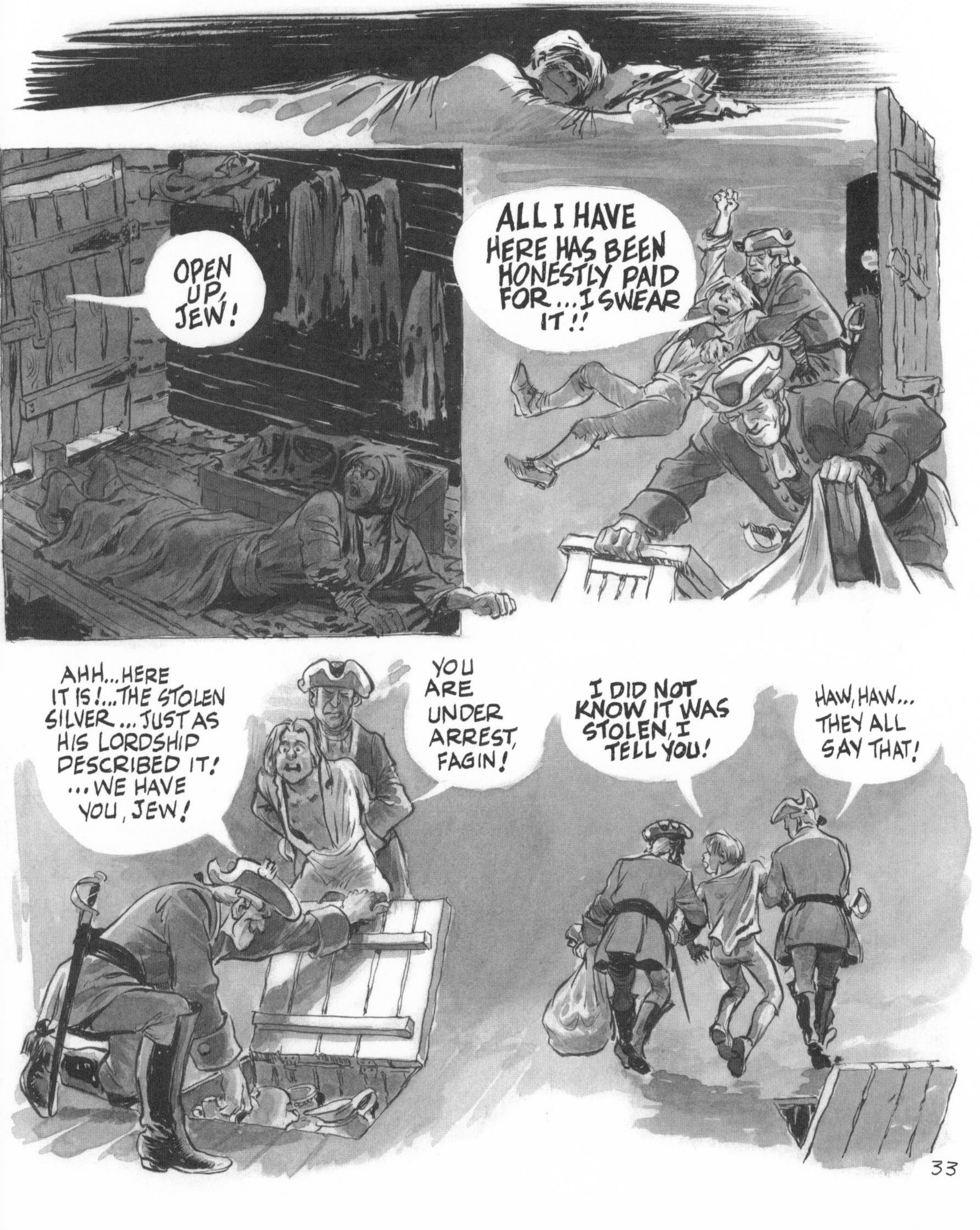
OPEN UP, JEW!
ALL I HAVE HERE HAS BEEN HONESTLY PAID FOR... I SWEAR IT!!
AHH... HERE IT IS!... THE STOLEN SILVER... JUST AS HIS LORDSHIP DESCRIBED IT! ...WE HAVE YOU, JEW!
YOU ARE UNDER ARREST, FAGIN!
I DID NOT KNOW IT WAS STOLEN, I TELL YOU!
HAW, HAW... THEY ALL SAY THAT!

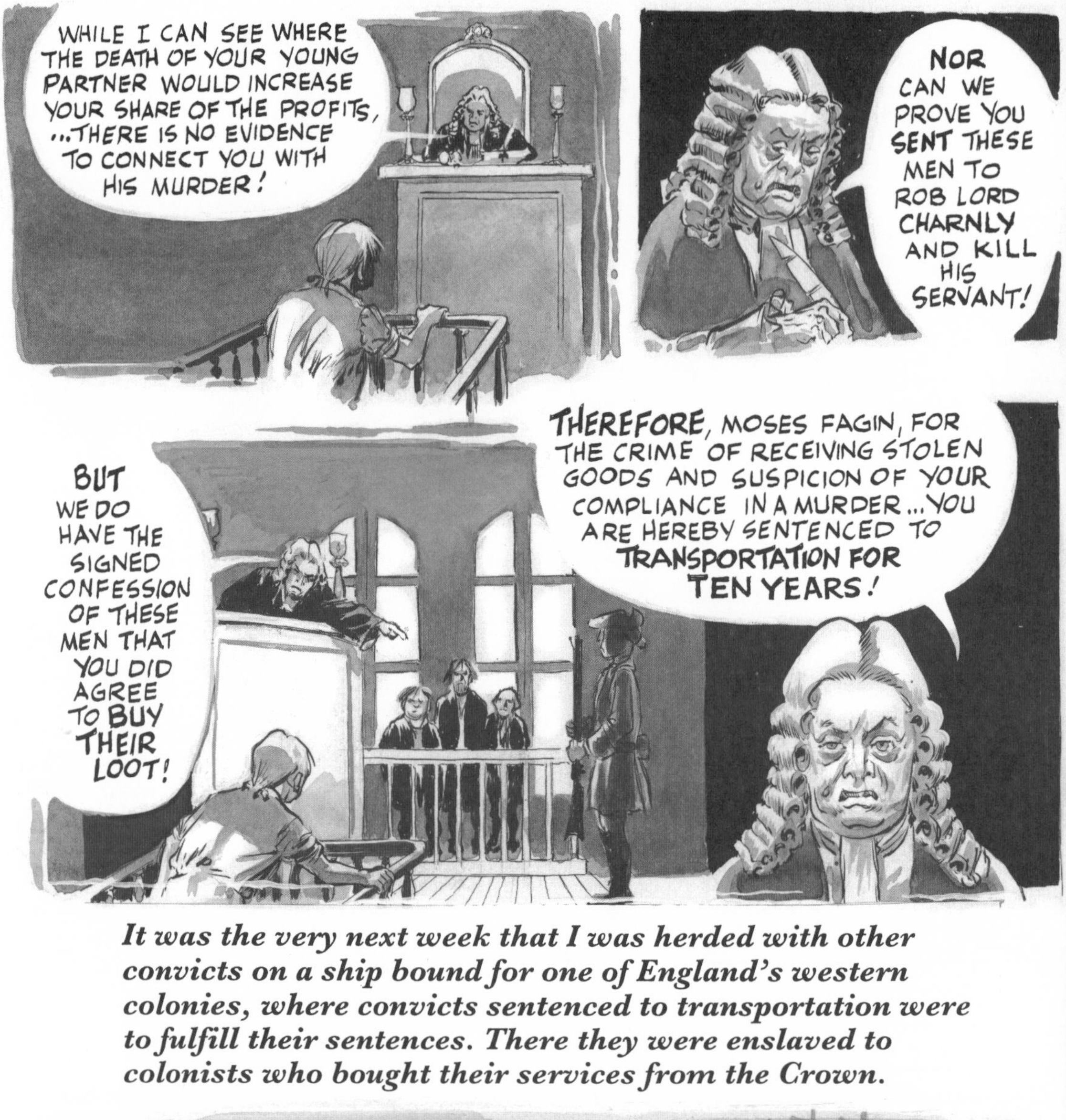
WHILE I CAN SEE WHERE THE DEATH OF YOUR YOUNG PARTNER WOULD INCREASE YOUR SHARE OF THE PROFITS, ...THERE IS NO EVIDENCE TO CONNECT YOU WITH HIS MURDER!
NOR CAN WE PROVE YOU SENT THESE MEN TO ROB LORD CHARNLY AND KILL HIS SERVANT!
BUT WE DO HAVE THE SIGNED CONFESSION OF THESE MEN THAT YOU DID AGREE TO BUY THEIR LOOT!
THEREFORE, MOSES FAGIN, FOR THE CRIME OF RECEIVING STOLEN GOODS AND SUSPICION OF YOUR COMPLIANCE IN A MURDER... YOU ARE HEREBY SENTENCED TO TRANSPORTATION FOR TEN YEARS!

It was the very next week that I was herded with other convicts on a ship bound for one of England's western colonies, where convicts sentenced to transportation were to fulfill their sentences. There they were enslaved to colonists who bought their services from the Crown.

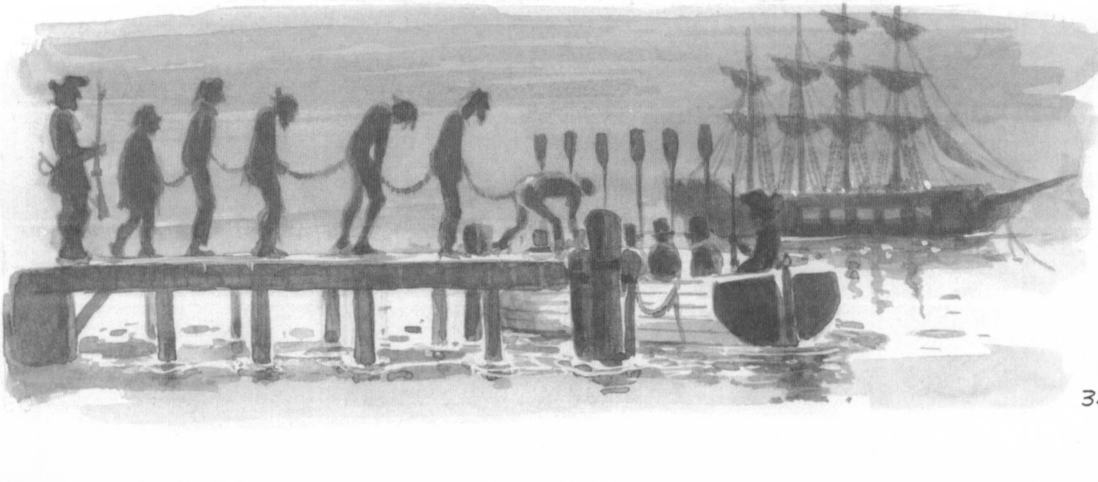

In the penal colony I was "bought" by a plantation owner, and for a year I was part of a gang clearing a swamp. There was little to eat and hard work from dawn to dusk… but I knew how to find food.

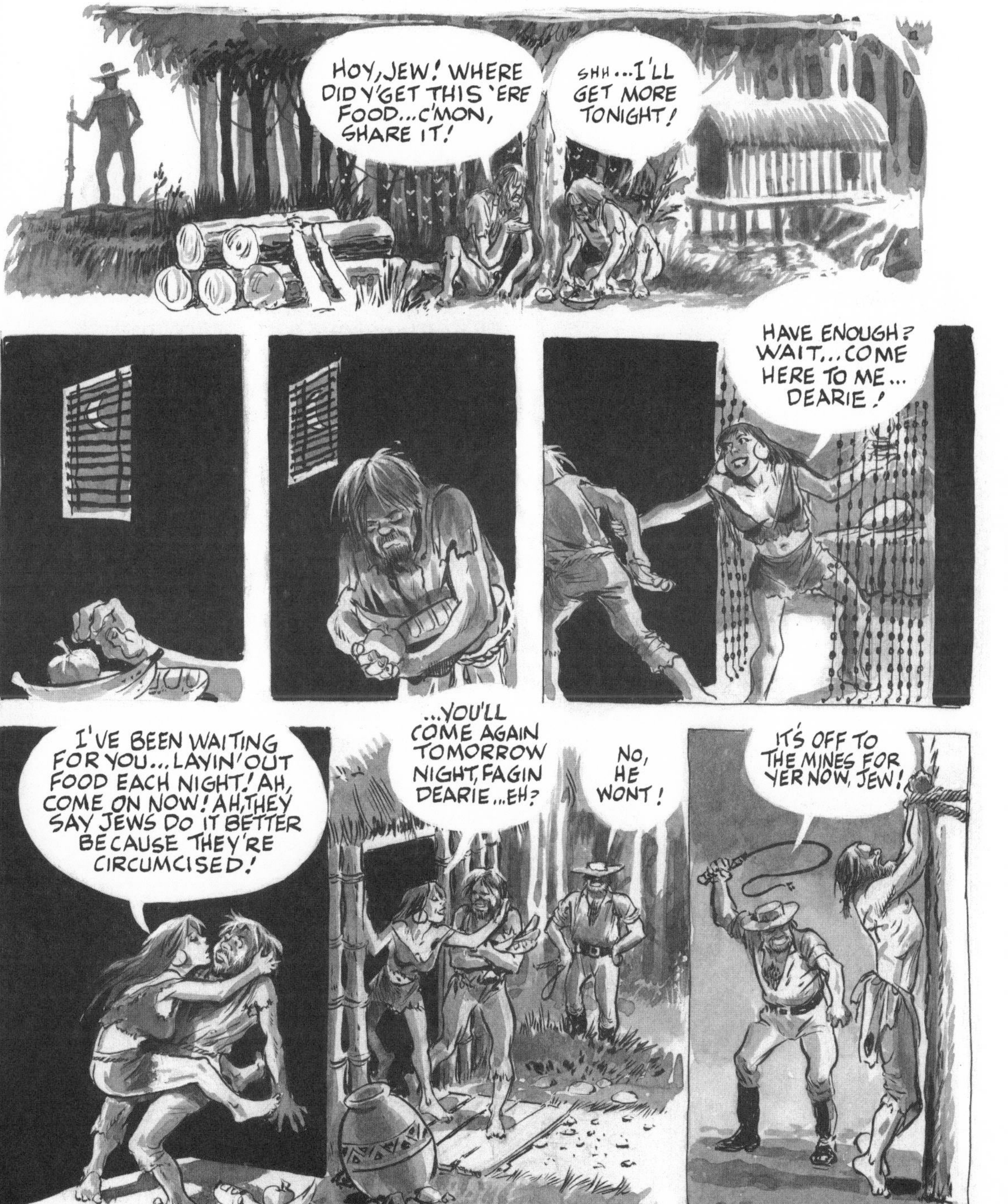

HOY, JEW! WHERE DID Y'GET THIS 'ERE FOOD...C'MON, SHARE IT!
SHH...I'LL GET MORE TONIGHT!
HAVE ENOUGH? WAIT...COME HERE TO ME... DEARIE!
I'VE BEEN WAITING FOR YOU...LAYIN' OUT FOOD EACH NIGHT! AH, COME ON NOW! AH, THEY SAY JEWS DO IT BETTER BECAUSE THEY'RE CIRCUMCISED!
...YOU'LL COME AGAIN TOMORROW NIGHT, FAGIN DEARIE...EH?
NO, HE WONT!
IT'S OFF TO THE MINES FOR YER NOW, JEW!

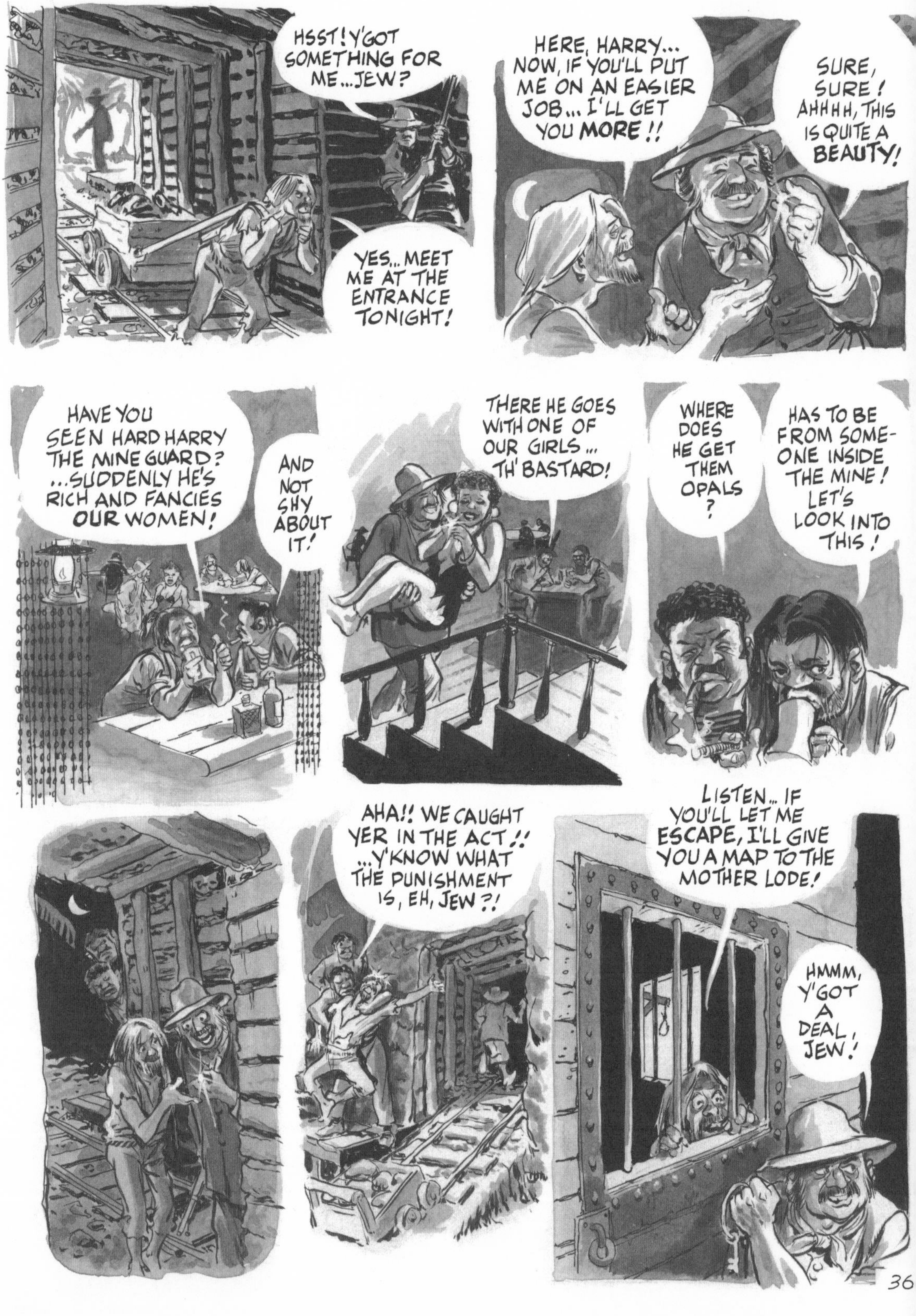
HSST! Y'GOT SOMETHING FOR ME...JEW?
YES... MEET ME AT THE ENTRANCE TONIGHT!
HERE, HARRY... NOW, IF YOU'LL PUT ME ON AN EASIER JOB... I'LL GET YOU MORE!!
SURE, SURE! AHHHH, THIS IS QUITE A BEAUTY!
HAVE YOU SEEN HARD HARRY THE MINE GUARD? ...SUDDENLY HE'S RICH AND FANCIES OUR WOMEN!
AND NOT SHY ABOUT IT!
THERE HE GOES WITH ONE OF OUR GIRLS ... TH' BASTARD!
WHERE DOES HE GET THEM OPALS?
HAS TO BE FROM SOMEONE INSIDE THE MINE! LET'S LOOK INTO THIS!
AHA!! WE CAUGHT YER IN THE ACT!! ...Y'KNOW WHAT THE PUNISHMENT IS, EH, JEW?!
LISTEN... IF YOU'LL LET ME ESCAPE, I'LL GIVE YOU A MAP TO THE MOTHER LODE!
HMMM, Y'GOT A DEAL, JEW!

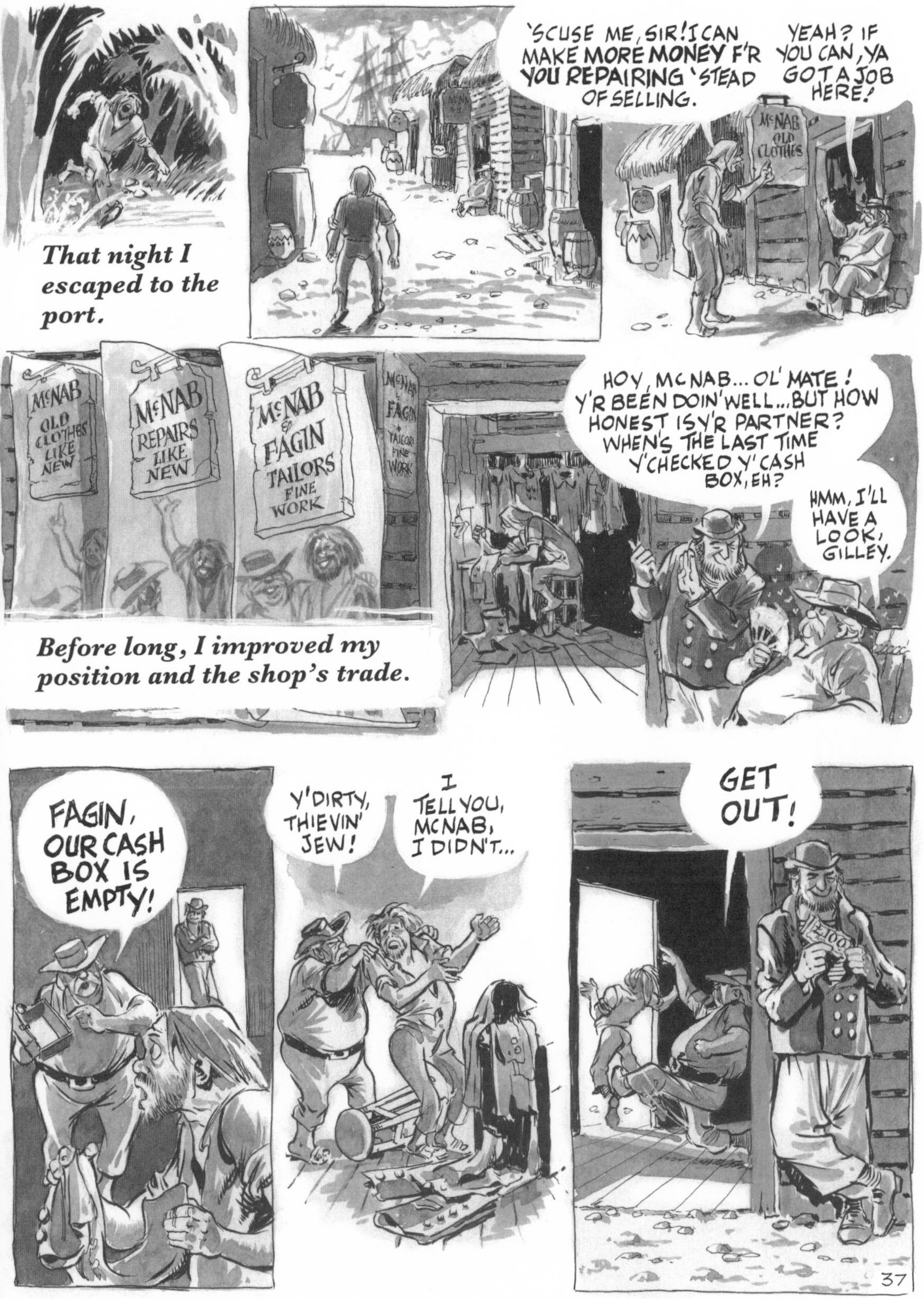
That night I escaped to the port.
'SCUSE ME, SIR! I CAN MAKE MORE MONEY F'R YOU REPAIRING 'STEAD OF SELLING.
YEAH? IF YOU CAN, YA GOT A JOB HERE!
McNAB OLD CLOTHES
McNAB OLD CLOTHES LIKE NEW
McNAB REPAIRS LIKE NEW
McNAB & FAGIN TAILORS FINE WORK
McNAB & FAGIN TAILORS FINE WORK
Before long, I improved my position and the shop's trade.
HOY, MCNAB... OL' MATE! Y'R BEEN DOIN' WELL... BUT HOW HONEST IS Y'R PARTNER? WHEN'S THE LAST TIME Y'CHECKED Y' CASH BOX, EH?
HMM, I'LL HAVE A LOOK, GILLEY.
FAGIN, OUR CASH BOX IS EMPTY!
Y'DIRTY, THIEVIN' JEW!
I TELL YOU, MCNAB, I DIDN'T...
GET OUT!
£100

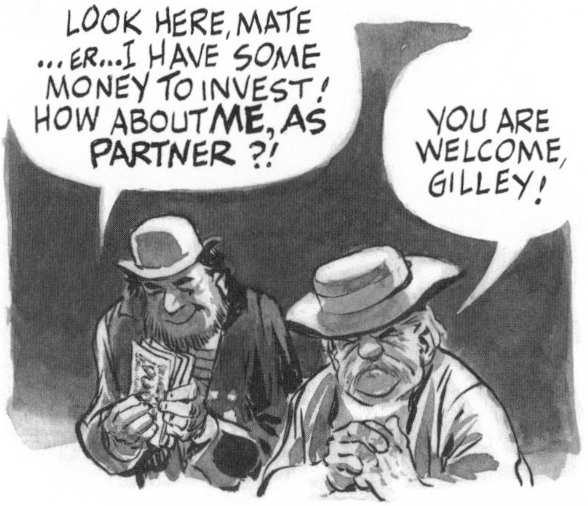
LOOK HERE, MATE ...ER...I HAVE SOME MONEY TO INVEST! HOW ABOUT ME, AS PARTNER ?!
YOU ARE WELCOME, GILLEY!

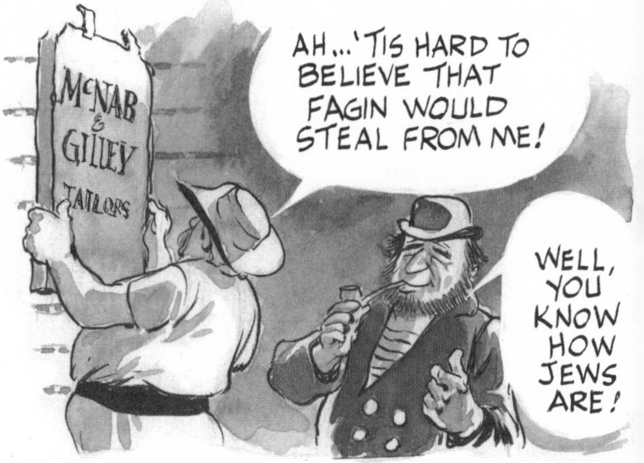
McNAB & GILLEY TAILORS
AH...'TIS HARD TO BELIEVE THAT FAGIN WOULD STEAL FROM ME!
WELL, YOU KNOW HOW JEWS ARE!

Once again I was at liberty, actually a prisoner-at-large. To avoid arrest I kept to the docks, hoping for any opportunity that would give me shelter.

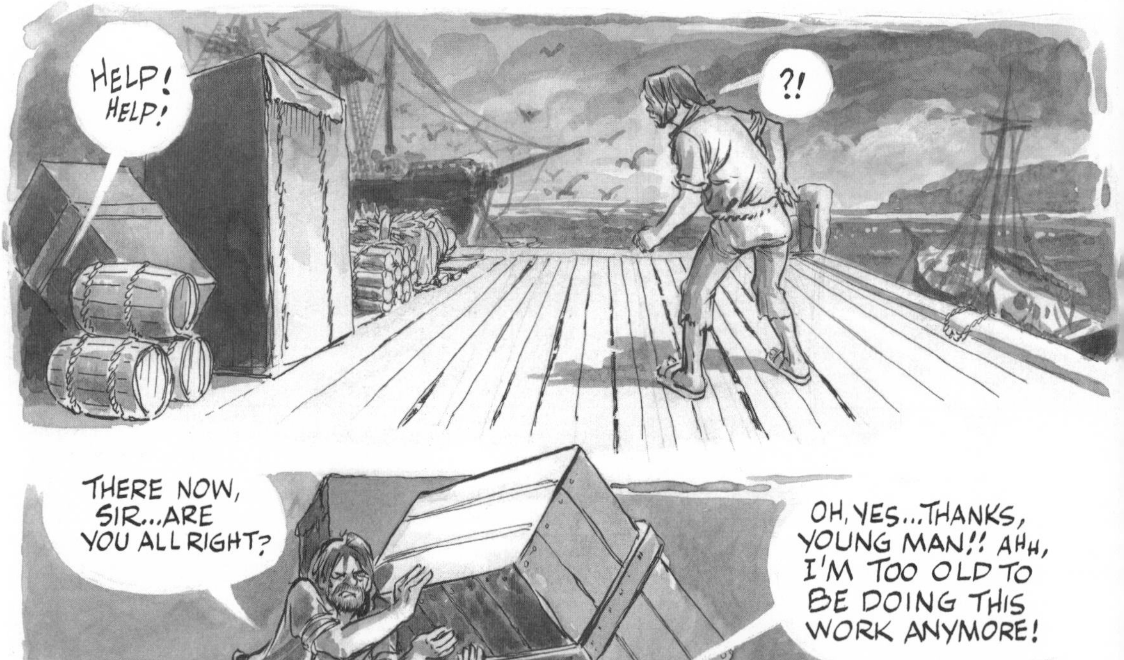
HELP! HELP!
?!

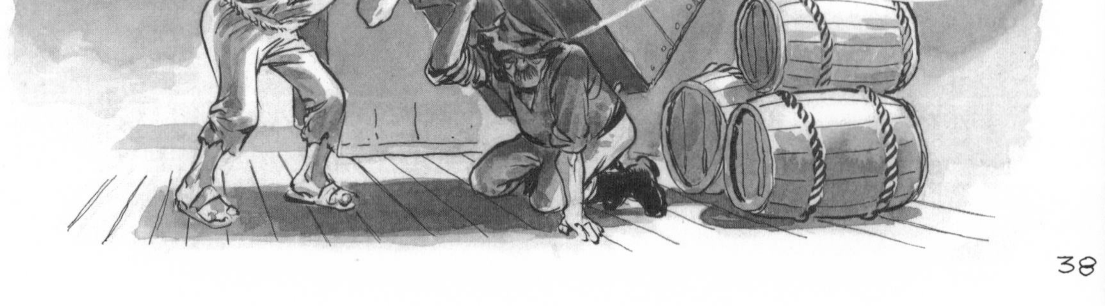
THERE NOW, SIR...ARE YOU ALL RIGHT?
OH, YES...THANKS, YOUNG MAN!! AHH, I'M TOO OLD TO BE DOING THIS WORK ANYMORE!

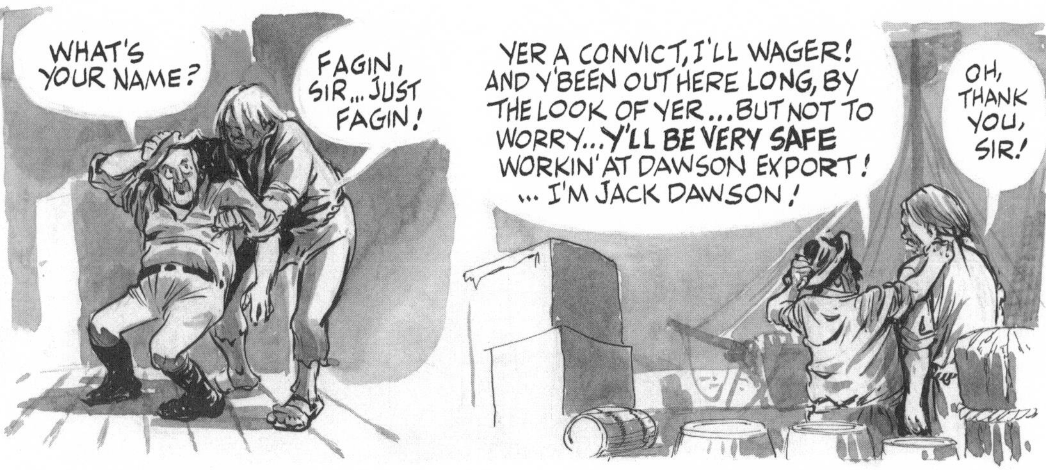
WHAT'S YOUR NAME?
FAGIN, SIR... JUST FAGIN!
YER A CONVICT, I'LL WAGER! AND Y'BEEN OUT HERE LONG, BY THE LOOK OF YER... BUT NOT TO WORRY... **Y'LL BE VERY SAFE** WORKIN' AT DAWSON EXPORT! ... I'M JACK DAWSON!
OH, THANK YOU, SIR!

Mr. Dawson was a good man, fair and kind, and he provided me with a safe haven. Meanwhile, my anger over the betrayal at McNab's kept boiling inside me, and before long I devised a plan to avenge myself.

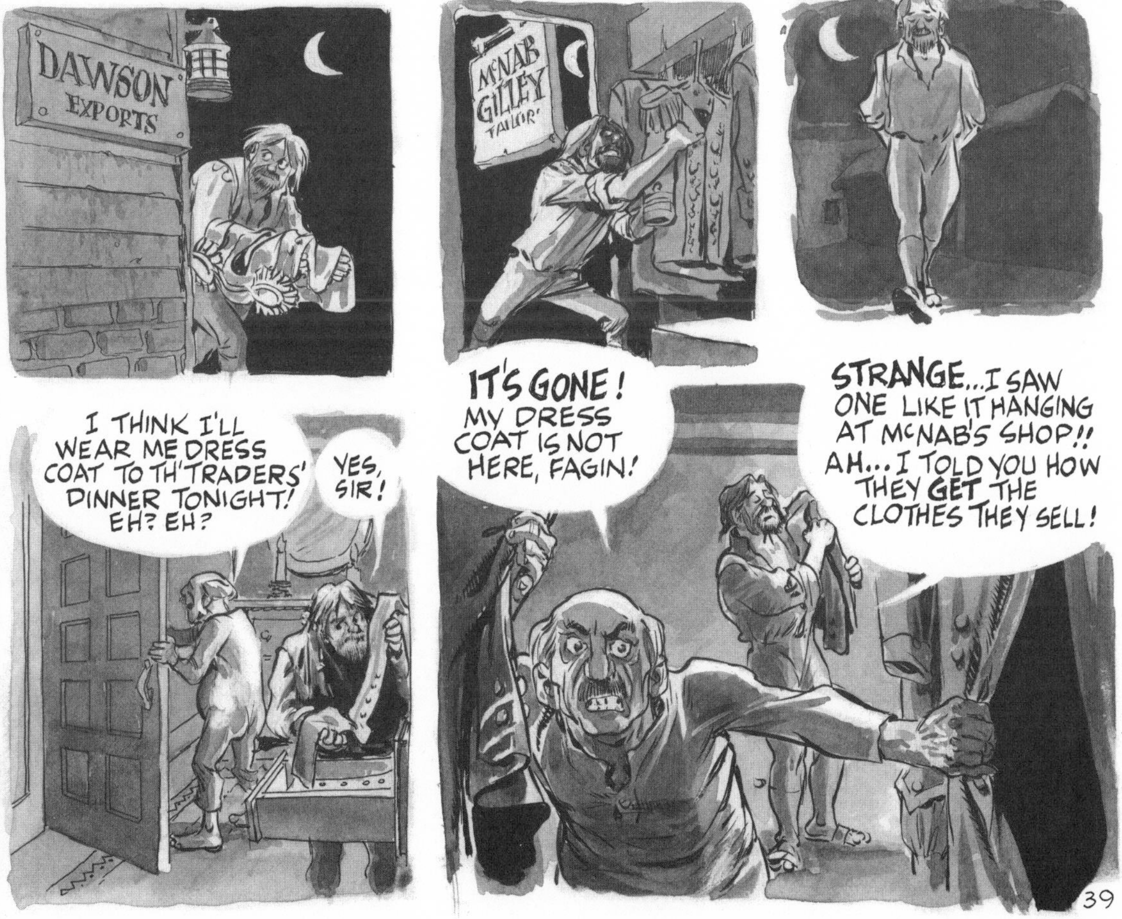
DAWSON EXPORTS
McNAB GILLEY TAILOR
I THINK I'LL WEAR ME DRESS COAT TO TH' TRADERS' DINNER TONIGHT! EH? EH?
YES, SIR!
IT'S GONE! MY DRESS COAT IS NOT HERE, FAGIN!
STRANGE... I SAW ONE LIKE IT HANGING AT McNAB'S SHOP!! AH... I TOLD YOU HOW THEY **GET** THE CLOTHES THEY SELL!

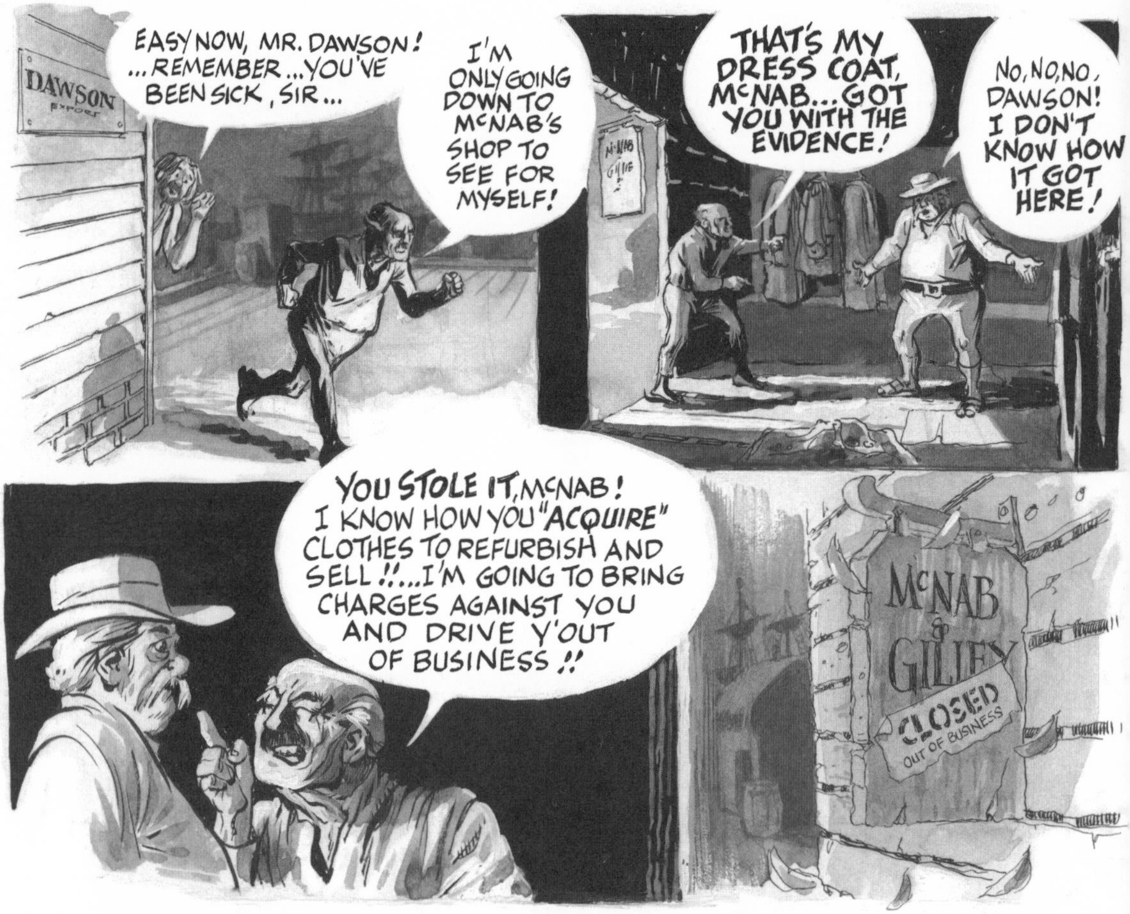
DAWSON
EXPORT
EASY NOW, MR. DAWSON! ...REMEMBER...YOU'VE BEEN SICK, SIR...
I'M ONLY GOING DOWN TO McNAB'S SHOP TO SEE FOR MYSELF!
THAT'S MY DRESS COAT, McNAB... GOT YOU WITH THE EVIDENCE!
NO, NO, NO, DAWSON! I DON'T KNOW HOW IT GOT HERE!
YOU STOLE IT, McNAB! I KNOW HOW YOU "ACQUIRE" CLOTHES TO REFURBISH AND SELL !!...I'M GOING TO BRING CHARGES AGAINST YOU AND DRIVE Y'OUT OF BUSINESS !!
McNAB & GILLEY
CLOSED
OUT OF BUSINESS

My plan worked perfectly... now at last I had a chance to establish myself. It was possible for convicts to do this if they had someone to "stake" them.

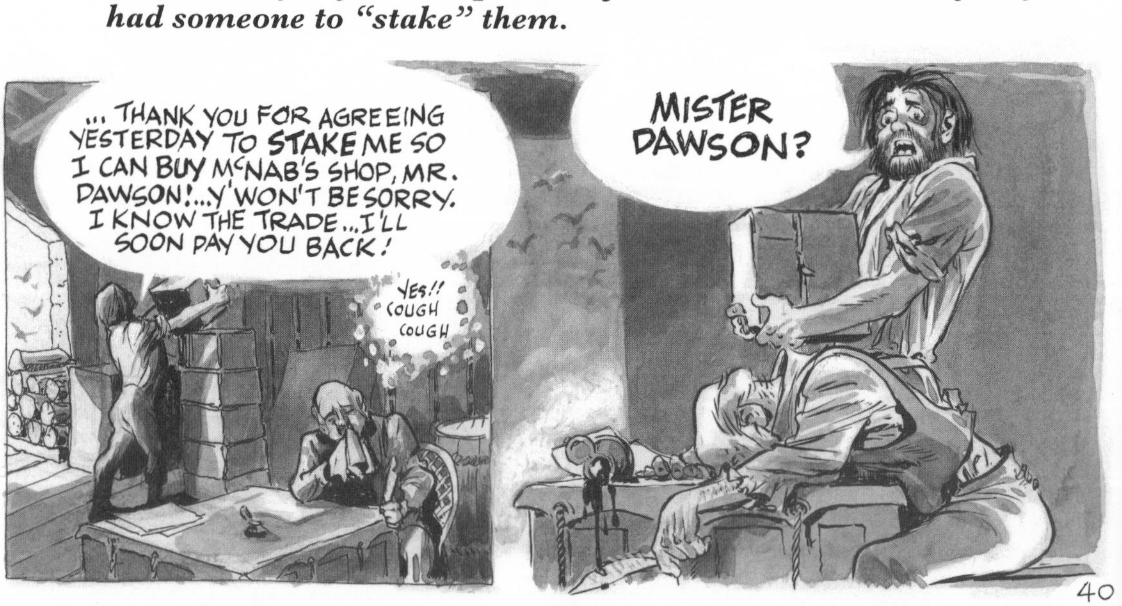
... THANK YOU FOR AGREEING YESTERDAY TO STAKE ME SO I CAN BUY McNAB'S SHOP, MR. DAWSON!...Y'WON'T BE SORRY. I KNOW THE TRADE...I'LL SOON PAY YOU BACK!
YES!! COUGH COUGH
MISTER DAWSON?

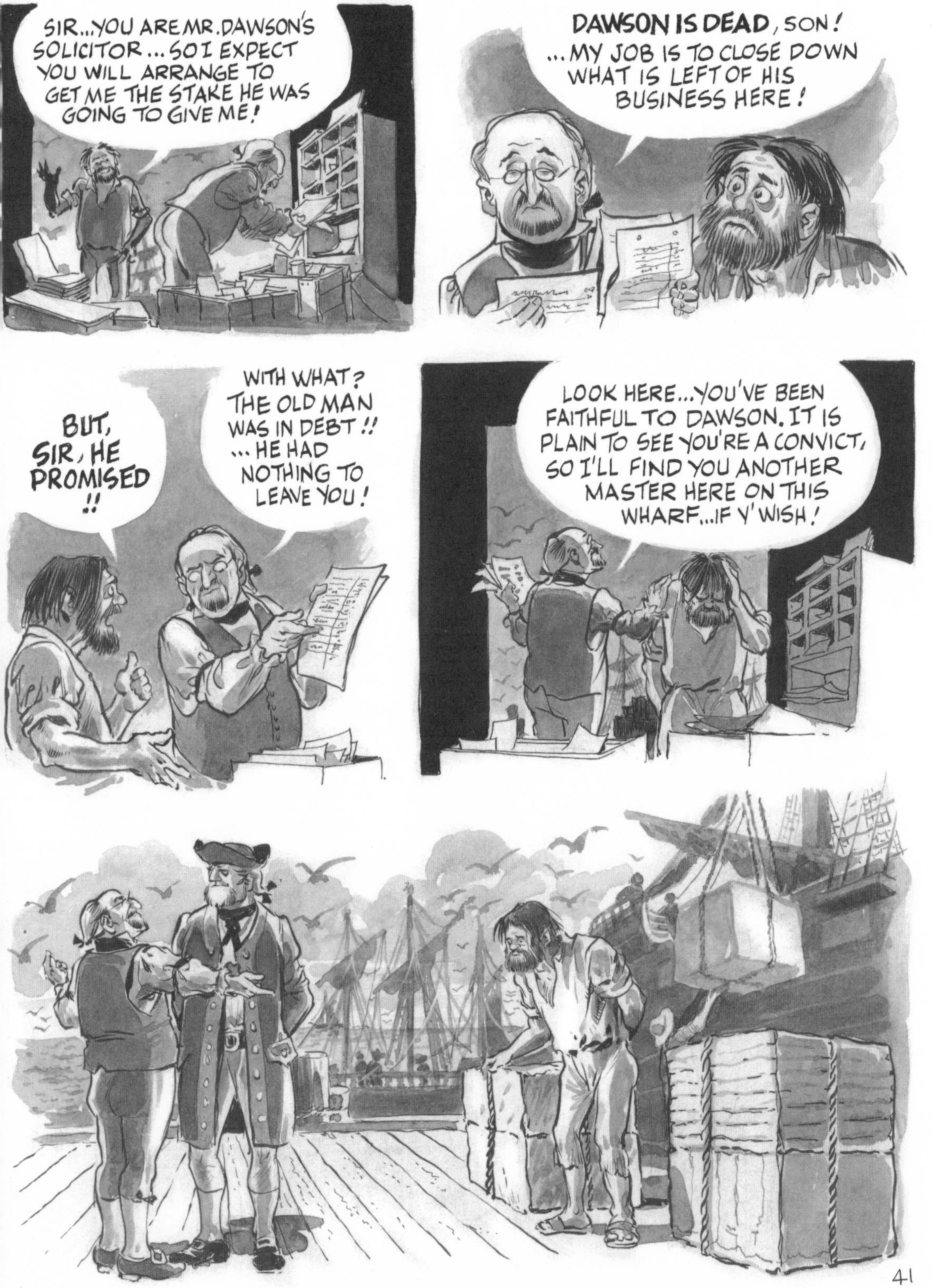
SIR...YOU ARE MR. DAWSON'S SOLICITOR... SO I EXPECT YOU WILL ARRANGE TO GET ME THE STAKE HE WAS GOING TO GIVE ME!
DAWSON IS DEAD, SON! ...MY JOB IS TO CLOSE DOWN WHAT IS LEFT OF HIS BUSINESS HERE!
BUT, SIR, HE PROMISED!!
WITH WHAT? THE OLD MAN WAS IN DEBT!! ...HE HAD NOTHING TO LEAVE YOU!
LOOK HERE...YOU'VE BEEN FAITHFUL TO DAWSON. IT IS PLAIN TO SEE YOU'RE A CONVICT, SO I'LL FIND YOU ANOTHER MASTER HERE ON THIS WHARF...IF Y' WISH!

So I remained there, working out the rest of my sentence, a slave indentured to an honest harbor master, until one day…

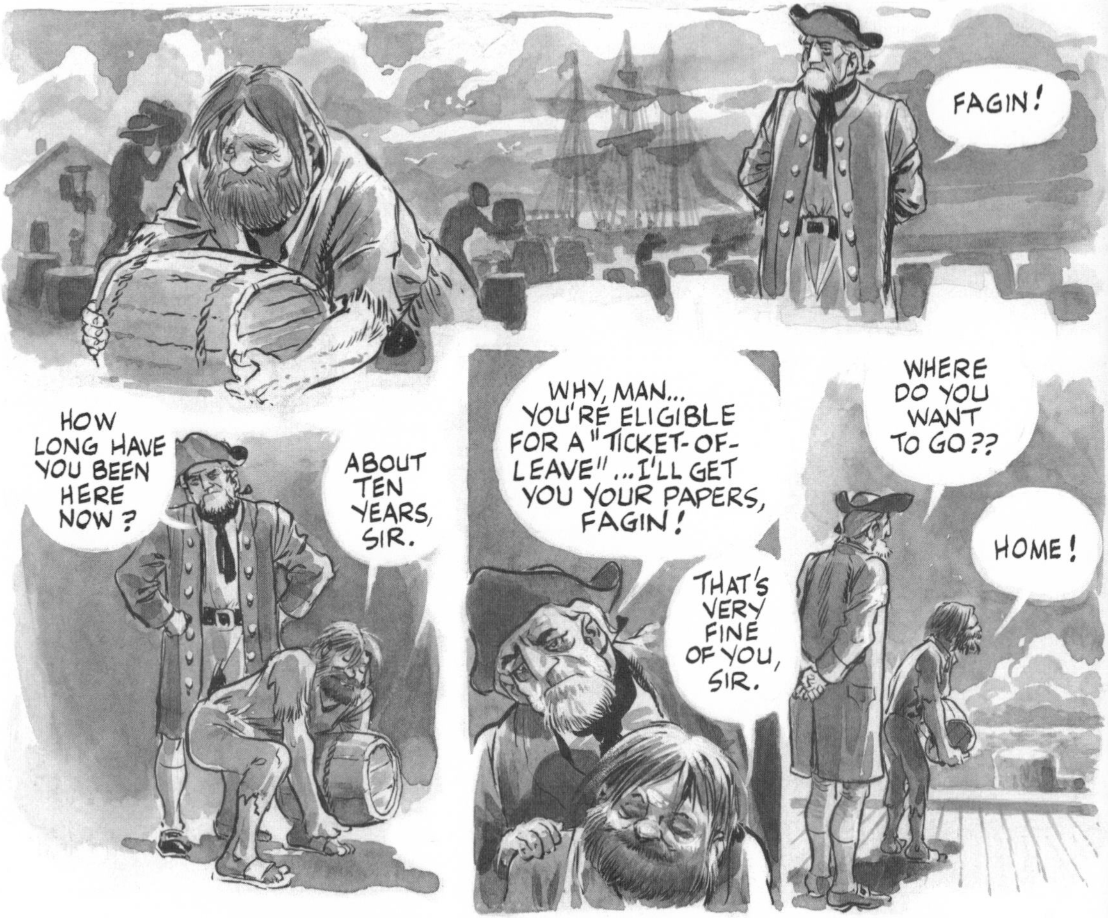

FAGIN!
HOW LONG HAVE YOU BEEN HERE NOW?
ABOUT TEN YEARS, SIR.
WHY, MAN... YOU'RE ELIGIBLE FOR A "TICKET-OF-LEAVE"... I'LL GET YOU YOUR PAPERS, FAGIN!
THAT'S VERY FINE OF YOU, SIR.
WHERE DO YOU WANT TO GO??
HOME!

And so it was, within the month, I returned to the world I really understood… London.

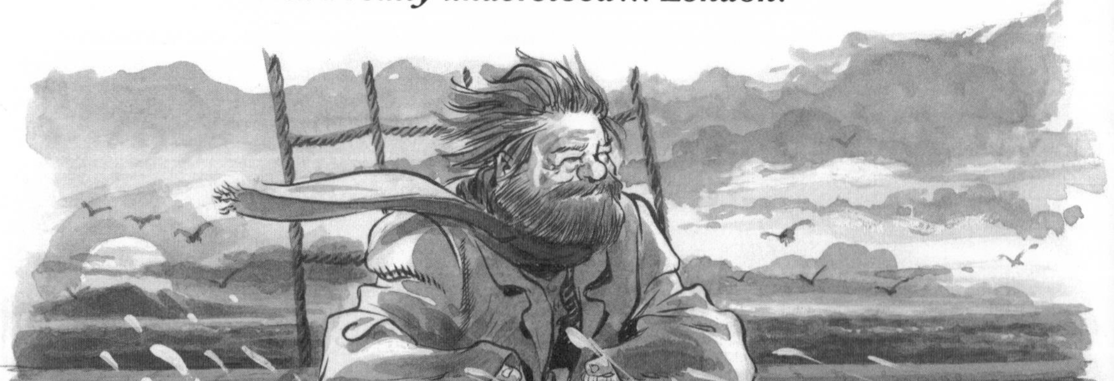

When at last I returned to London, I was aged beyond my years. Broken in body, in fragile health, I was in appearance a shuffling graybeard, the result of the horrors of penal life and imprisonment.

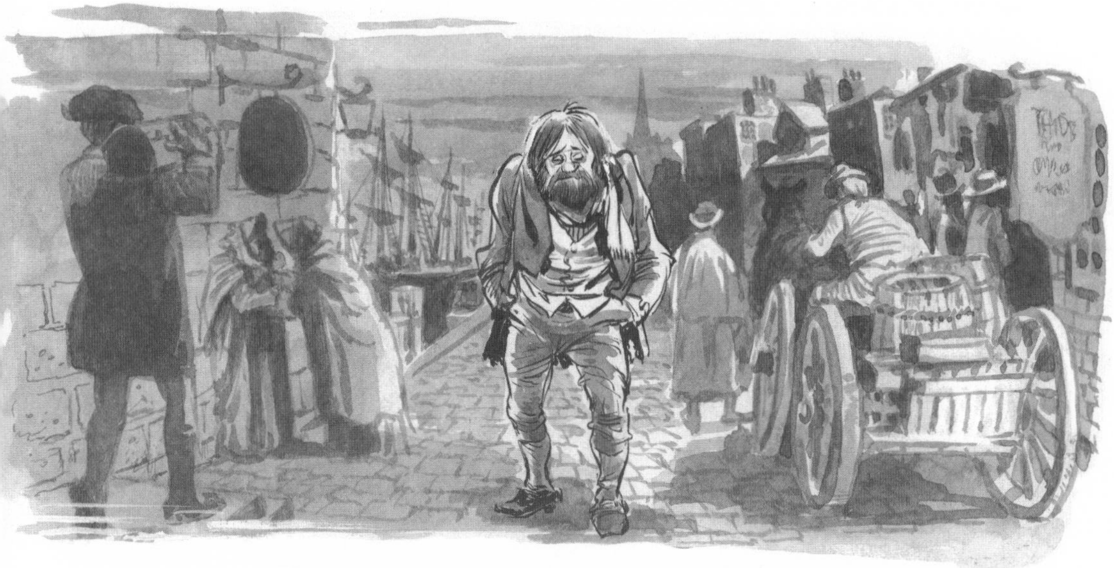

However, I still had my wits about me. Sharper than ever were my skills, which had been honed in the penal colonies.

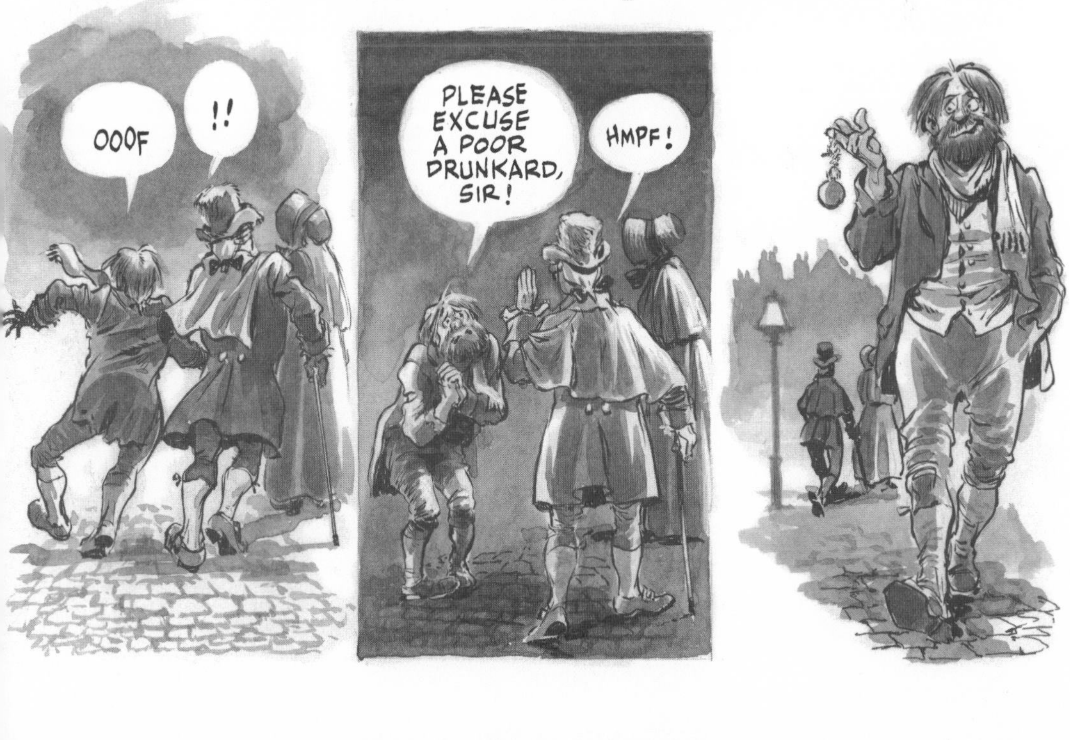
OOOF
!!
PLEASE EXCUSE A POOR DRUNKARD, SIR!
HMPF!

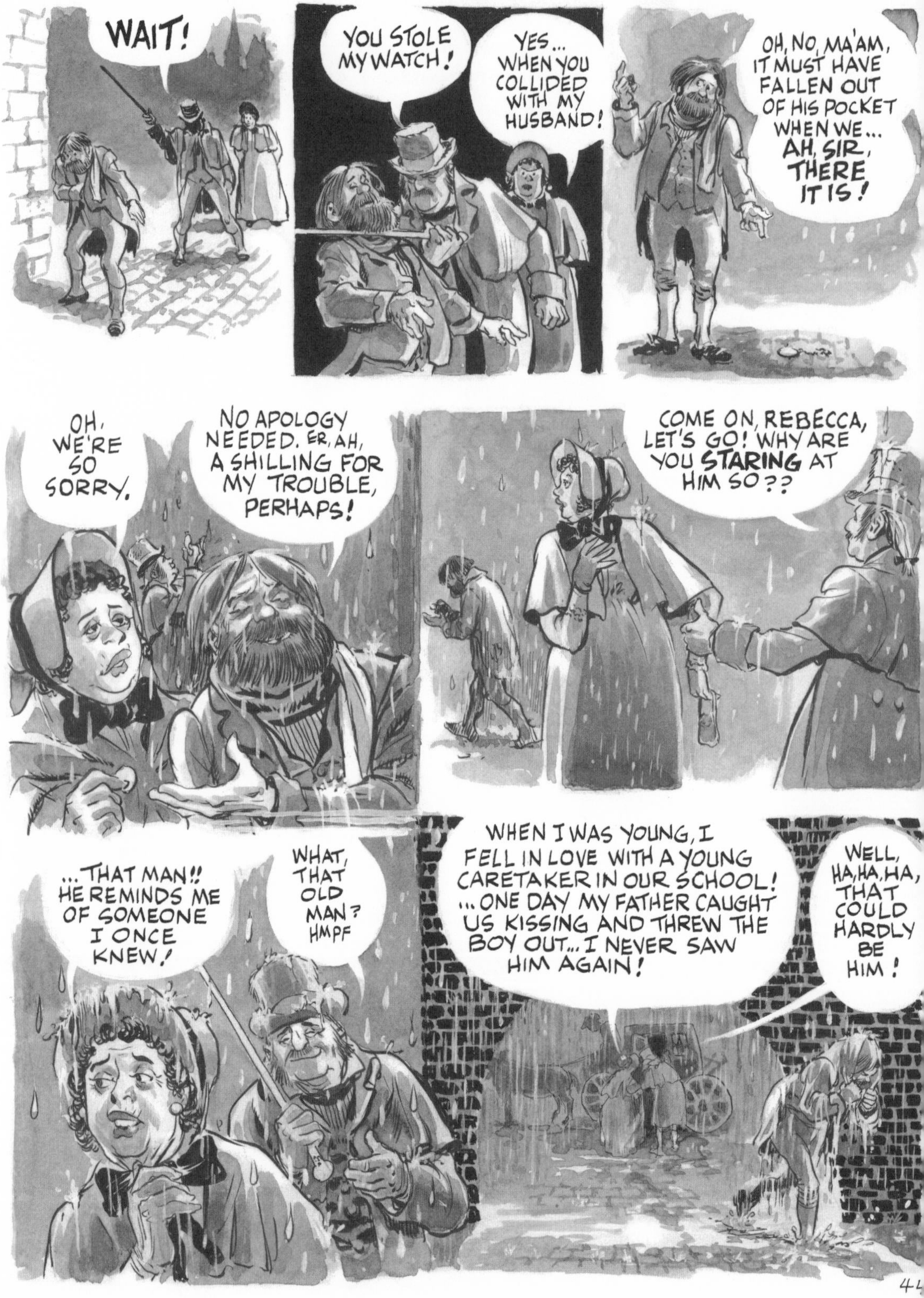
WAIT!
YOU STOLE MY WATCH!
YES... WHEN YOU COLLIDED WITH MY HUSBAND!
OH, NO, MA'AM, IT MUST HAVE FALLEN OUT OF HIS POCKET WHEN WE... AH, SIR, THERE IT IS!
OH. WE'RE SO SORRY.
NO APOLOGY NEEDED. ER, AH, A SHILLING FOR MY TROUBLE, PERHAPS!
COME ON, REBECCA, LET'S GO! WHY ARE YOU STARING AT HIM SO??
...THAT MAN!! HE REMINDS ME OF SOMEONE I ONCE KNEW!
WHAT, THAT OLD MAN? HMPF
WHEN I WAS YOUNG, I FELL IN LOVE WITH A YOUNG CARETAKER IN OUR SCHOOL! ...ONE DAY MY FATHER CAUGHT US KISSING AND THREW THE BOY OUT... I NEVER SAW HIM AGAIN!
WELL, HA, HA, HA, THAT COULD HARDLY BE HIM!

In London, I finally established myself. I was no longer naive; gone was the promise that fueled my hope of a grand future. I was what the urchins who worked for me would one day become.

Who knows, were I not a Jew... had I not lost opportunities or suffered the misfortune of imprisonment, or had I been able to stay in Mr. Salomon's employ, I might not be standing here in a knot of people in a London street, operating a street game with a new partner, a ruffian named Sikes.

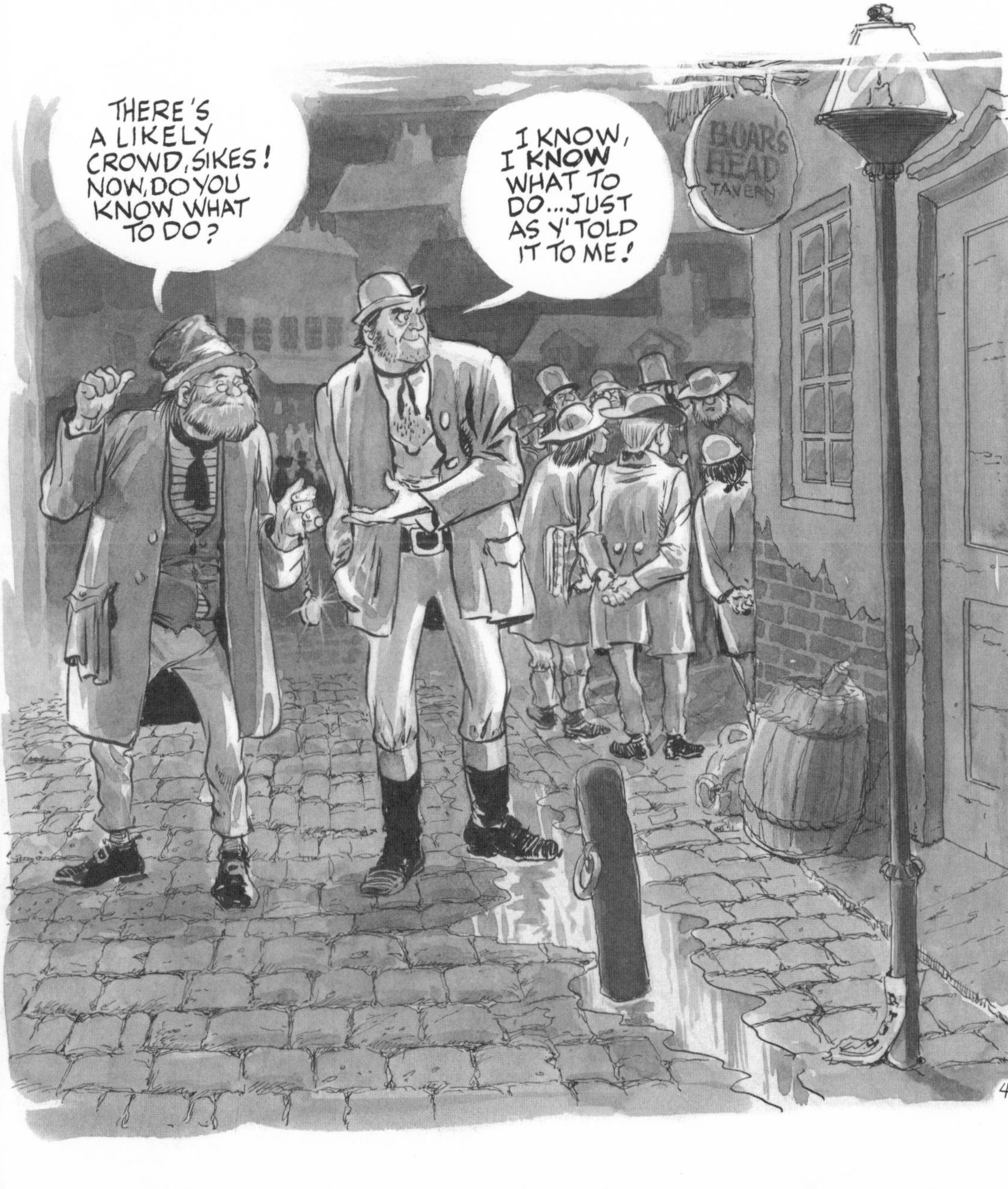

THERE'S A LIKELY CROWD, SIKES! NOW, DO YOU KNOW WHAT TO DO?
I KNOW, I KNOW WHAT TO DO... JUST AS Y' TOLD IT TO ME!
BOAR'S HEAD TAVERN

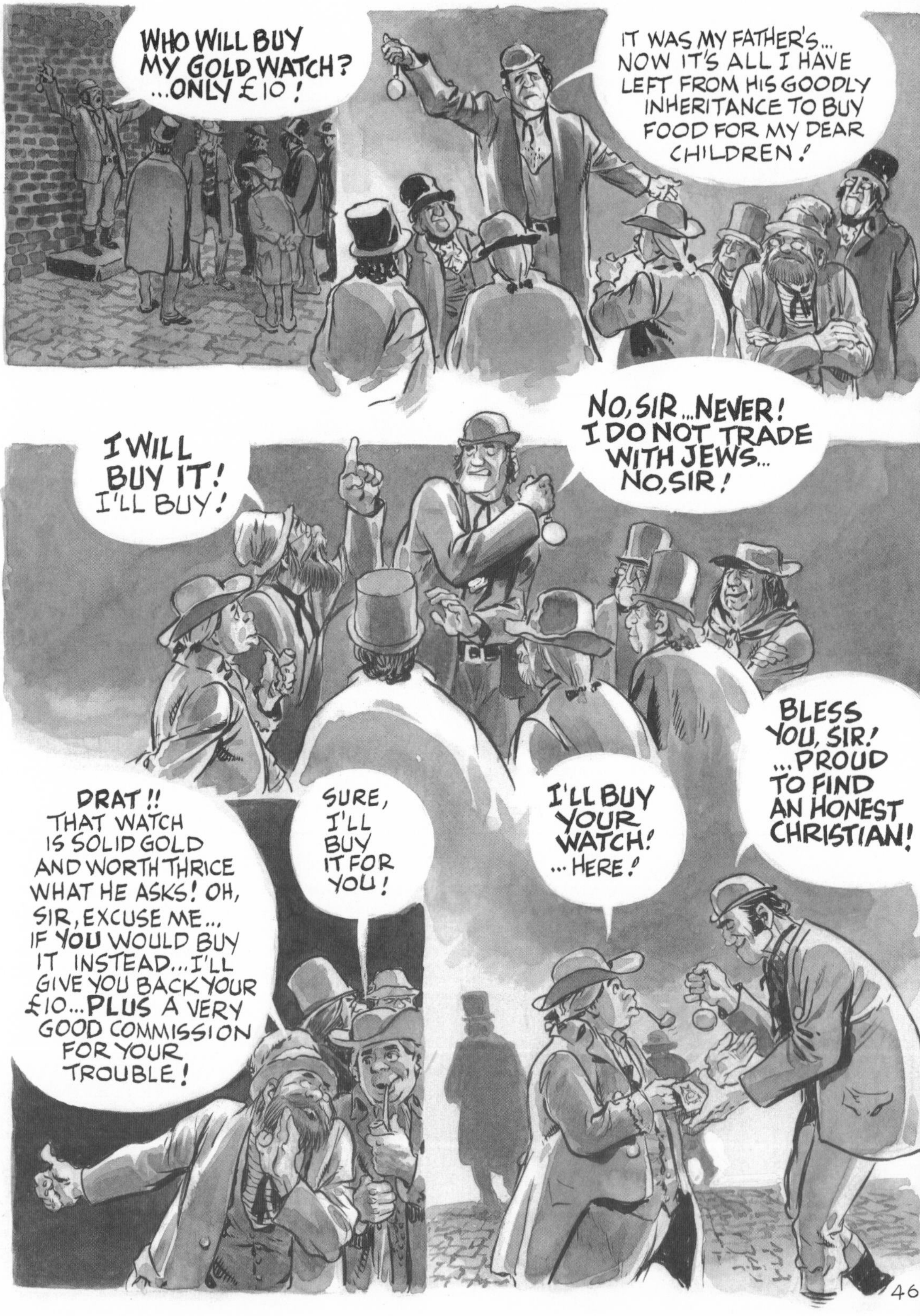
WHO WILL BUY MY GOLD WATCH? ...ONLY £10!
IT WAS MY FATHER'S... NOW IT'S ALL I HAVE LEFT FROM HIS GOODLY INHERITANCE TO BUY FOOD FOR MY DEAR CHILDREN!
I WILL BUY IT! I'LL BUY!
NO, SIR...NEVER! I DO NOT TRADE WITH JEWS... NO, SIR!
DRAT!! THAT WATCH IS SOLID GOLD AND WORTH THRICE WHAT HE ASKS! OH, SIR, EXCUSE ME... IF YOU WOULD BUY IT INSTEAD...I'LL GIVE YOU BACK YOUR £10...PLUS A VERY GOOD COMMISSION FOR YOUR TROUBLE!
SURE, I'LL BUY IT FOR YOU!
I'LL BUY YOUR WATCH! ...HERE!
BLESS YOU, SIR! ...PROUD TO FIND AN HONEST CHRISTIAN!

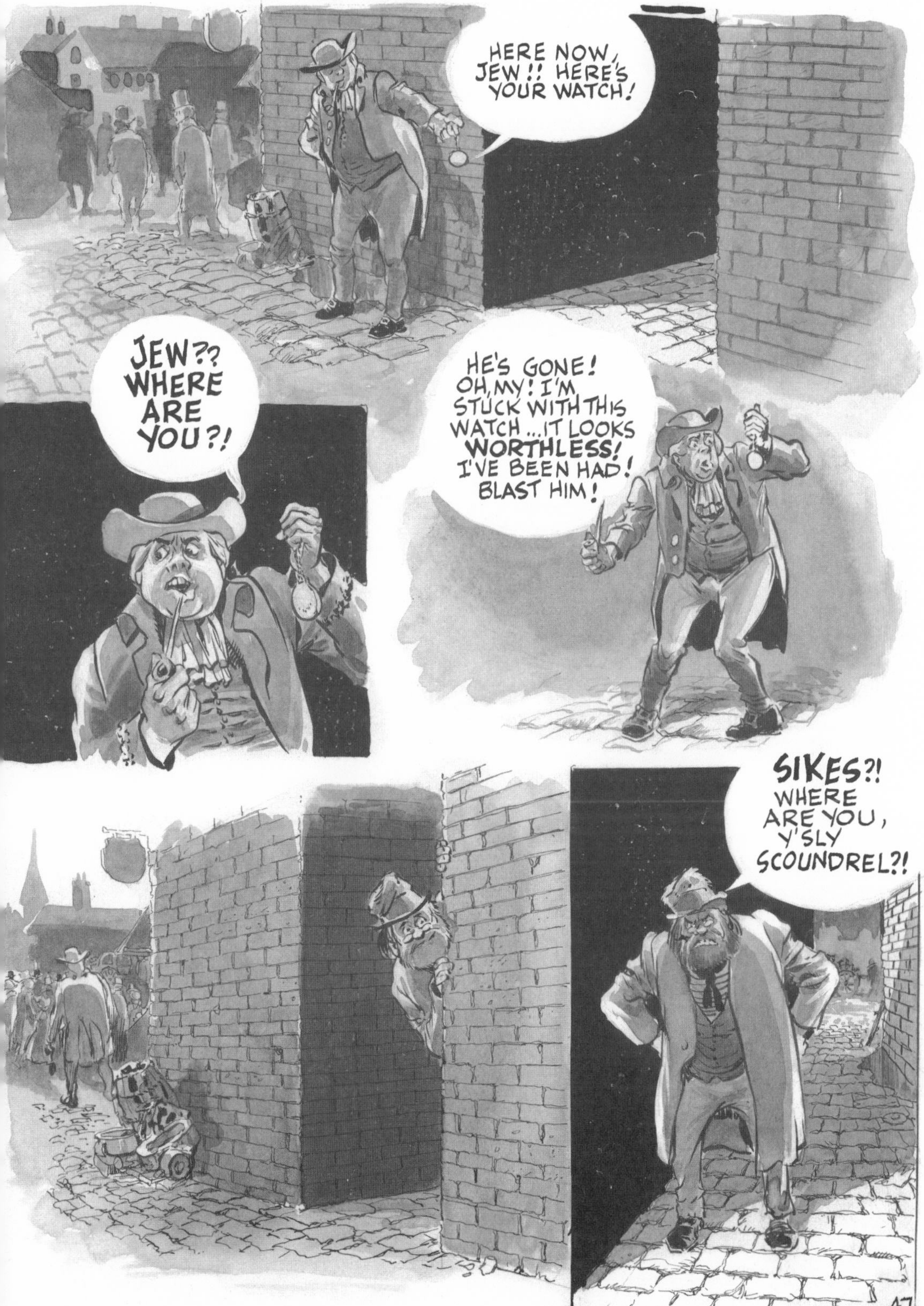
HERE NOW, JEW!! HERE'S YOUR WATCH!
JEW?? WHERE ARE YOU?!
HE'S GONE! OH, MY! I'M STUCK WITH THIS WATCH ...IT LOOKS WORTHLESS! I'VE BEEN HAD! BLAST HIM!
SIKES?! WHERE ARE YOU, Y'SLY SCOUNDREL?!

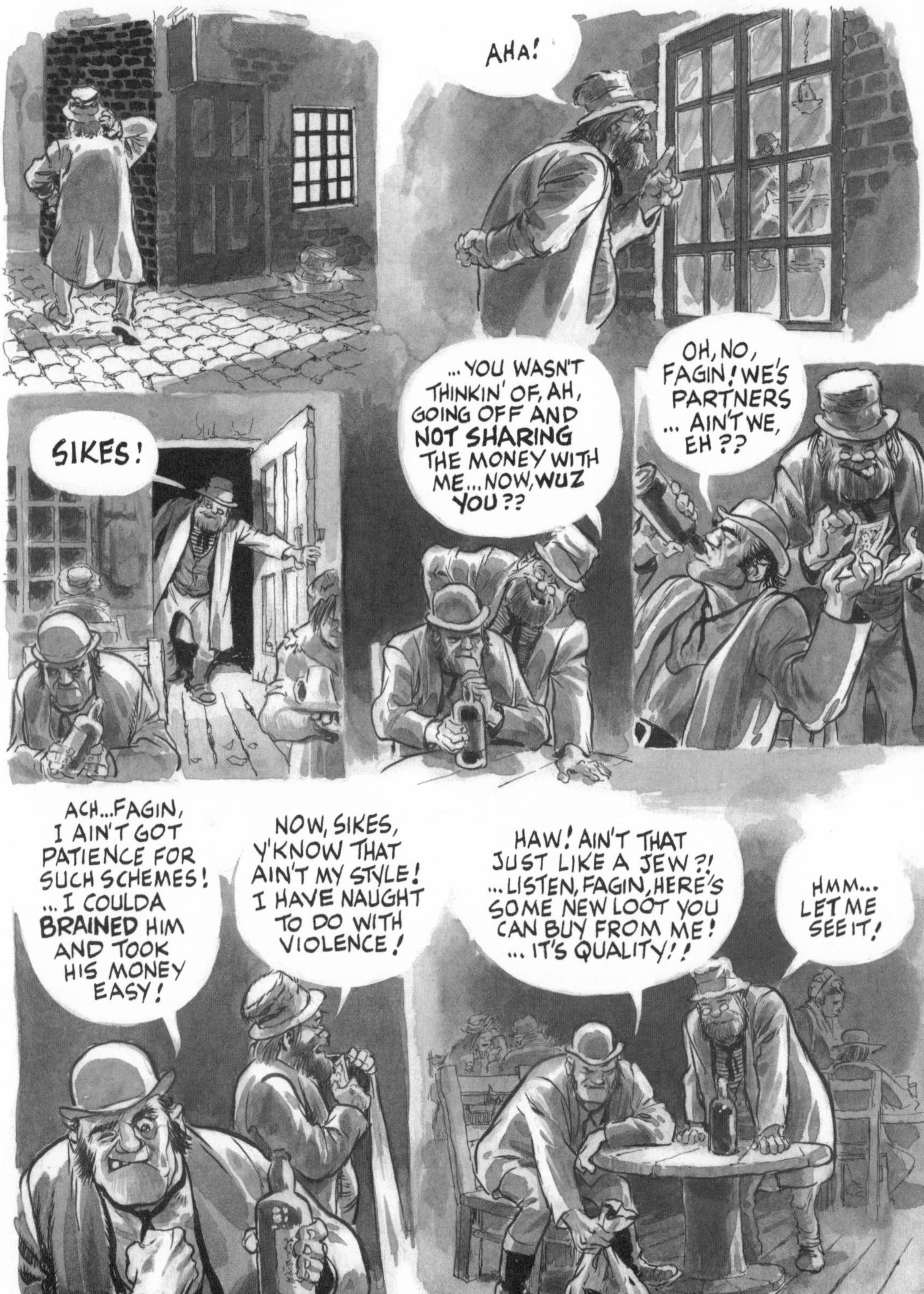
AHA!
SIKES!
... YOU WASN'T THINKIN' OF, AH, GOING OFF AND NOT SHARING THE MONEY WITH ME... NOW, WUZ YOU??
OH, NO, FAGIN! WE'S PARTNERS ... AIN'T WE, EH??
ACH... FAGIN, I AIN'T GOT PATIENCE FOR SUCH SCHEMES! ... I COULDA BRAINED HIM AND TOOK HIS MONEY EASY!
NOW, SIKES, Y'KNOW THAT AIN'T MY STYLE! I HAVE NAUGHT TO DO WITH VIOLENCE!
HAW! AIN'T THAT JUST LIKE A JEW?! ... LISTEN, FAGIN, HERE'S SOME NEW LOOT YOU CAN BUY FROM ME! ... IT'S QUALITY!!
HMM... LET ME SEE IT!

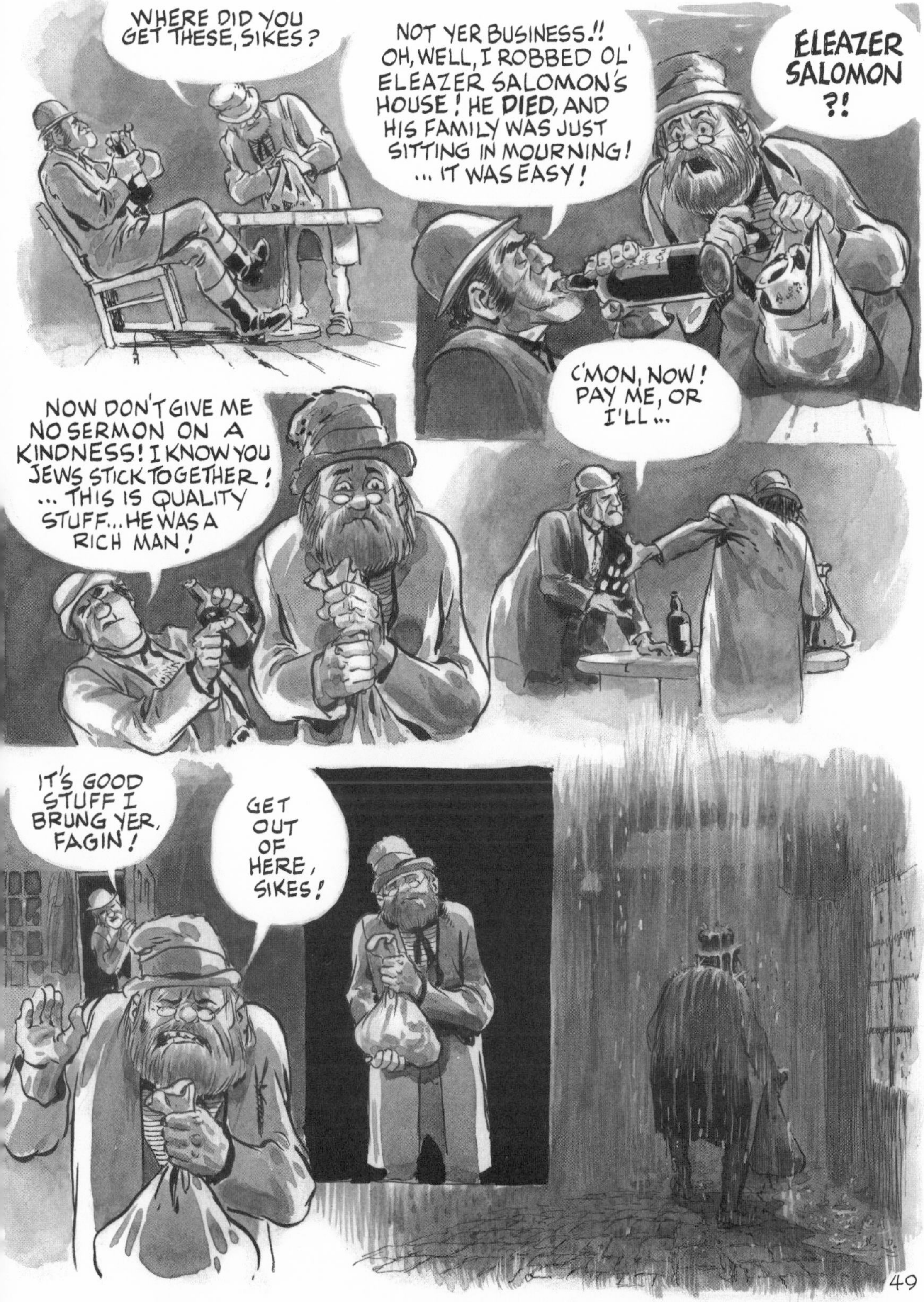
WHERE DID YOU GET THESE, SIKES?
NOT YER BUSINESS.!! OH, WELL, I ROBBED OL' ELEAZER SALOMON'S HOUSE! HE DIED, AND HIS FAMILY WAS JUST SITTING IN MOURNING! ... IT WAS EASY!
ELEAZER SALOMON ?!
NOW DON'T GIVE ME NO SERMON ON A KINDNESS! I KNOW YOU JEWS STICK TOGETHER! ... THIS IS QUALITY STUFF... HE WAS A RICH MAN!
C'MON, NOW! PAY ME, OR I'LL...
IT'S GOOD STUFF I BRUNG YER, FAGIN!
GET OUT OF HERE, SIKES!

I returned the loot to Mr. Salomon's home, where, for a few moments, I mourned over what my life... what I might have been, had Mr. Lopez not thrown me out of that school so many years ago.

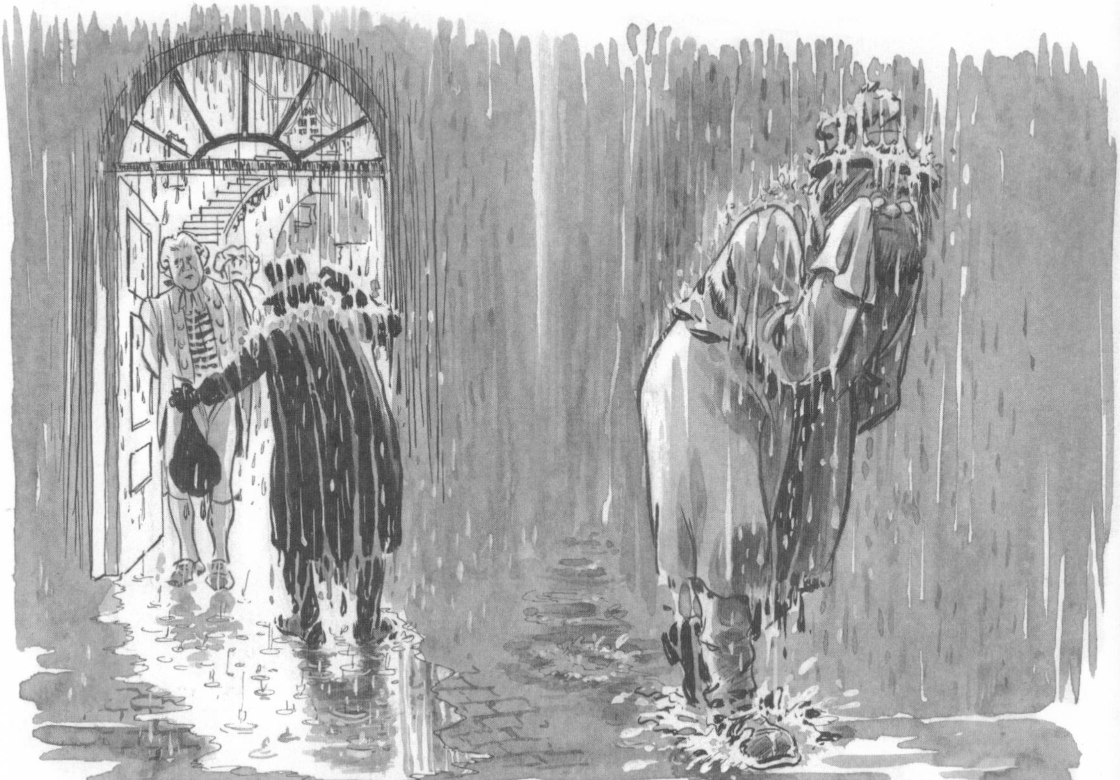

The following years were spent at the only trade I knew... buying and selling whatever came to hand. I became a haven for the ragged urchins of the street.

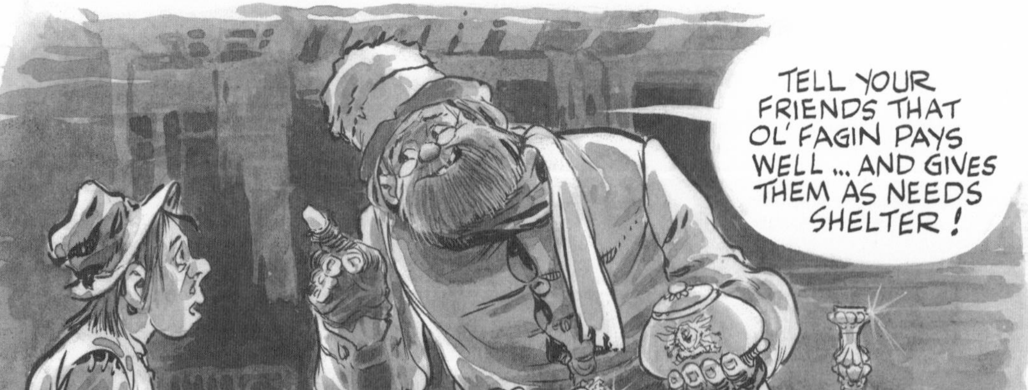
TELL YOUR FRIENDS THAT OL' FAGIN PAYS WELL ... AND GIVES THEM AS NEEDS SHELTER!

And my reputation among the little derelicts soon spread. I became known as a teacher of street arts...

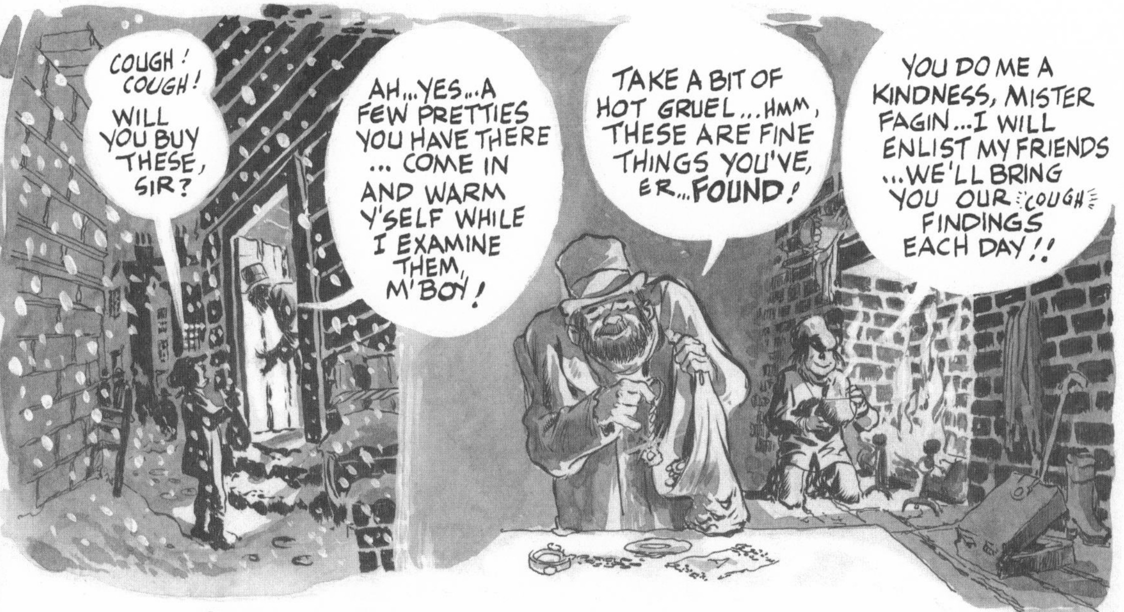

COUGH! COUGH! WILL YOU BUY THESE, SIR?
AH...YES...A FEW PRETTIES YOU HAVE THERE ... COME IN AND WARM Y'SELF WHILE I EXAMINE THEM, M'BOY!
TAKE A BIT OF HOT GRUEL ...HMM, THESE ARE FINE THINGS YOU'VE, ER...FOUND!
YOU DO ME A KINDNESS, MISTER FAGIN...I WILL ENLIST MY FRIENDS ...WE'LL BRING YOU OUR COUGH FINDINGS EACH DAY!!

Soon my dwelling, such as it was, filled with adept ragamuffins who provided me with an ample source of merchandise I could resell.

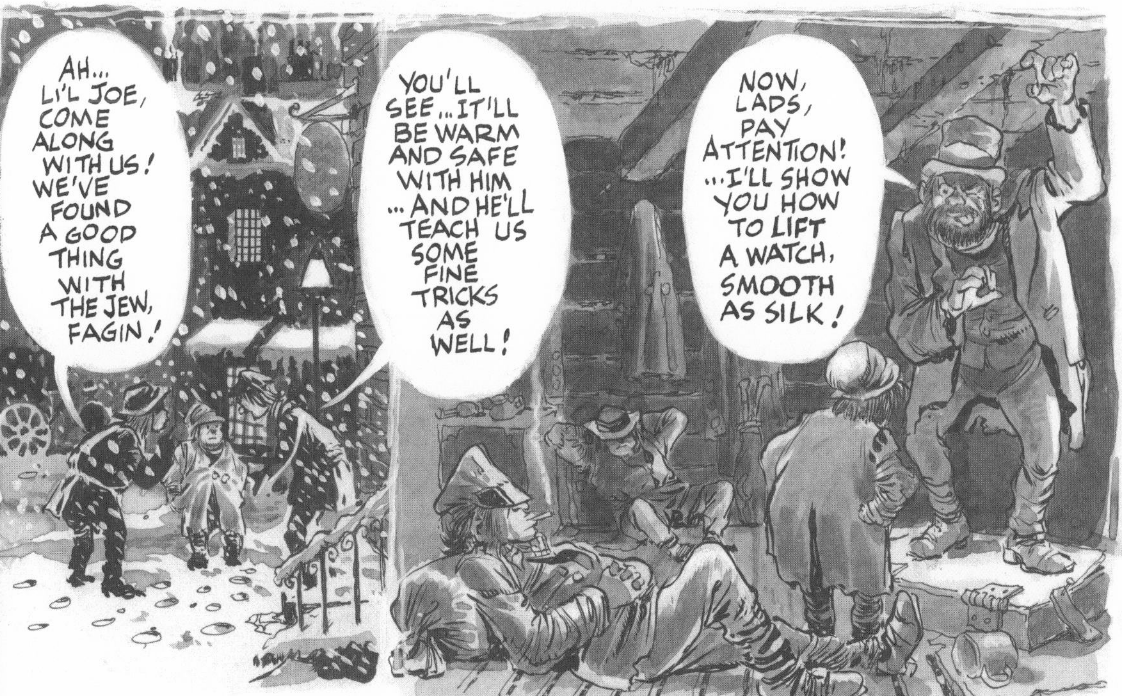

AH... LI'L JOE, COME ALONG WITH US! WE'VE FOUND A GOOD THING WITH THE JEW, FAGIN!
YOU'LL SEE...IT'LL BE WARM AND SAFE WITH HIM ...AND HE'LL TEACH US SOME FINE TRICKS AS WELL!
NOW, LADS, PAY ATTENTION! ...I'LL SHOW YOU HOW TO LIFT A WATCH, SMOOTH AS SILK!

I bought and sold what I could from whatever my boys brought me. Ah, but they required a bit of discipline.

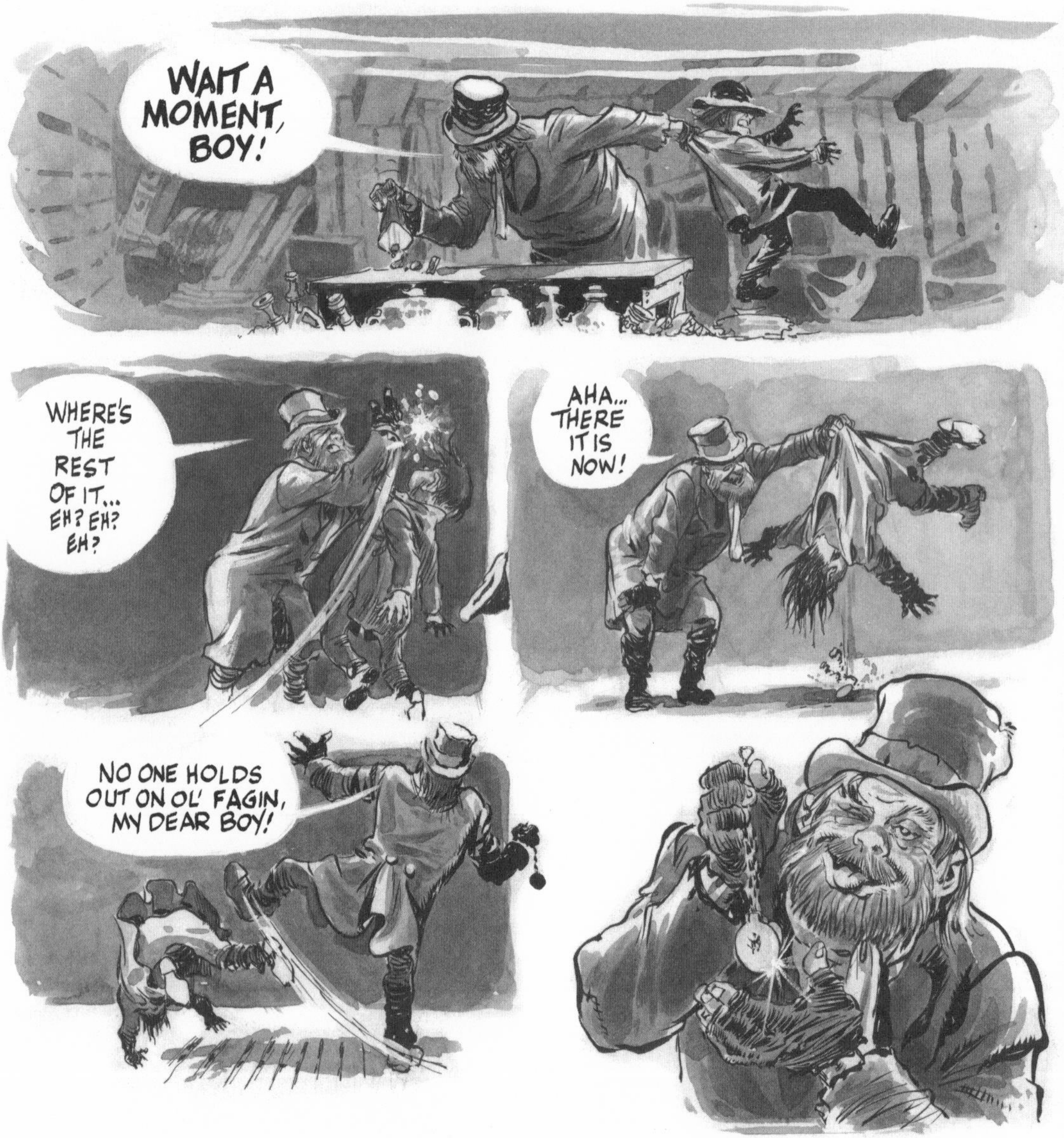
WAIT A MOMENT, BOY!
WHERE'S THE REST OF IT... EH? EH? EH?
AHA... THERE IT IS NOW!
NO ONE HOLDS OUT ON OL' FAGIN, MY DEAR BOY!

So the years went by. I never did prosper, nor was I able to advance beyond the grimy life on the streets of London. Still, I kept myself and my boys from the bitter refuge of workhouses.

It was in one of these houses of questionable charity that fate delivered a young companion for me in the last chapter of my life. He joined my "family" as usual, recruited by one of my steady boys. Years later, I learned of his origin from young Claypole, who was once employed with him at Sowerberry's. The rest came from hearsay and deduction. The boy was born out of grim circumstances not unusual for our society.

It was ten years ago. Late one evening a young woman appeared at the doorstep of one of these poorly maintained workhouses.

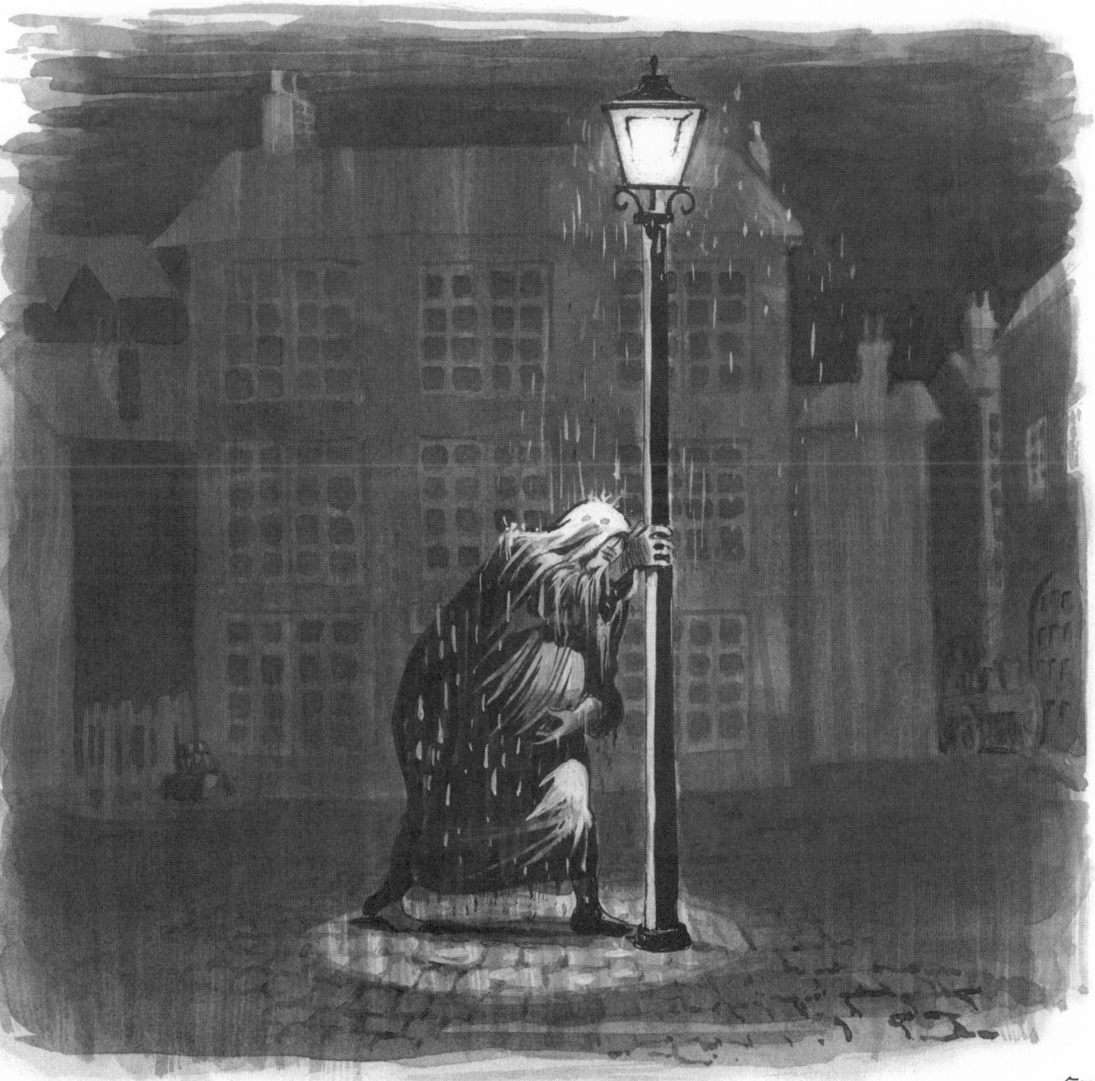

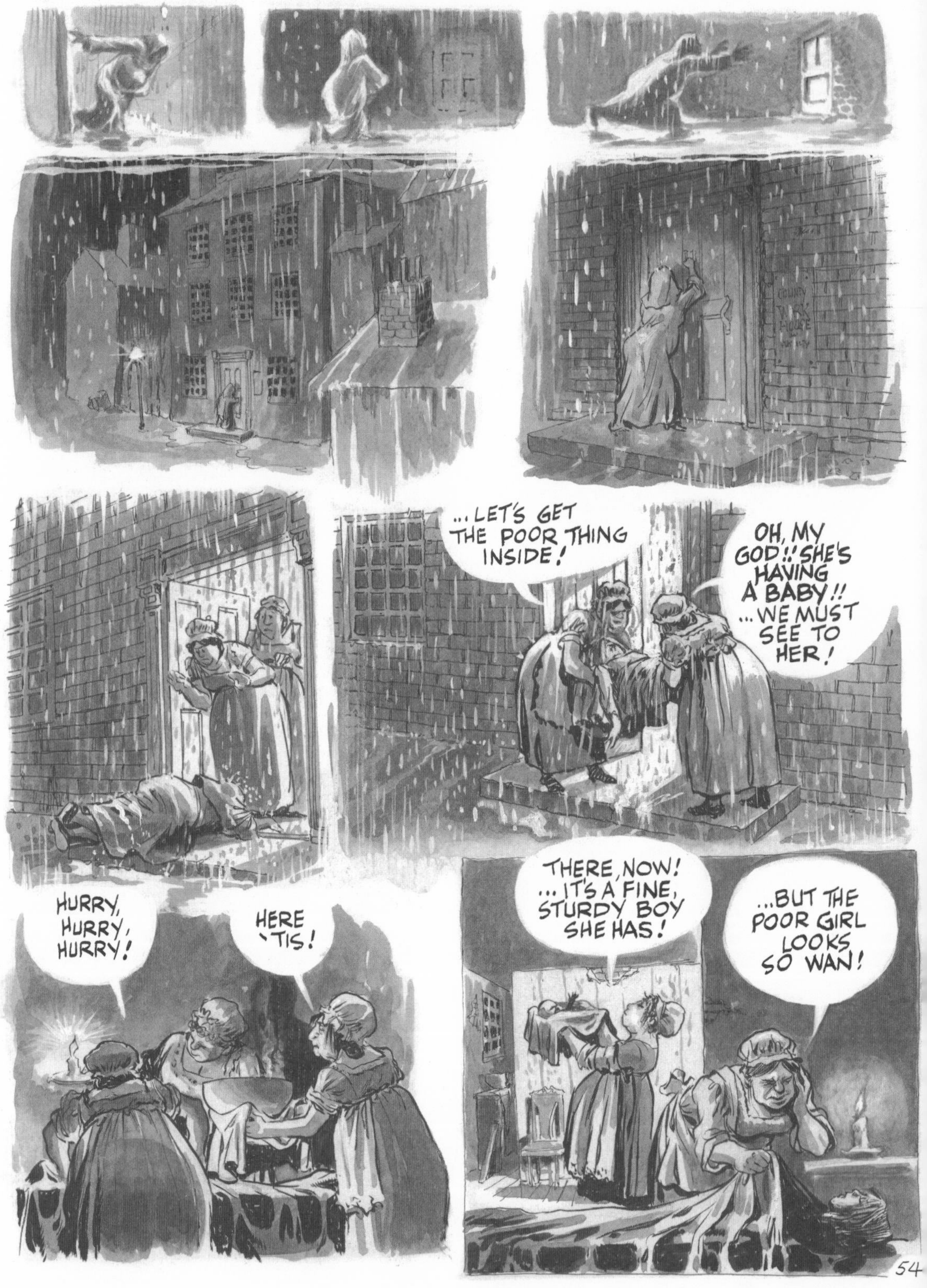
...LET'S GET THE POOR THING INSIDE!
OH, MY GOD!! SHE'S HAVING A BABY!! ...WE MUST SEE TO HER!
HURRY, HURRY, HURRY!
HERE 'TIS!
THERE, NOW! ... IT'S A FINE, STURDY BOY SHE HAS!
...BUT THE POOR GIRL LOOKS SO WAN!

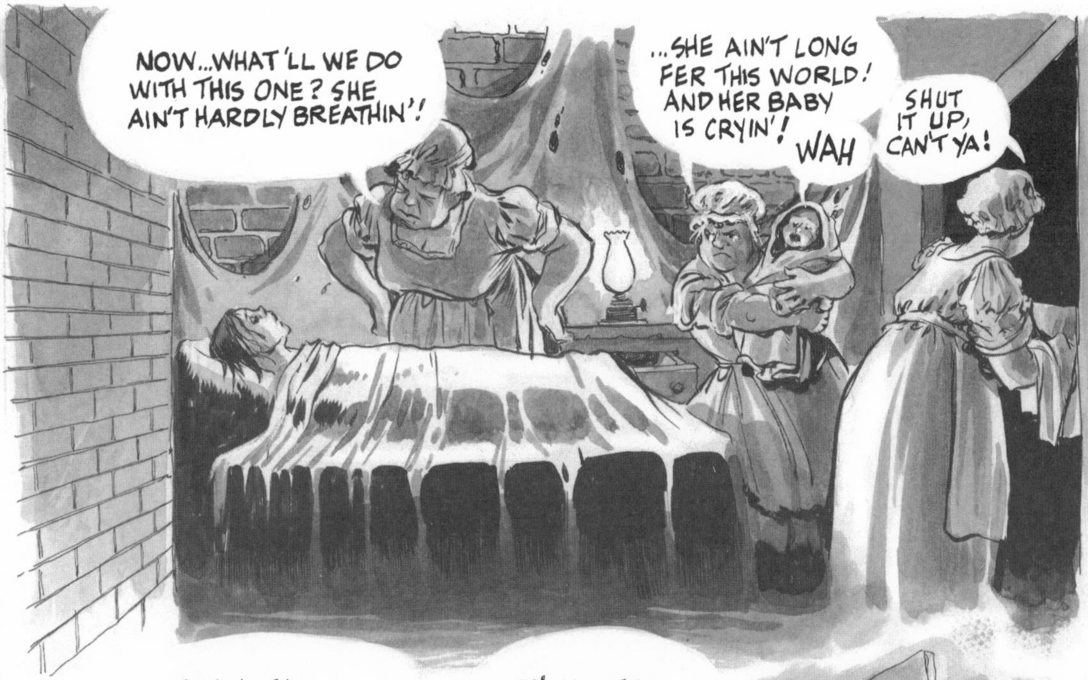
NOW...WHAT'LL WE DO WITH THIS ONE? SHE AIN'T HARDLY BREATHIN'!
...SHE AIN'T LONG FER THIS WORLD! AND HER BABY IS CRYIN'!
WAH
SHUT IT UP, CAN'T YA!

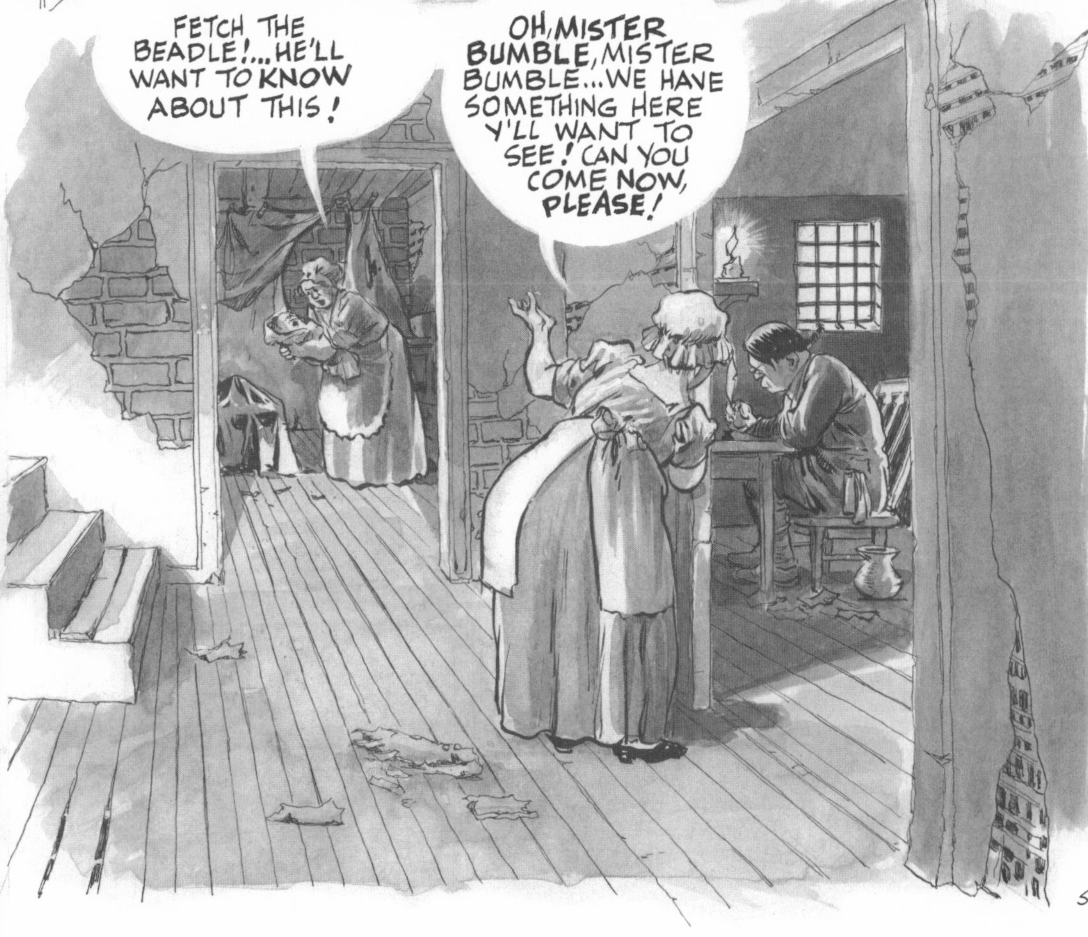
FETCH THE BEADLE!...HE'LL WANT TO KNOW ABOUT THIS!
OH, MISTER BUMBLE, MISTER BUMBLE...WE HAVE SOMETHING HERE Y'LL WANT TO SEE! CAN YOU COME NOW, PLEASE!

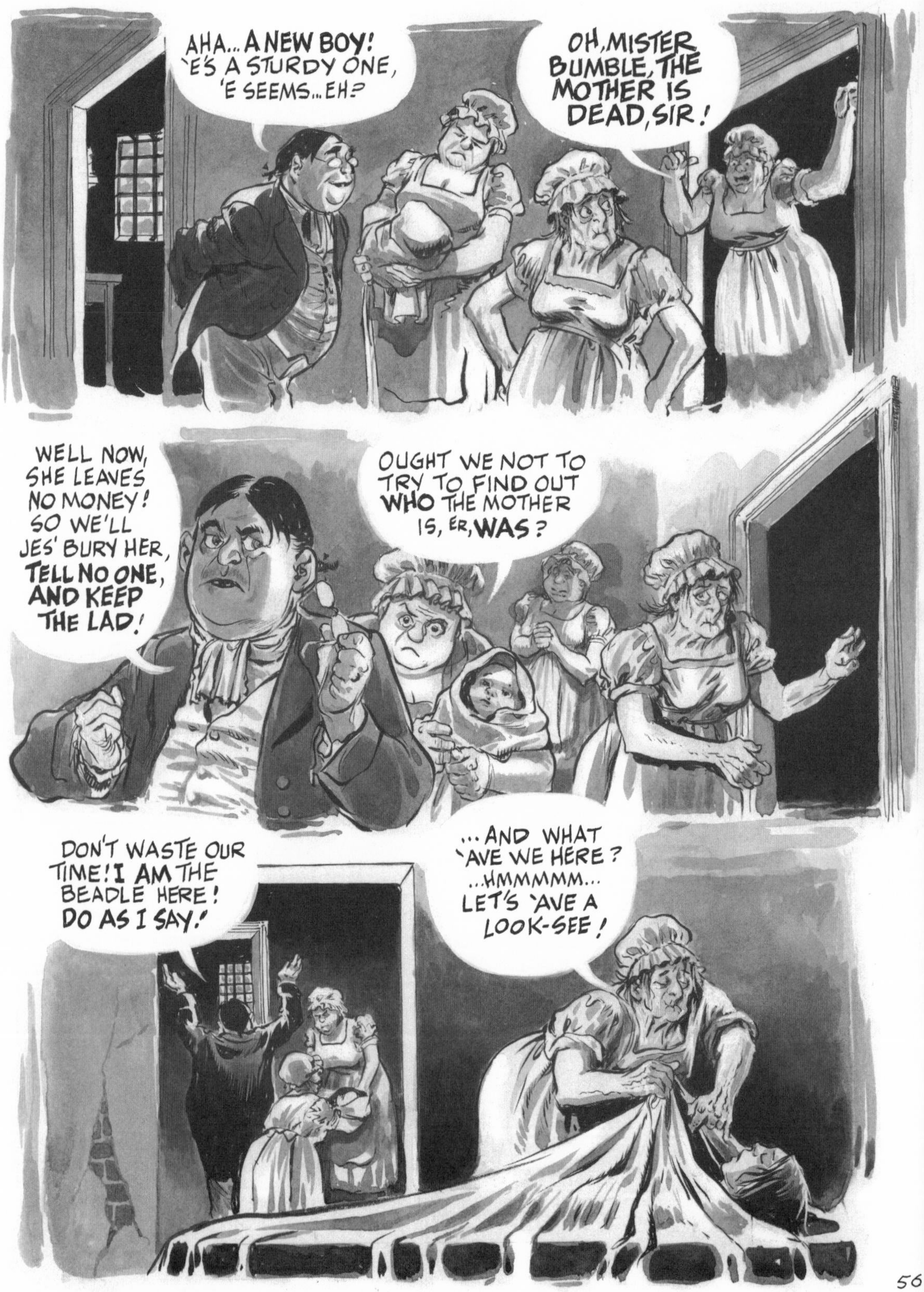
AHA... A NEW BOY! `E'S A STURDY ONE, 'E SEEMS... EH?
OH, MISTER BUMBLE, THE MOTHER IS DEAD, SIR!
WELL NOW, SHE LEAVES NO MONEY! SO WE'LL JES' BURY HER, TELL NO ONE, AND KEEP THE LAD!
OUGHT WE NOT TO TRY TO FIND OUT WHO THE MOTHER IS, ER, WAS?
DON'T WASTE OUR TIME! I AM THE BEADLE HERE! DO AS I SAY!
...AND WHAT `AVE WE HERE? ...HMMMMM... LET'S `AVE A LOOK-SEE!

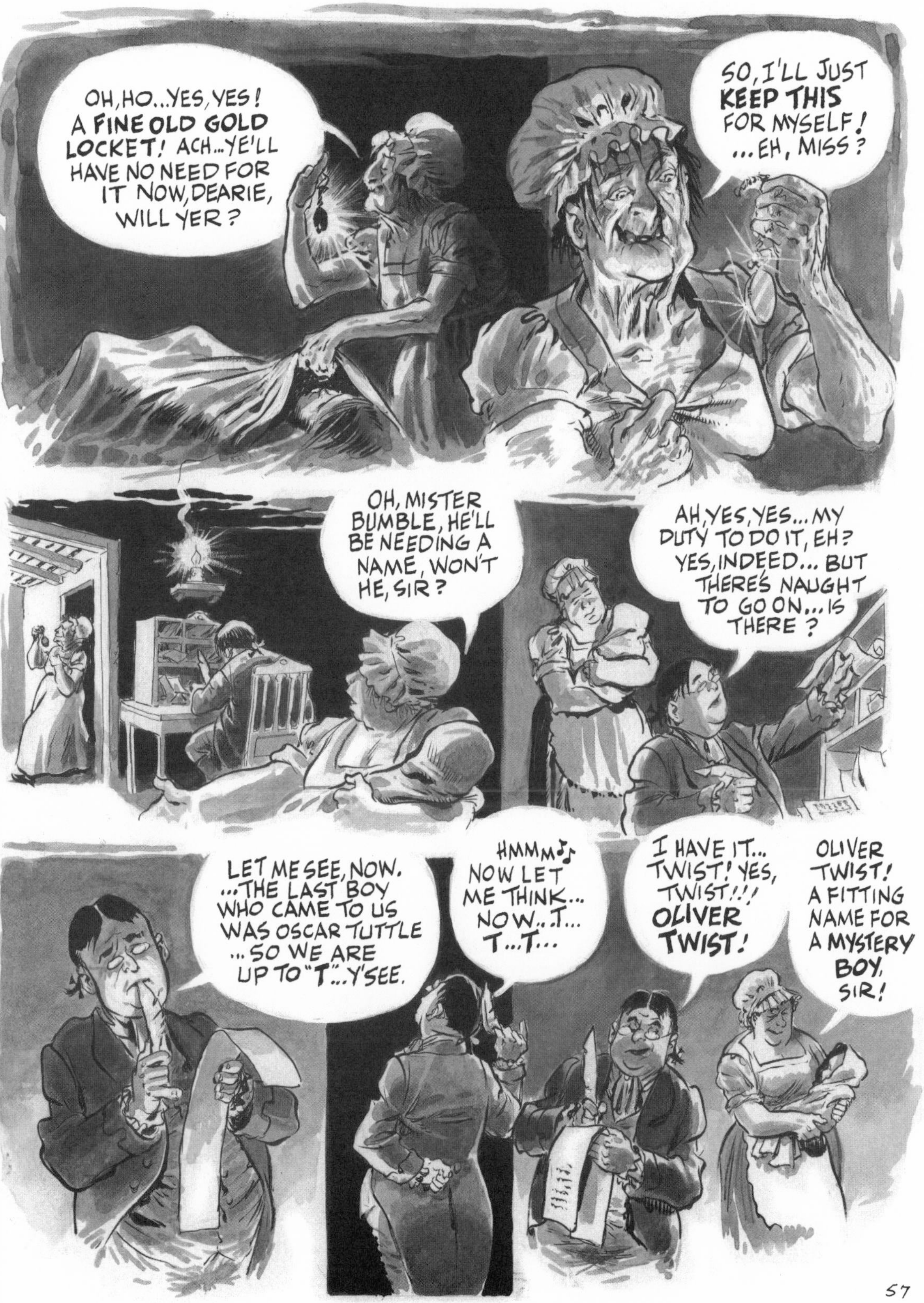
OH, HO... YES, YES! A FINE OLD GOLD LOCKET! ACH... YE'LL HAVE NO NEED FOR IT NOW, DEARIE, WILL YER?
SO, I'LL JUST KEEP THIS FOR MYSELF! ...EH, MISS?
OH, MISTER BUMBLE, HE'LL BE NEEDING A NAME, WON'T HE, SIR?
AH, YES, YES... MY DUTY TO DO IT, EH? YES, INDEED... BUT THERE'S NAUGHT TO GO ON... IS THERE?
LET ME SEE, NOW. ...THE LAST BOY WHO CAME TO US WAS OSCAR TUTTLE ...SO WE ARE UP TO "T"... Y'SEE.
HMMM NOW LET ME THINK... NOW.. T... T...T...
I HAVE IT... TWIST! YES, TWIST!!! OLIVER TWIST!
OLIVER TWIST! A FITTING NAME FOR A MYSTERY BOY, SIR!

Growing up in a workhouse, as you may have heard, is not easy. In these places, largesse or charity is doled out with a cruel economy by the people who operate the workhouse, for they seek to profit from the money they receive out of its management. Oh, I know well enough what Oliver's life was like there, and what he had to endure.

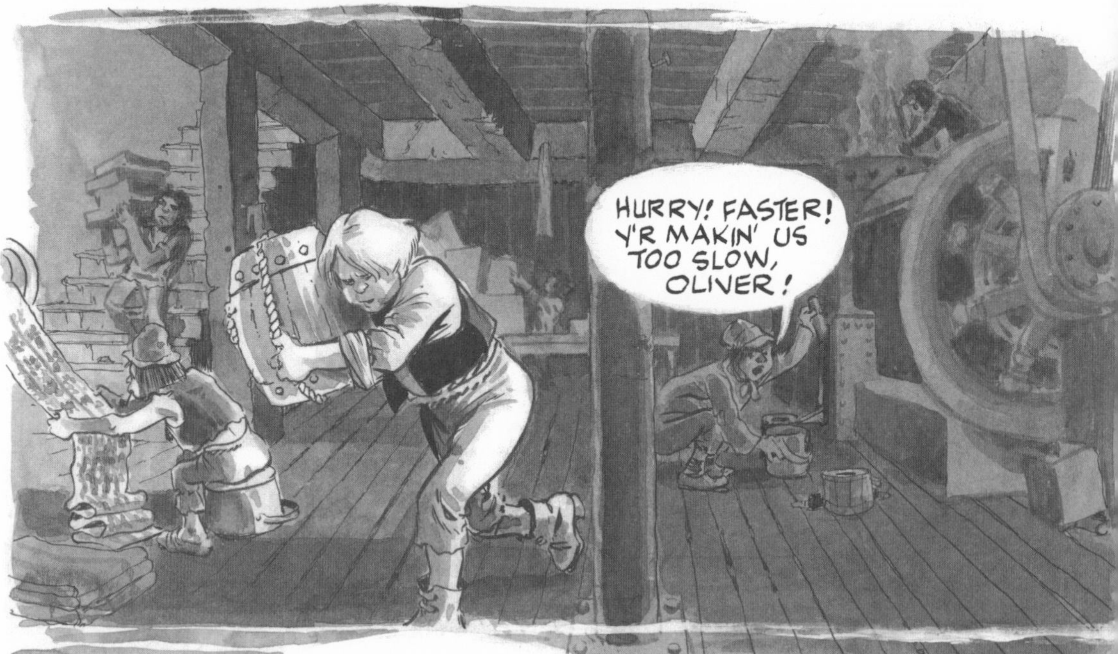
HURRY! FASTER! Y'R MAKIN' US TOO SLOW, OLIVER!

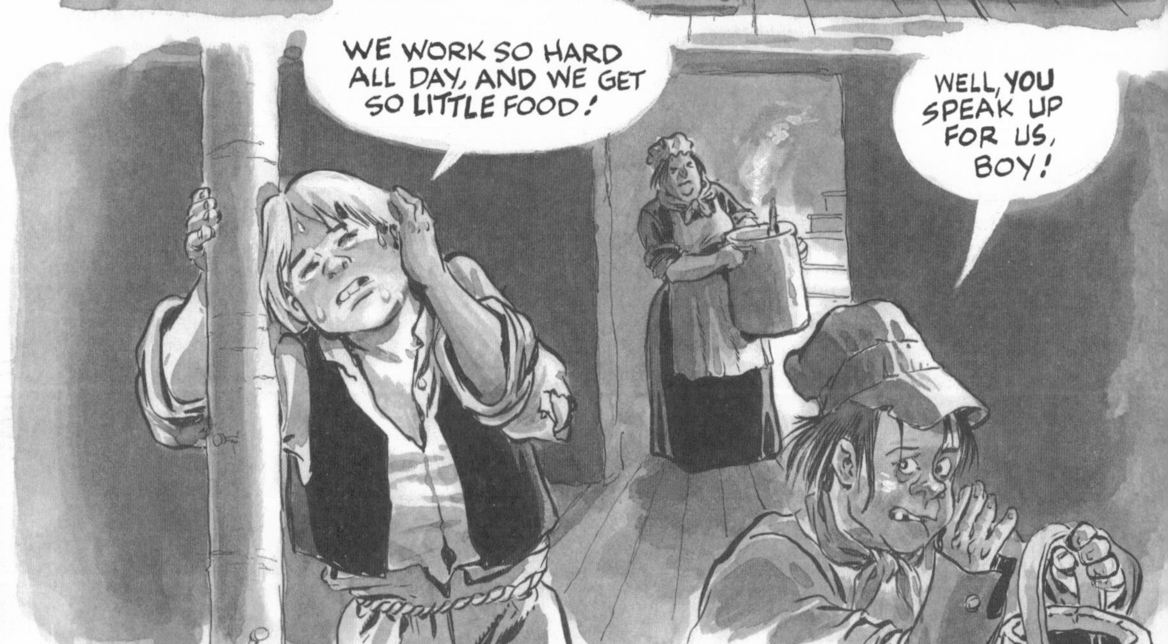
WE WORK SO HARD ALL DAY, AND WE GET SO LITTLE FOOD!
WELL, YOU SPEAK UP FOR US, BOY!

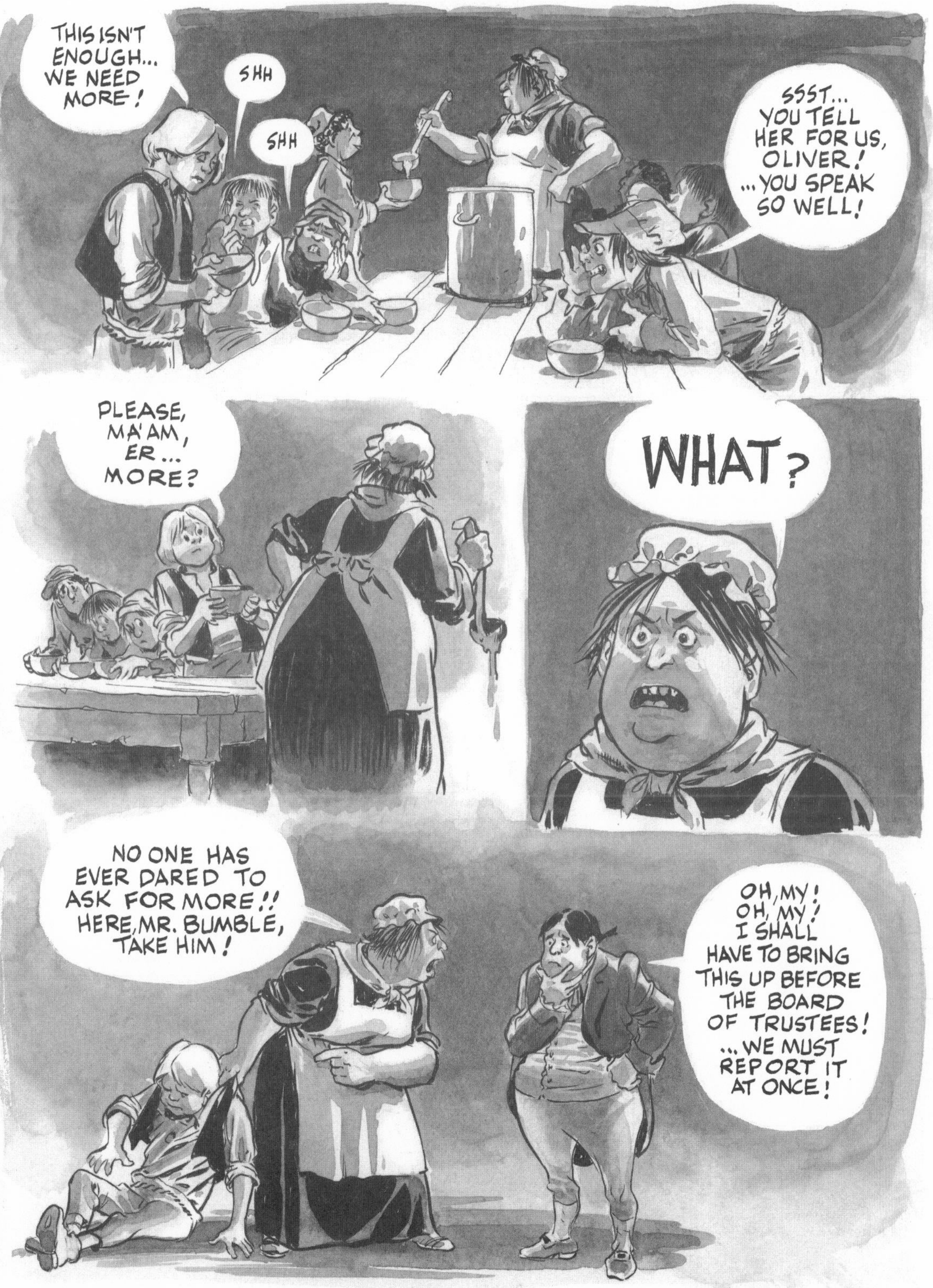
THIS ISN'T ENOUGH... WE NEED MORE!
SHH
SHH
SSST... YOU TELL HER FOR US, OLIVER! ...YOU SPEAK SO WELL!
PLEASE, MA'AM, ER... MORE?
WHAT?
NO ONE HAS EVER DARED TO ASK FOR MORE!! HERE, MR. BUMBLE, TAKE HIM!
OH, MY! OH, MY! I SHALL HAVE TO BRING THIS UP BEFORE THE BOARD OF TRUSTEES! ...WE MUST REPORT IT AT ONCE!

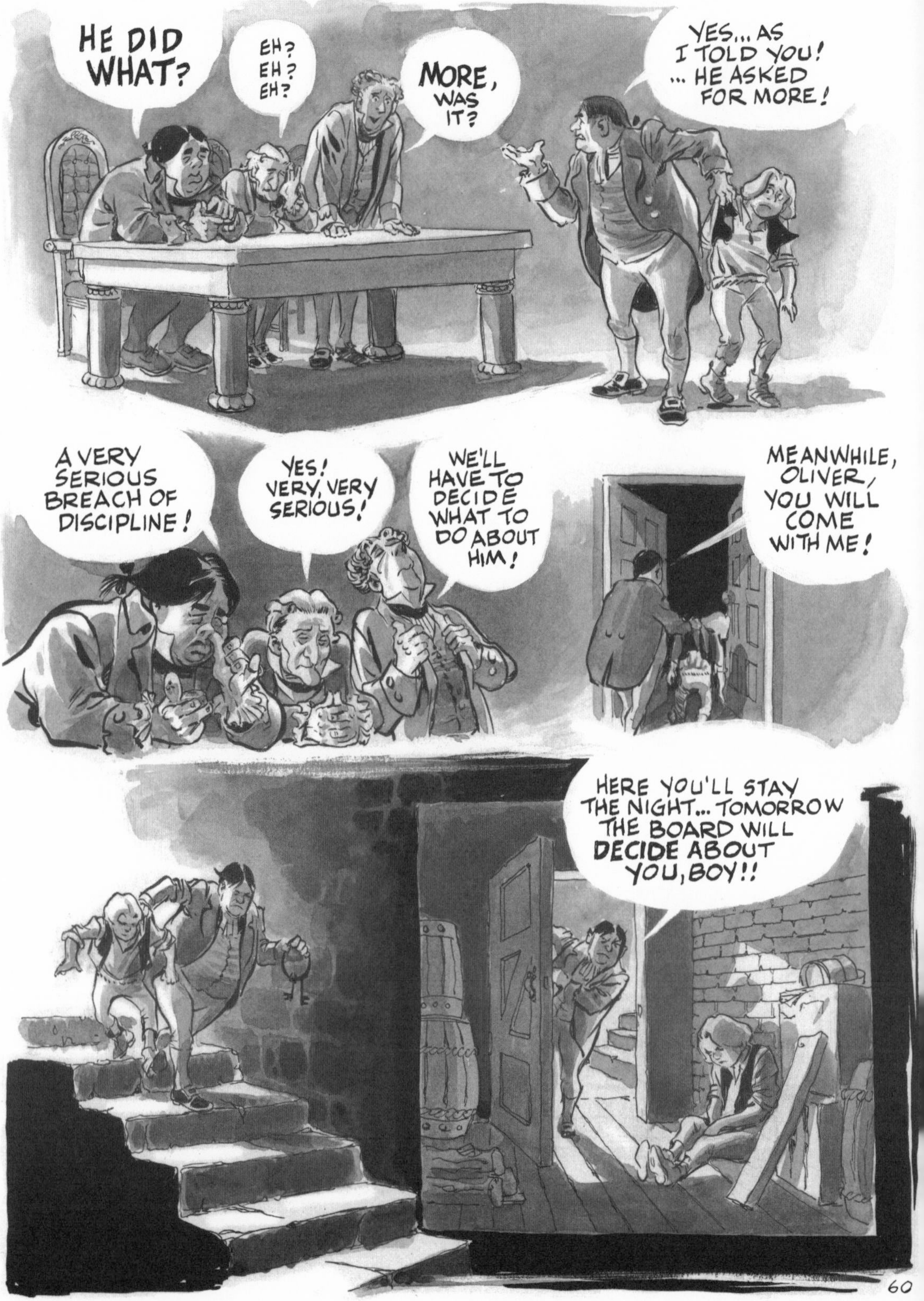
HE DID WHAT?
EH? EH? EH?
MORE, WAS IT?
YES... AS I TOLD YOU! ... HE ASKED FOR MORE!
A VERY SERIOUS BREACH OF DISCIPLINE!
YES! VERY, VERY SERIOUS!
WE'LL HAVE TO DECIDE WHAT TO DO ABOUT HIM!
MEANWHILE, OLIVER, YOU WILL COME WITH ME!
HERE YOU'LL STAY THE NIGHT... TOMORROW THE BOARD WILL DECIDE ABOUT YOU, BOY!!

The next day the trustees met again. It was their duty as custodians of this charitable institution to sit in judgment on all matters of discipline.

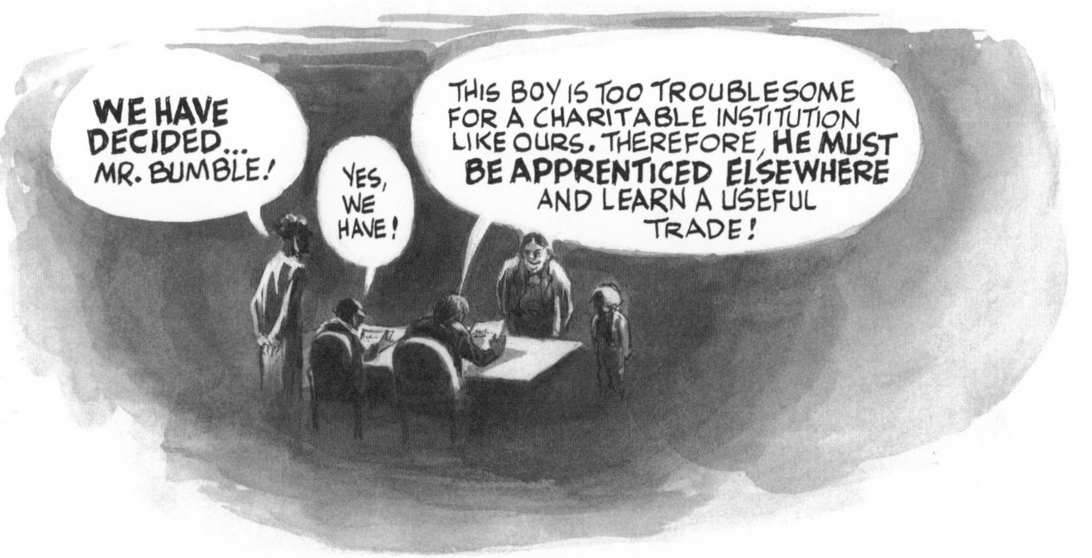
WE HAVE DECIDED... MR. BUMBLE!
YES, WE HAVE!
THIS BOY IS TOO TROUBLESOME FOR A CHARITABLE INSTITUTION LIKE OURS. THEREFORE, HE MUST BE APPRENTICED ELSEWHERE AND LEARN A USEFUL TRADE!

So Mr. Bumble undertook this task of finding a suitable apprenticeship for Oliver.

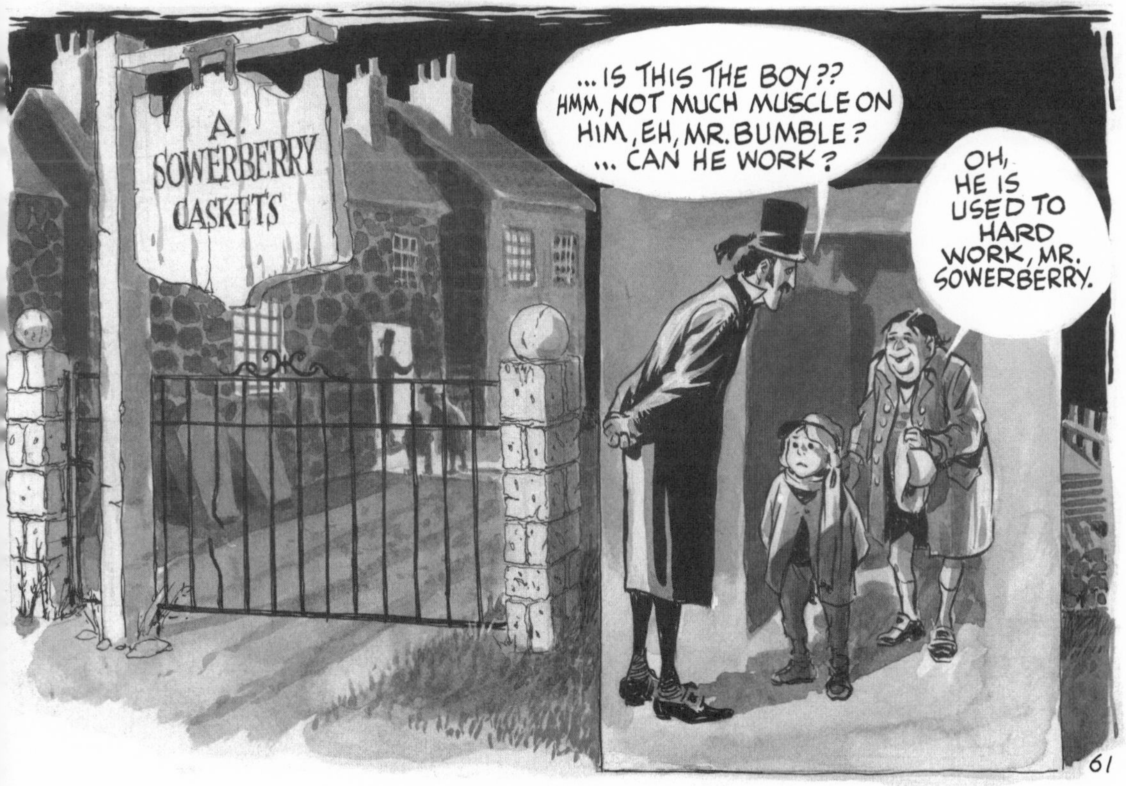
A. SOWERBERRY CASKETS
...IS THIS THE BOY?? HMM, NOT MUCH MUSCLE ON HIM, EH, MR. BUMBLE? ... CAN HE WORK?
OH, HE IS USED TO HARD WORK, MR. SOWERBERRY.

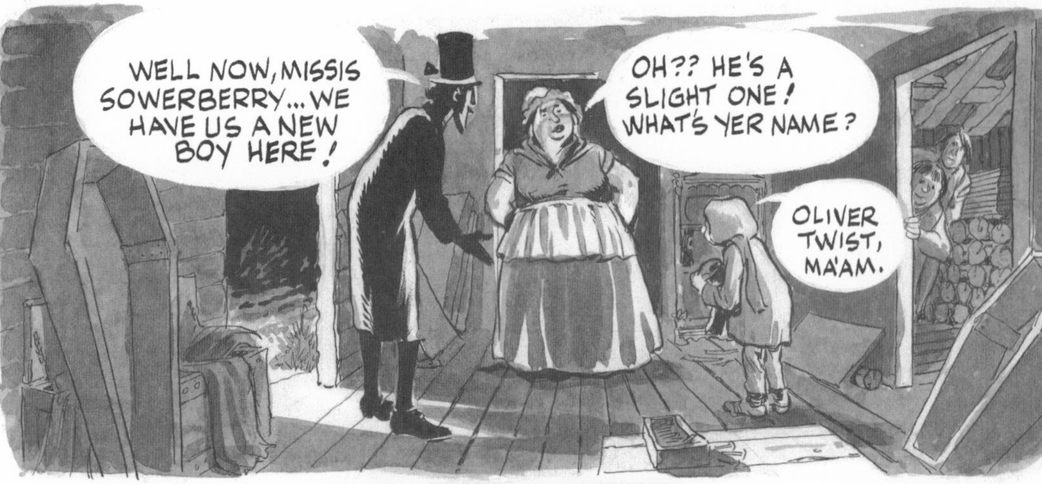
WELL NOW, MISSIS SOWERBERRY... WE HAVE US A NEW BOY HERE!
OH?? HE'S A SLIGHT ONE! WHAT'S YER NAME?
OLIVER TWIST, MA'AM.

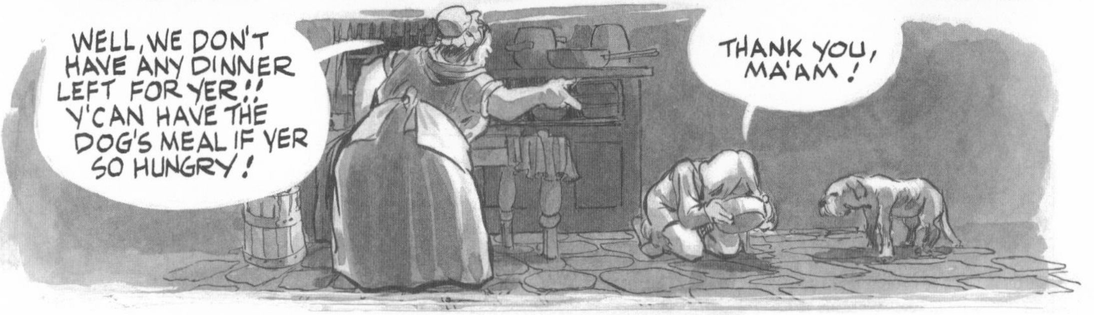
WELL, WE DON'T HAVE ANY DINNER LEFT FOR YER!! Y'CAN HAVE THE DOG'S MEAL IF YER SO HUNGRY!
THANK YOU, MA'AM!

As my boys who have also experienced employment in similar circumstances tell me, finding a place here is always a challenge.

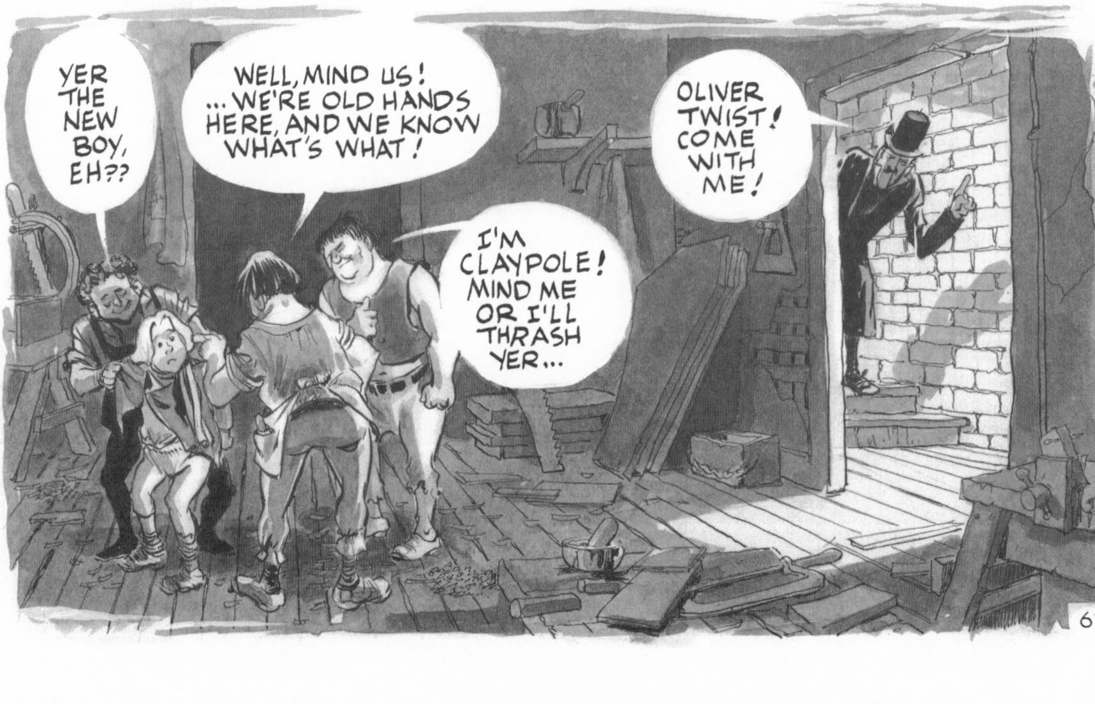
YER THE NEW BOY, EH??
WELL, MIND US! ...WE'RE OLD HANDS HERE, AND WE KNOW WHAT'S WHAT!
I'M CLAYPOLE! MIND ME OR I'LL THRASH YER...
OLIVER TWIST! COME WITH ME!

A rise in position in such a place is a splendid opportunity, as I can tell you.

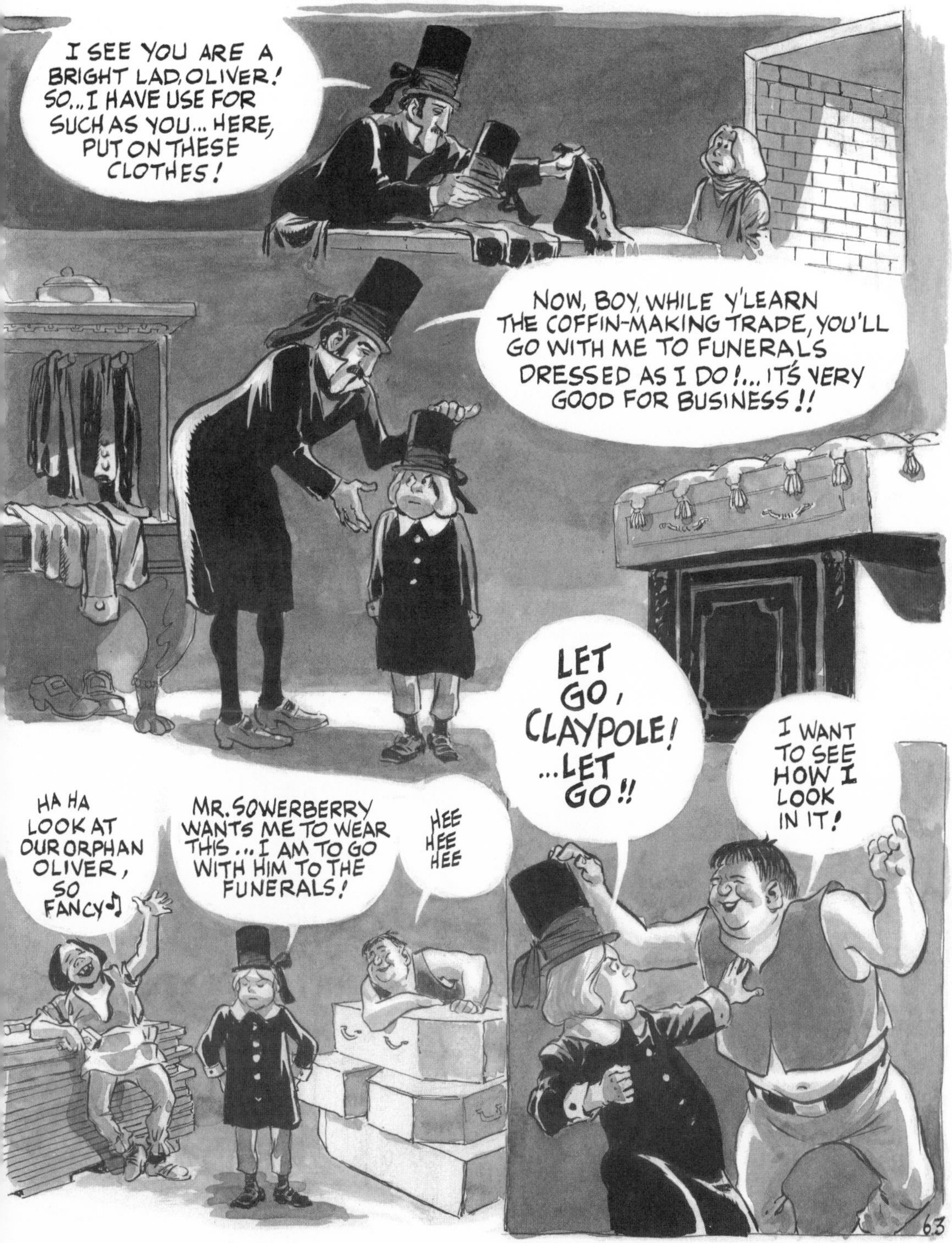
I SEE YOU ARE A BRIGHT LAD, OLIVER! SO...I HAVE USE FOR SUCH AS YOU... HERE, PUT ON THESE CLOTHES!
NOW, BOY, WHILE Y'LEARN THE COFFIN-MAKING TRADE, YOU'LL GO WITH ME TO FUNERALS DRESSED AS I DO!... IT'S VERY GOOD FOR BUSINESS!!
HA HA LOOK AT OUR ORPHAN OLIVER, SO FANCY♫
MR. SOWERBERRY WANTS ME TO WEAR THIS ... I AM TO GO WITH HIM TO THE FUNERALS!
HEE HEE HEE
LET GO, CLAYPOLE! ...LET GO!!
I WANT TO SEE HOW I LOOK IN IT!

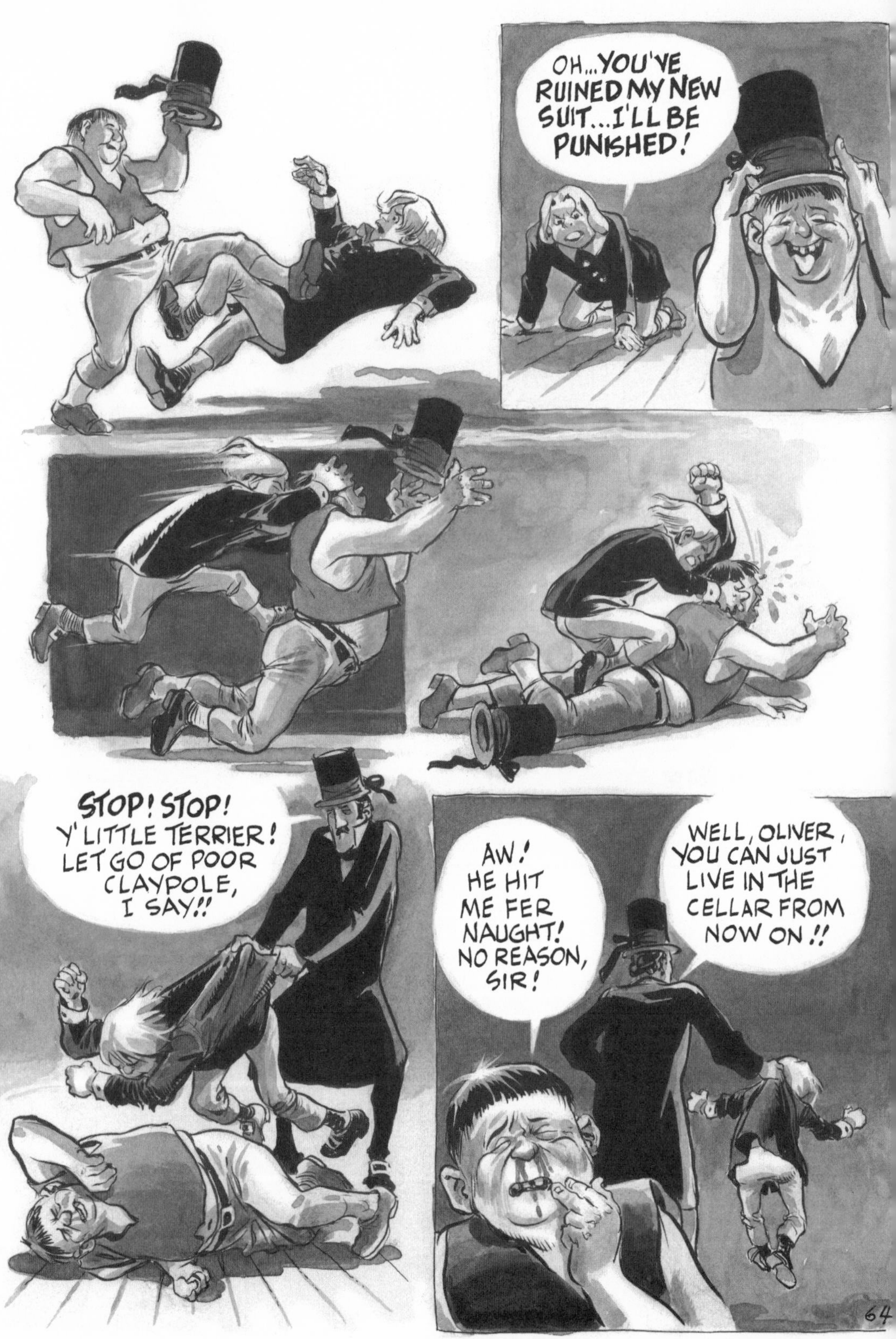
OH...YOU'VE RUINED MY NEW SUIT...I'LL BE PUNISHED!
STOP! STOP! Y' LITTLE TERRIER! LET GO OF POOR CLAYPOLE, I SAY!!
AW! HE HIT ME FER NAUGHT! NO REASON, SIR!
WELL, OLIVER, YOU CAN JUST LIVE IN THE CELLAR FROM NOW ON!!

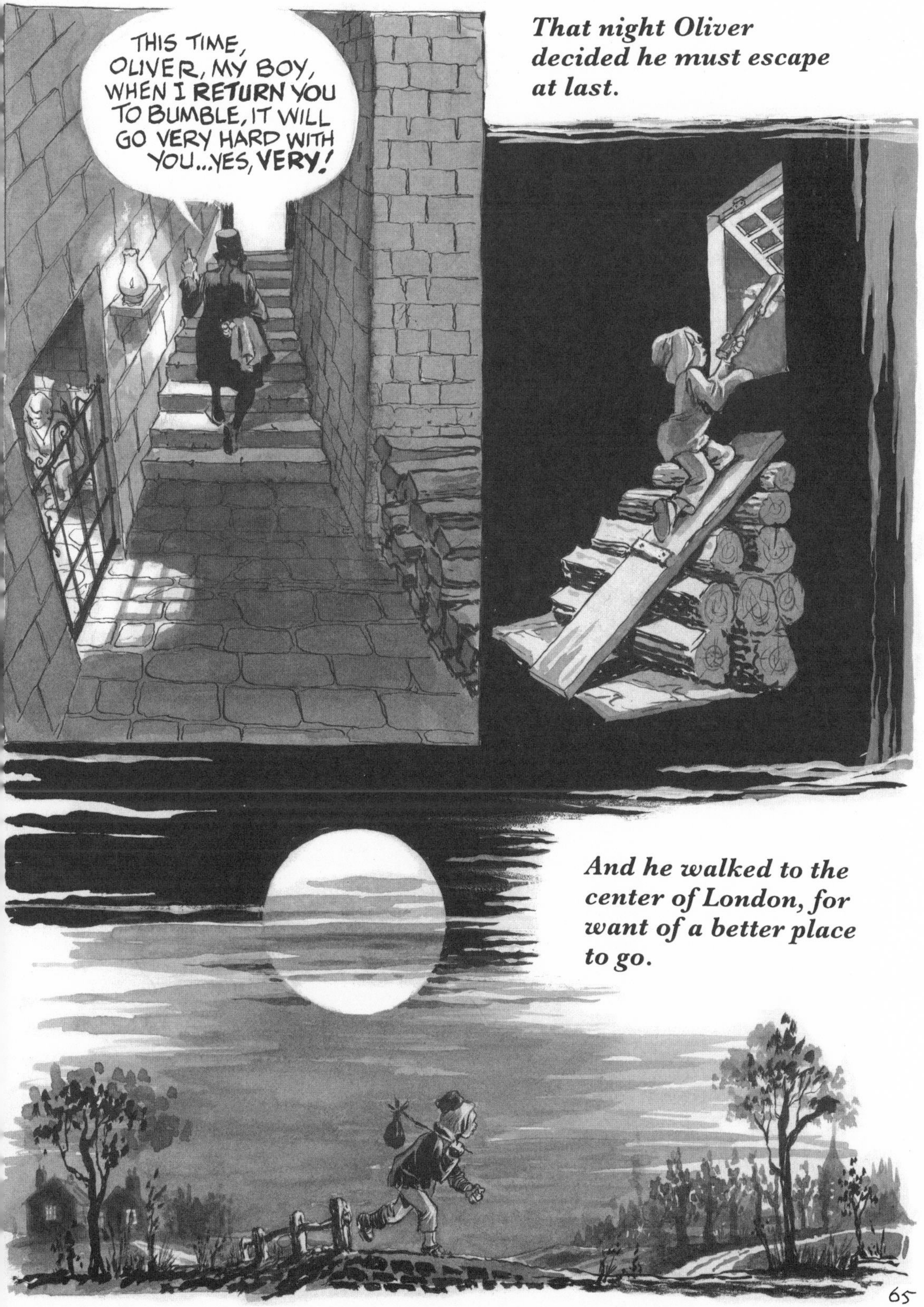
THIS TIME, OLIVER, MY BOY, WHEN I RETURN YOU TO BUMBLE, IT WILL GO VERY HARD WITH YOU...YES, VERY!
That night Oliver decided he must escape at last.
And he walked to the center of London, for want of a better place to go.

So began my relationship with a child of destiny, as they say... and with it the circumstances that defined my own encounter with fate. My affairs were taking a troubling turn, and I had a meeting with my best boy, Jack Dawkins.

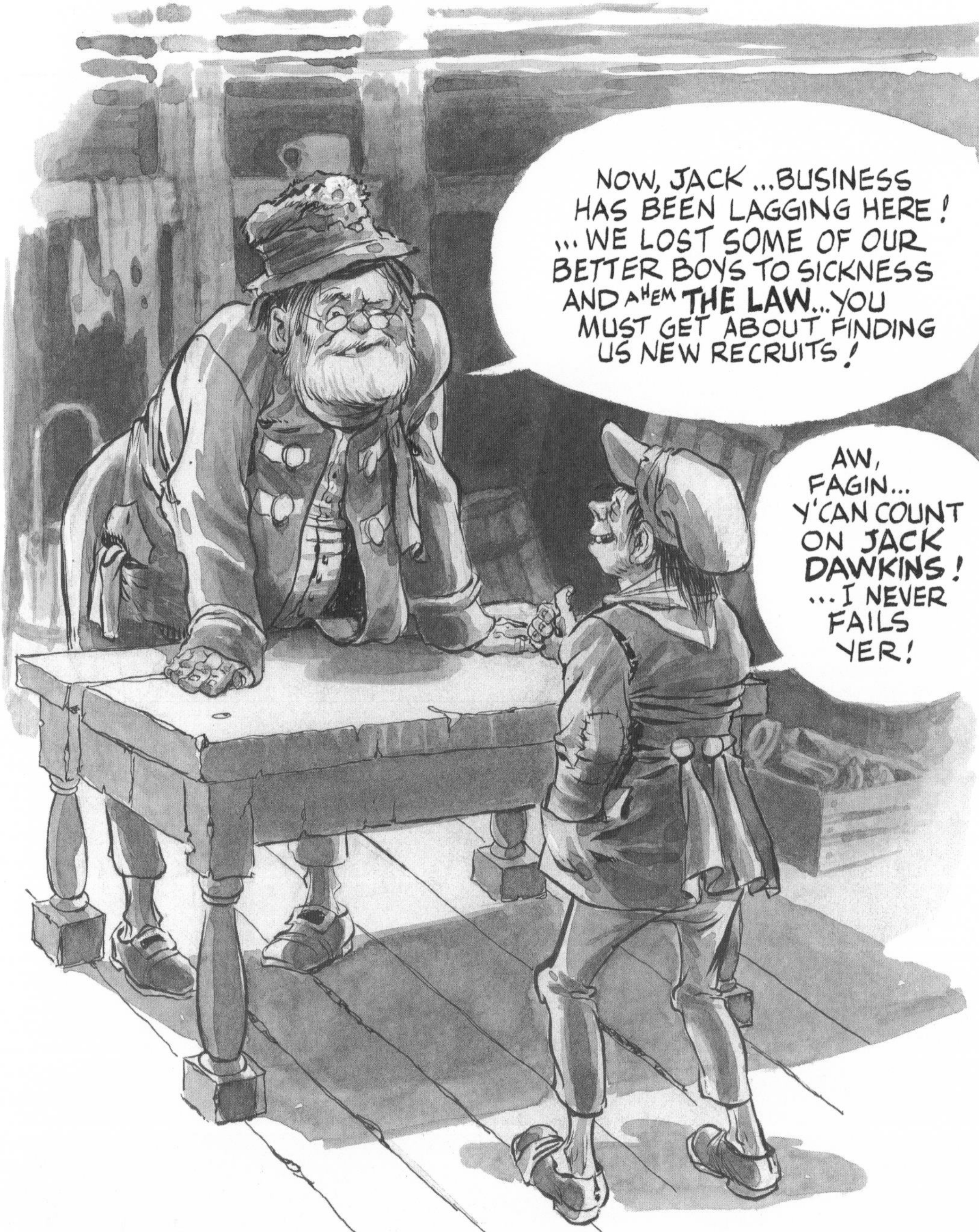
NOW, JACK ...BUSINESS HAS BEEN LAGGING HERE! ...WE LOST SOME OF OUR BETTER BOYS TO SICKNESS AND AHEM THE LAW...YOU MUST GET ABOUT FINDING US NEW RECRUITS!
AW, FAGIN... Y'CAN COUNT ON JACK DAWKINS! ...I NEVER FAILS YER!

And as fate would have it, that was the very day young Oliver arrived in London.

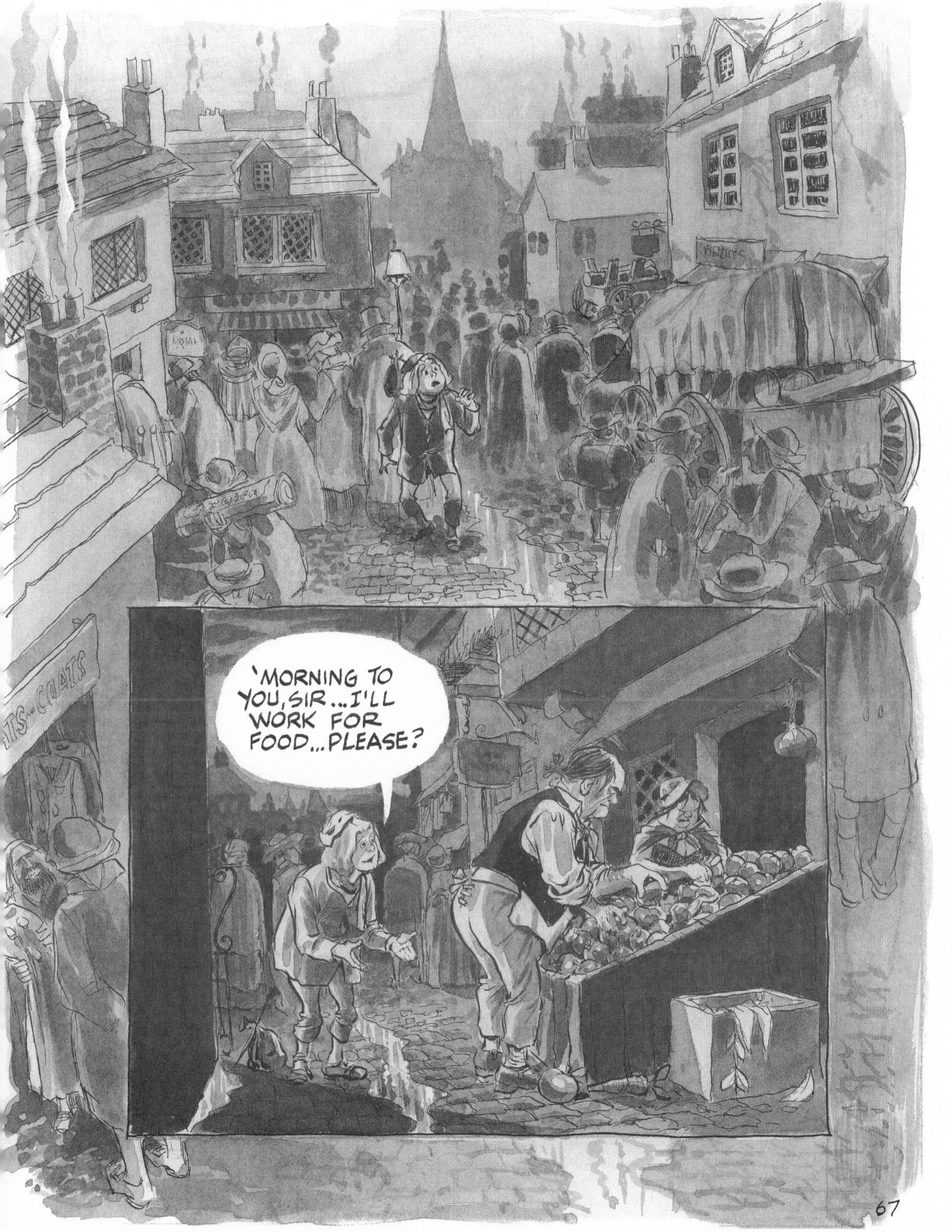
'MORNING TO YOU, SIR...I'LL WORK FOR FOOD...PLEASE?

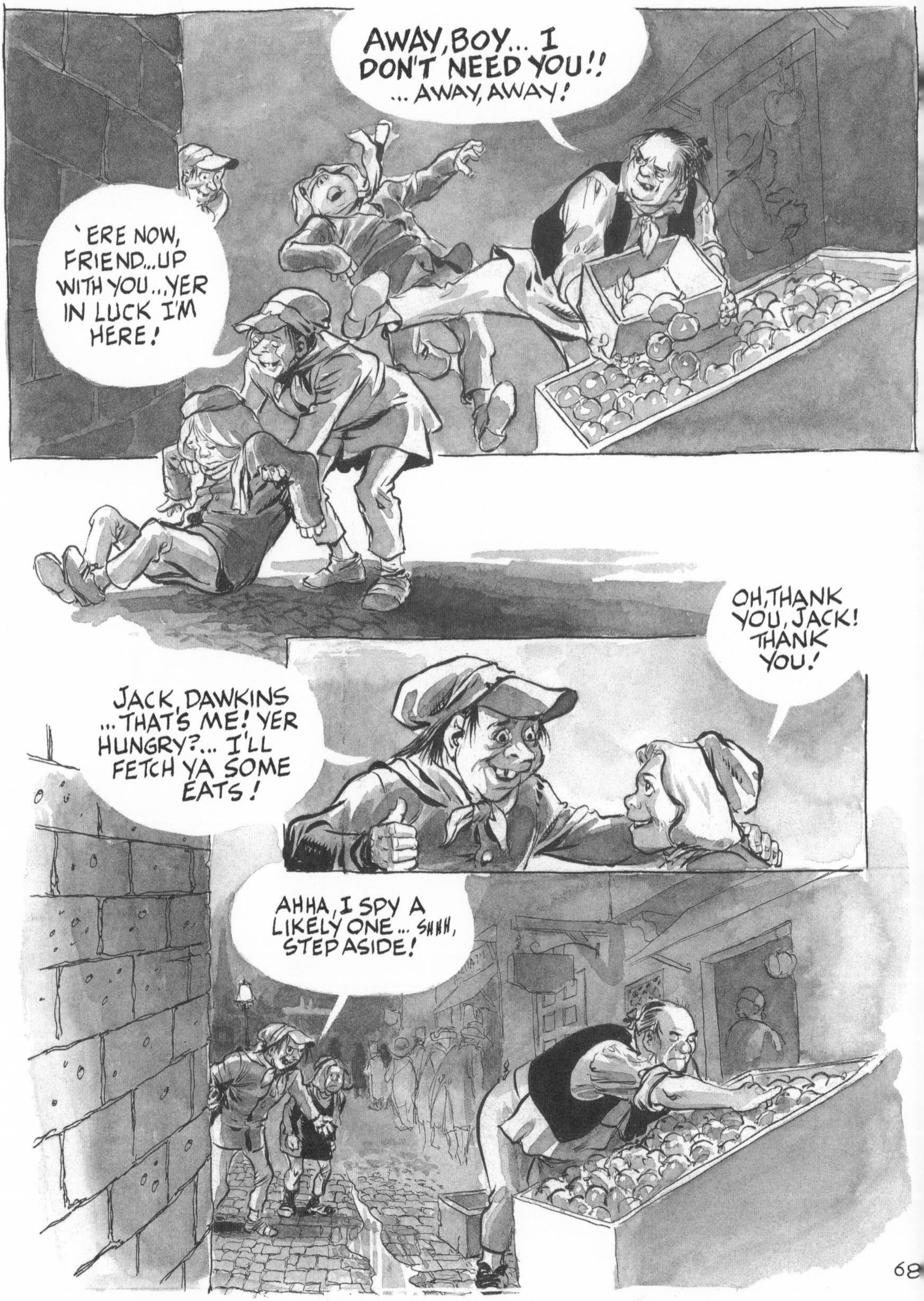
AWAY, BOY... I DON'T NEED YOU!! ...AWAY, AWAY!
'ERE NOW, FRIEND...UP WITH YOU...YER IN LUCK I'M HERE!
JACK DAWKINS ...THAT'S ME! YER HUNGRY?... I'LL FETCH YA SOME EATS!
OH, THANK YOU, JACK! THANK YOU!
AHHA, I SPY A LIKELY ONE... SHHH, STEP ASIDE!

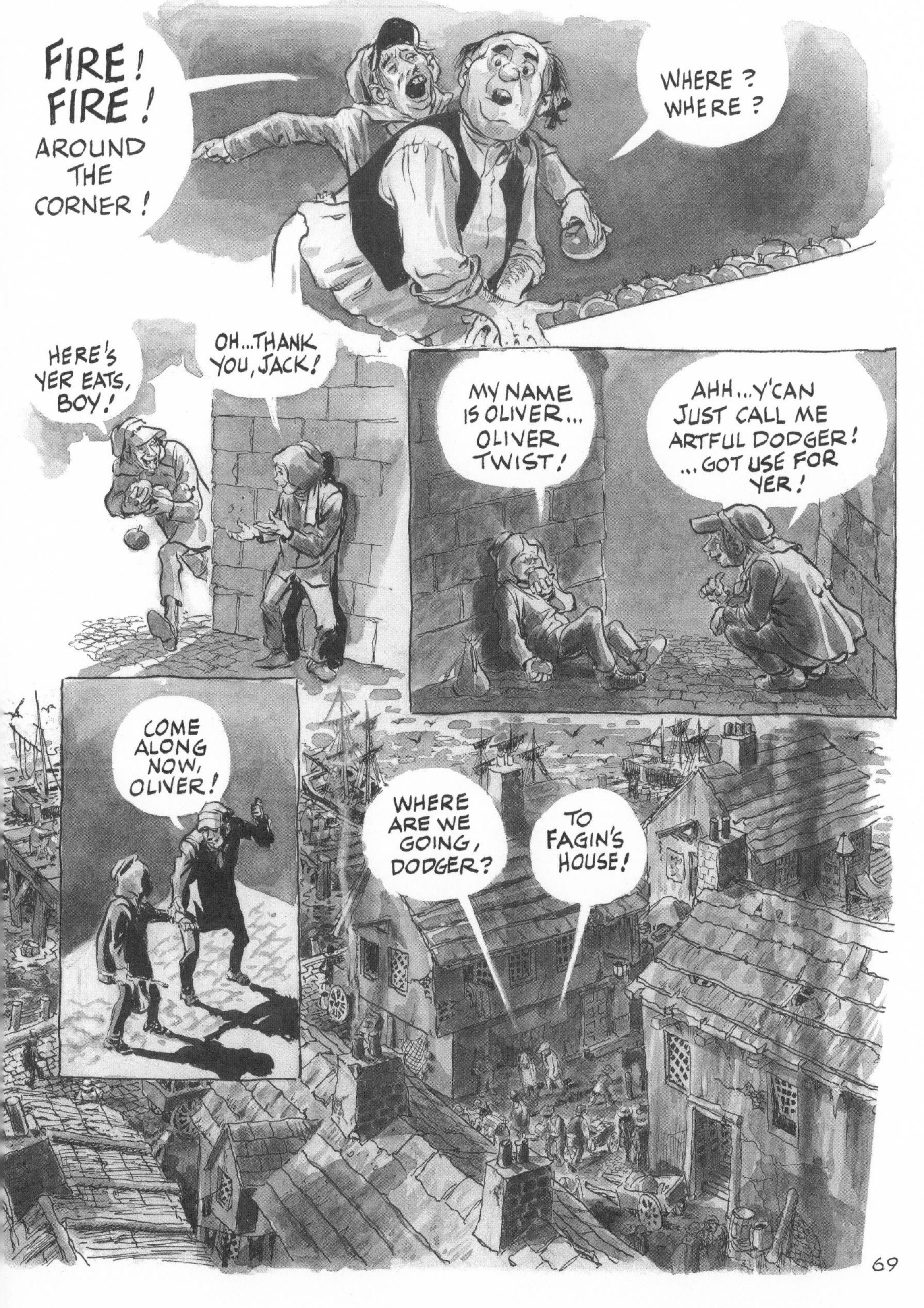
FIRE! FIRE! AROUND THE CORNER!
WHERE? WHERE?
HERE'S YER EATS, BOY!
OH...THANK YOU, JACK!
MY NAME IS OLIVER... OLIVER TWIST!
AHH...Y'CAN JUST CALL ME ARTFUL DODGER! ...GOT USE FOR YER!
COME ALONG NOW, OLIVER!
WHERE ARE WE GOING, DODGER?
TO FAGIN'S HOUSE!

Ah, well do I remember him… clearly a lad of quality… rare indeed in those days, I can assure you.

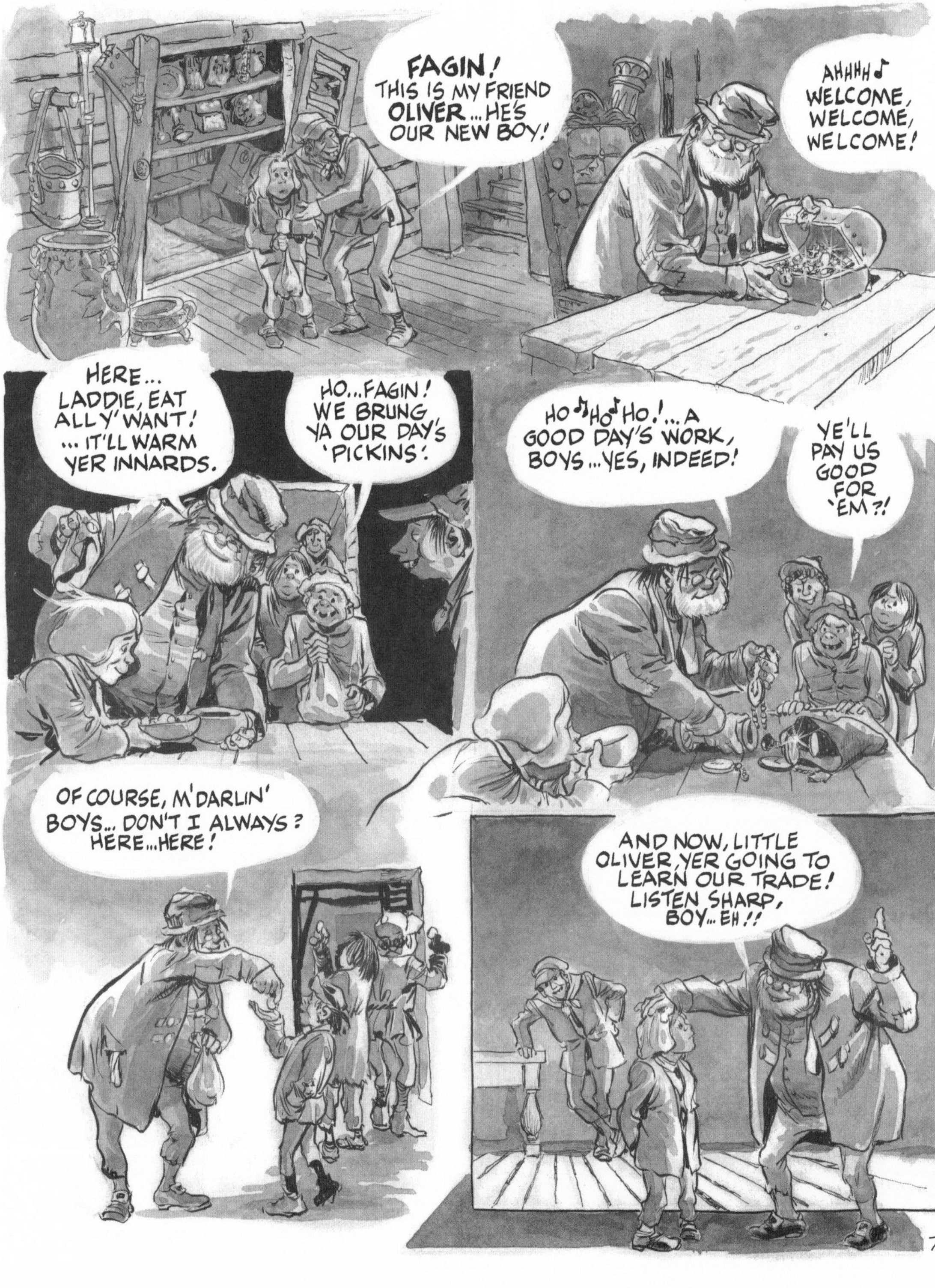

FAGIN! THIS IS MY FRIEND OLIVER… HE'S OUR NEW BOY!
AHHHH♪ WELCOME, WELCOME, WELCOME!
HERE… LADDIE, EAT ALL Y' WANT! … IT'LL WARM YER INNARDS.
HO… FAGIN! WE BRUNG YA OUR DAY'S 'PICKINS'.
HO♪HO♪HO!… A GOOD DAY'S WORK, BOYS… YES, INDEED!
YE'LL PAY US GOOD FOR 'EM?!
OF COURSE, M'DARLIN' BOYS… DON'T I ALWAYS? HERE… HERE!
AND NOW, LITTLE OLIVER, YER GOING TO LEARN OUR TRADE! LISTEN SHARP, BOY… EH!!

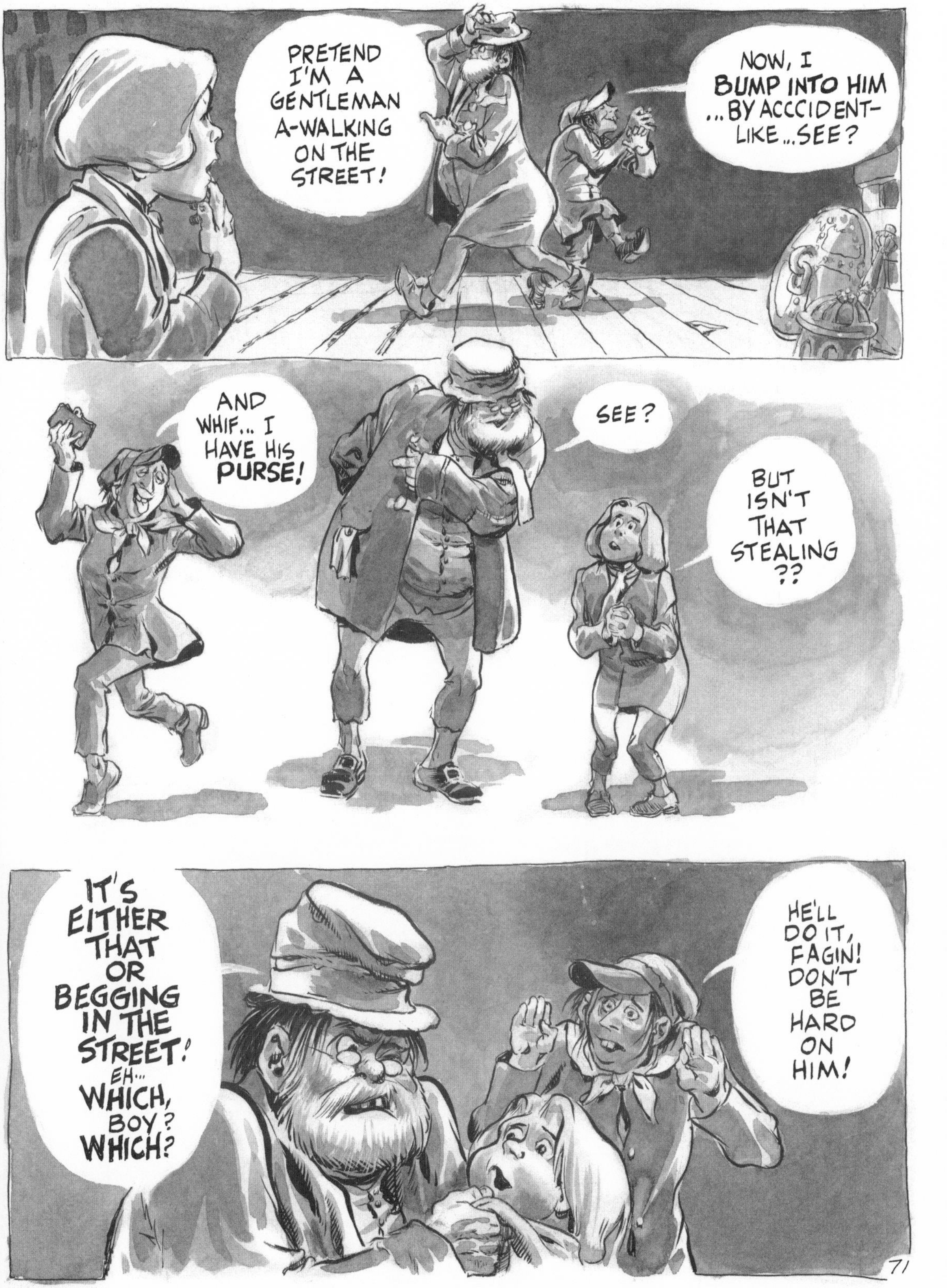
PRETEND I'M A GENTLEMAN A-WALKING ON THE STREET!
NOW, I BUMP INTO HIM ...BY ACCCIDENT-LIKE...SEE?
AND WHIF... I HAVE HIS PURSE!
SEE?
BUT ISN'T THAT STEALING??
IT'S EITHER THAT OR BEGGING IN THE STREET! EH... WHICH, BOY? WHICH?
HE'LL DO IT, FAGIN! DON'T BE HARD ON HIM!

Well, Oliver was recruited… oh, yes! In just a week he was working the street with the Artful Dodger.

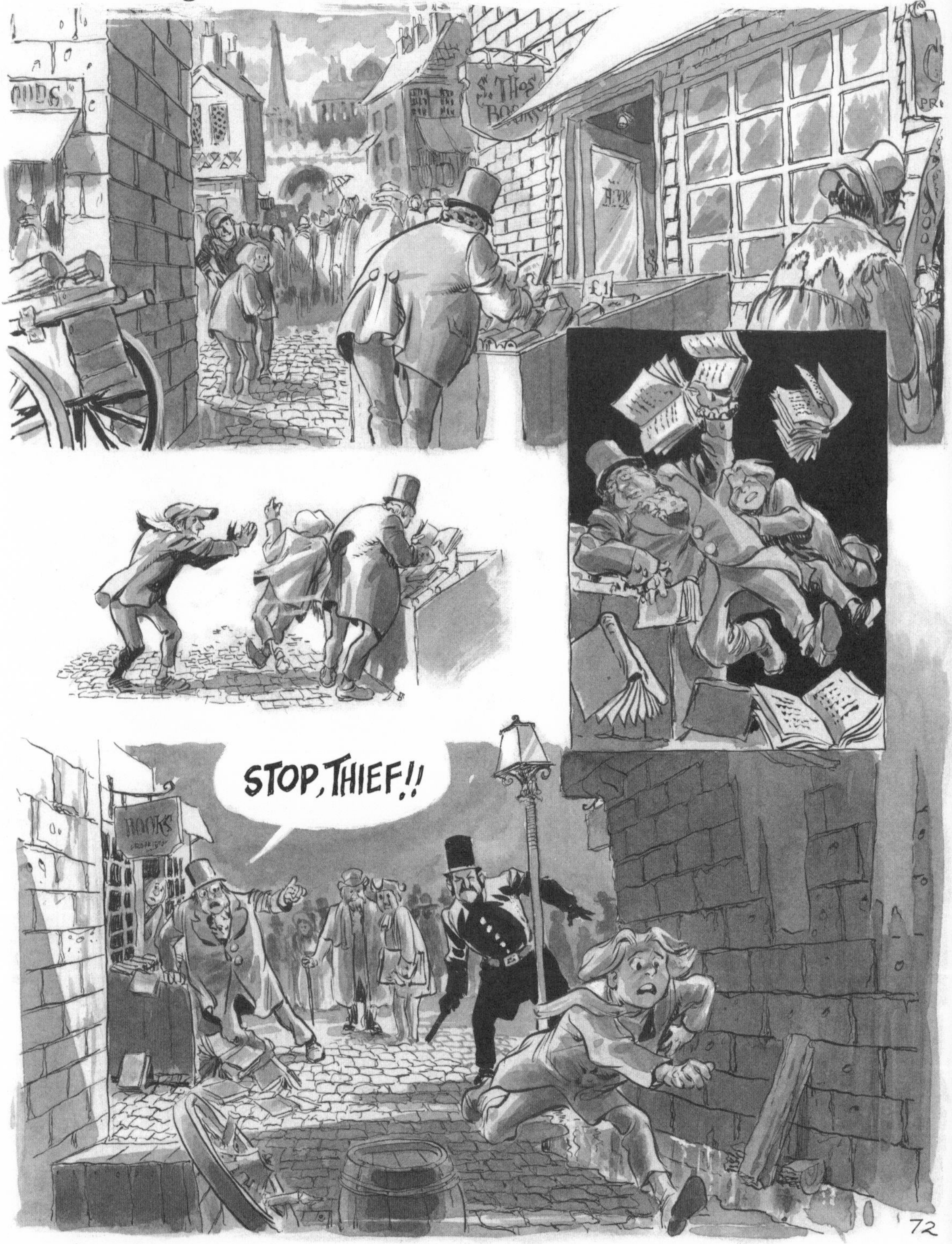
STOP, THIEF!!

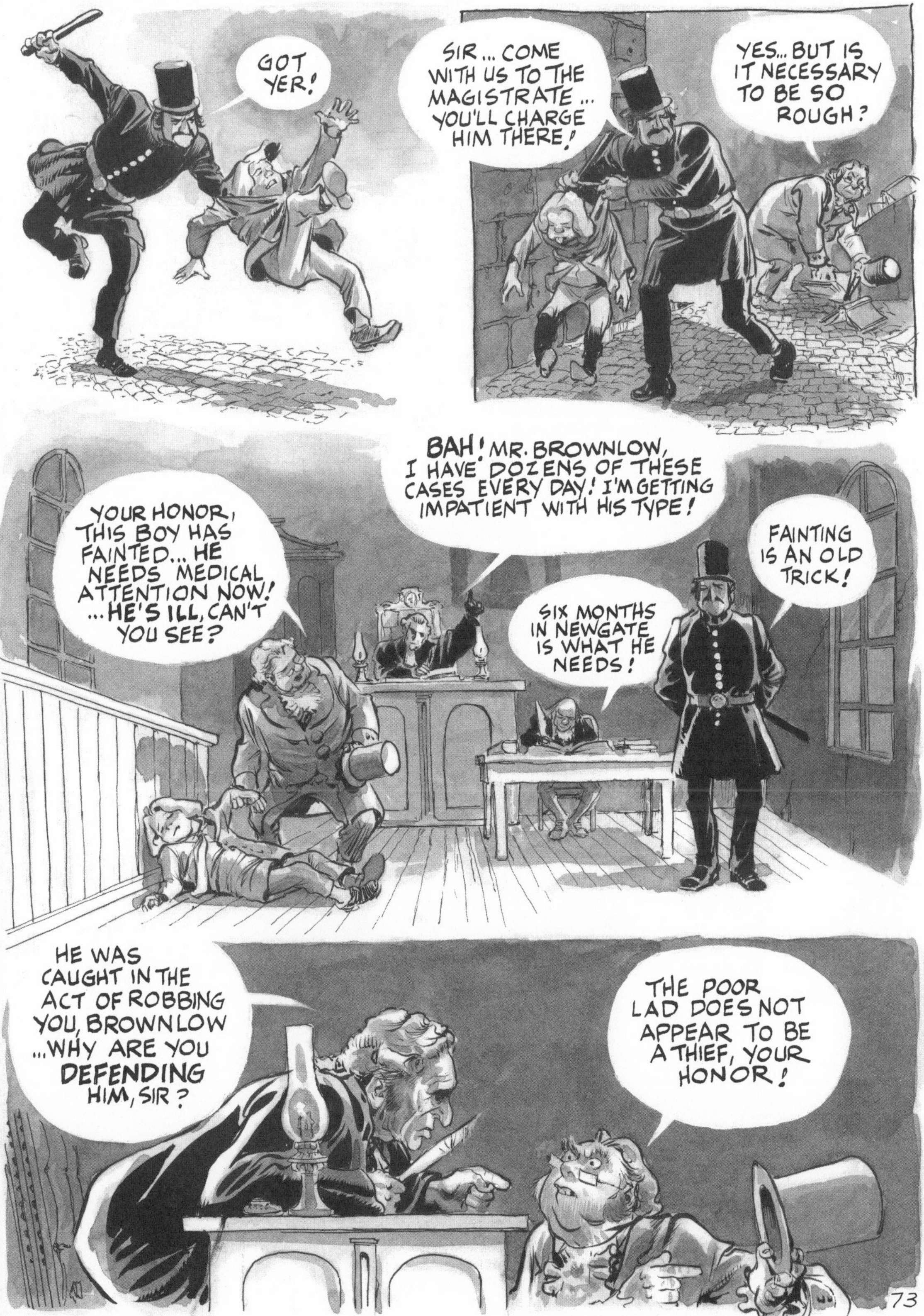
GOT YER!
SIR... COME WITH US TO THE MAGISTRATE... YOU'LL CHARGE HIM THERE!
YES... BUT IS IT NECESSARY TO BE SO ROUGH?
YOUR HONOR, THIS BOY HAS FAINTED... HE NEEDS MEDICAL ATTENTION NOW! ...HE'S ILL, CAN'T YOU SEE?
BAH! MR. BROWNLOW, I HAVE DOZENS OF THESE CASES EVERY DAY! I'M GETTING IMPATIENT WITH HIS TYPE!
SIX MONTHS IN NEWGATE IS WHAT HE NEEDS!
FAINTING IS AN OLD TRICK!
HE WAS CAUGHT IN THE ACT OF ROBBING YOU, BROWNLOW ...WHY ARE YOU DEFENDING HIM, SIR?
THE POOR LAD DOES NOT APPEAR TO BE A THIEF, YOUR HONOR!

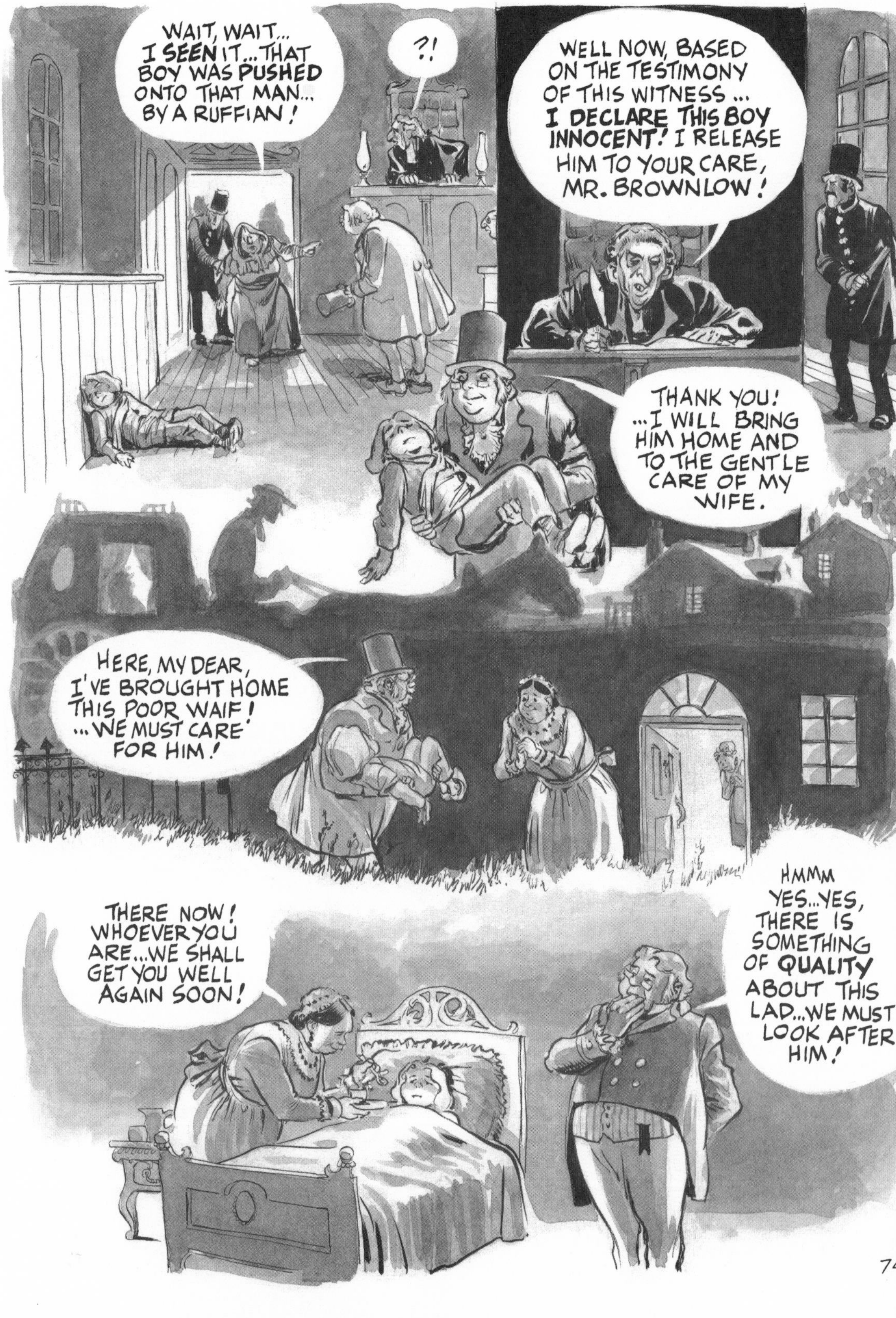
WAIT, WAIT... I SEEN IT... THAT BOY WAS PUSHED ONTO THAT MAN... BY A RUFFIAN!
?!
WELL NOW, BASED ON THE TESTIMONY OF THIS WITNESS... I DECLARE THIS BOY INNOCENT! I RELEASE HIM TO YOUR CARE, MR. BROWNLOW!
THANK YOU! ...I WILL BRING HIM HOME AND TO THE GENTLE CARE OF MY WIFE.
HERE, MY DEAR, I'VE BROUGHT HOME THIS POOR WAIF! ...WE MUST CARE FOR HIM!
THERE NOW! WHOEVER YOU ARE... WE SHALL GET YOU WELL AGAIN SOON!
HMMM YES... YES, THERE IS SOMETHING OF QUALITY ABOUT THIS LAD... WE MUST LOOK AFTER HIM!

Oliver was out of our hands. I knew not where until later, when I found out he was at the Brownlows, quite safe. Then my partner, Sikes, returned. He was always in fear of betrayal.

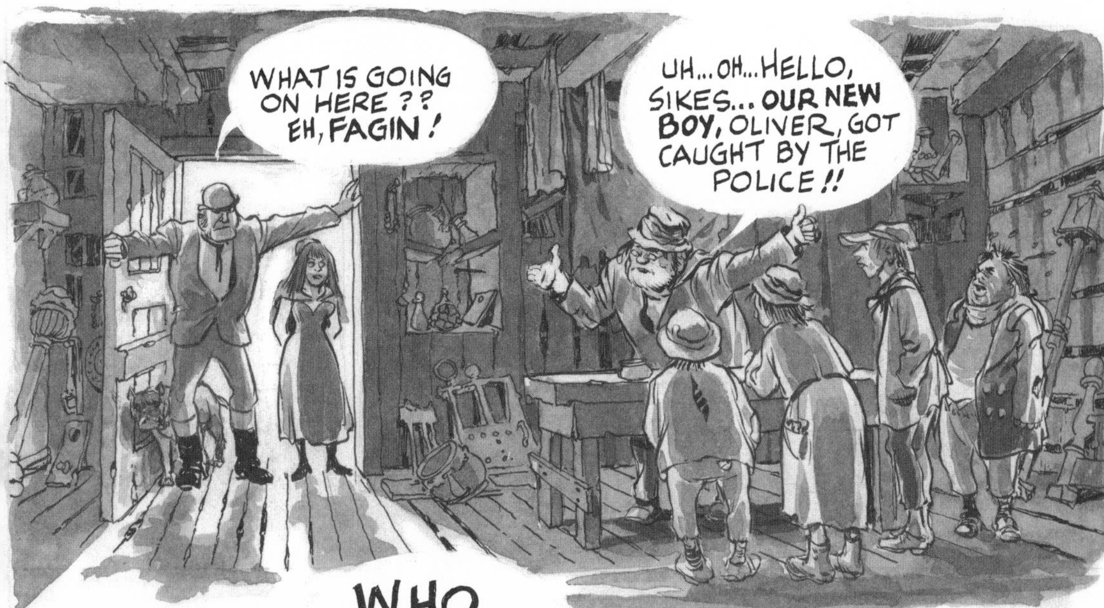
WHAT IS GOING ON HERE ?? EH, FAGIN !
UH... OH... HELLO, SIKES... OUR NEW BOY, OLIVER, GOT CAUGHT BY THE POLICE !!

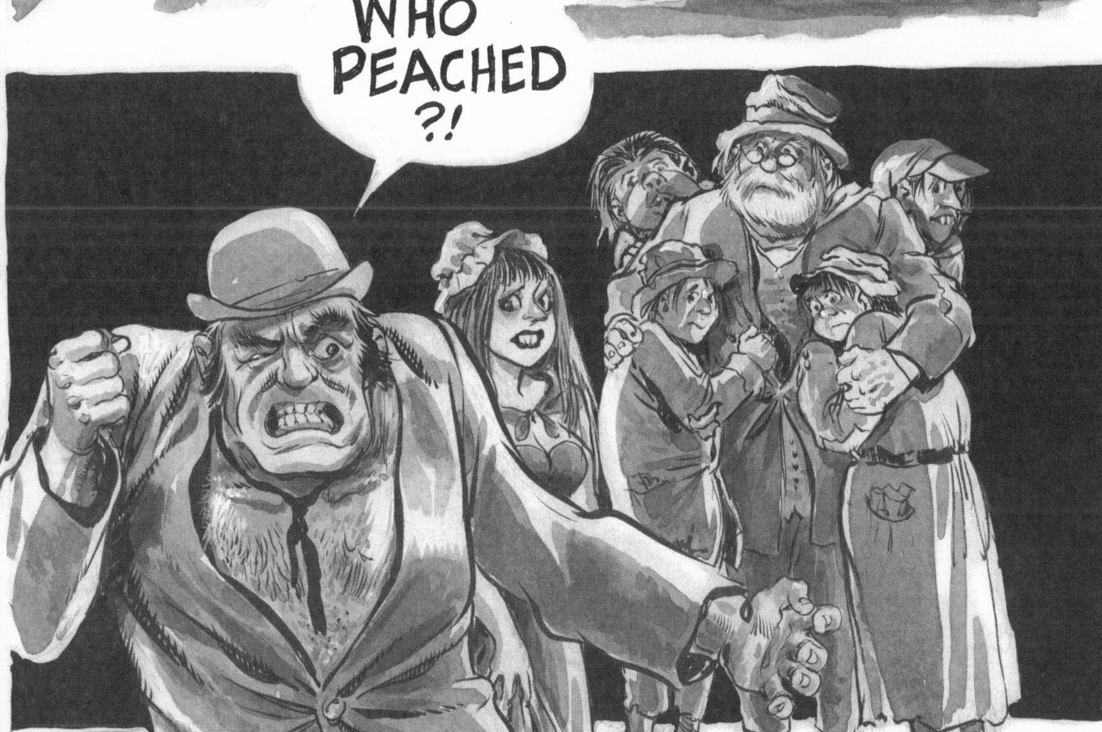
WHO PEACHED ?!

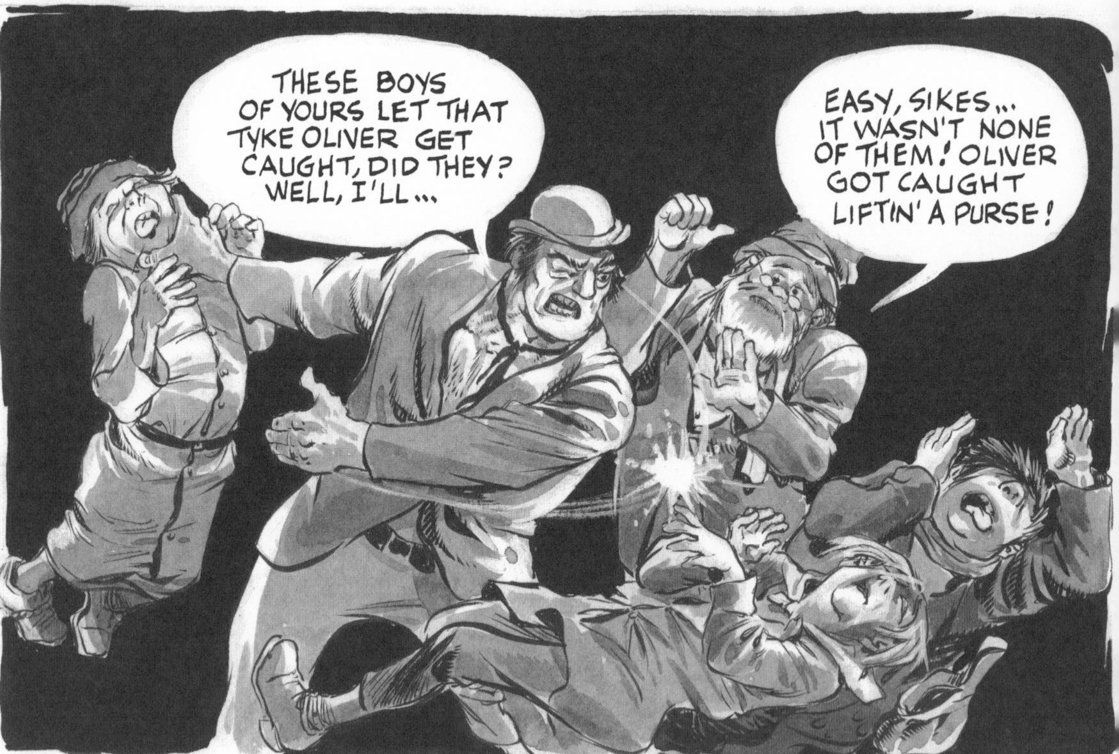
THESE BOYS OF YOURS LET THAT TYKE OLIVER GET CAUGHT, DID THEY? WELL, I'LL...
EASY, SIKES... IT WASN'T NONE OF THEM! OLIVER GOT CAUGHT LIFTIN' A PURSE!

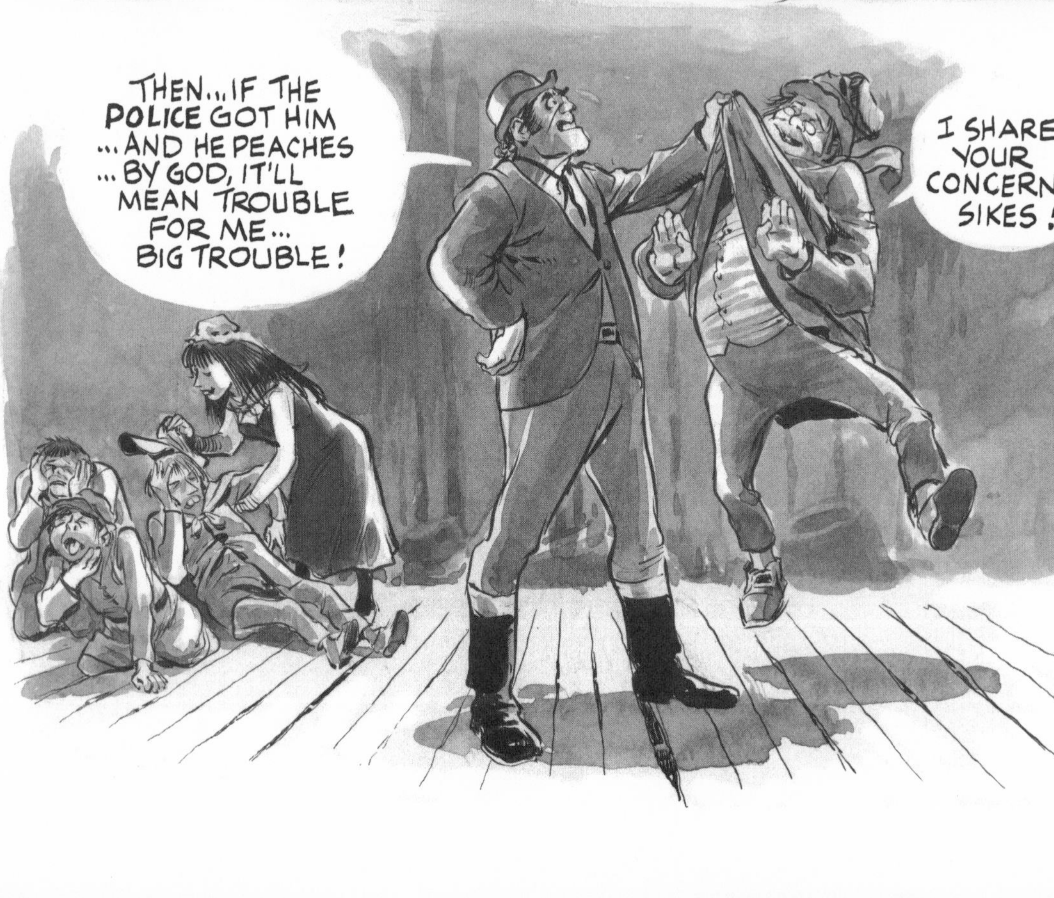
THEN...IF THE **POLICE** GOT HIM ...AND HE PEACHES ...BY GOD, IT'LL MEAN TROUBLE FOR ME... BIG TROUBLE!
I SHARE YOUR CONCERN, SIKES!

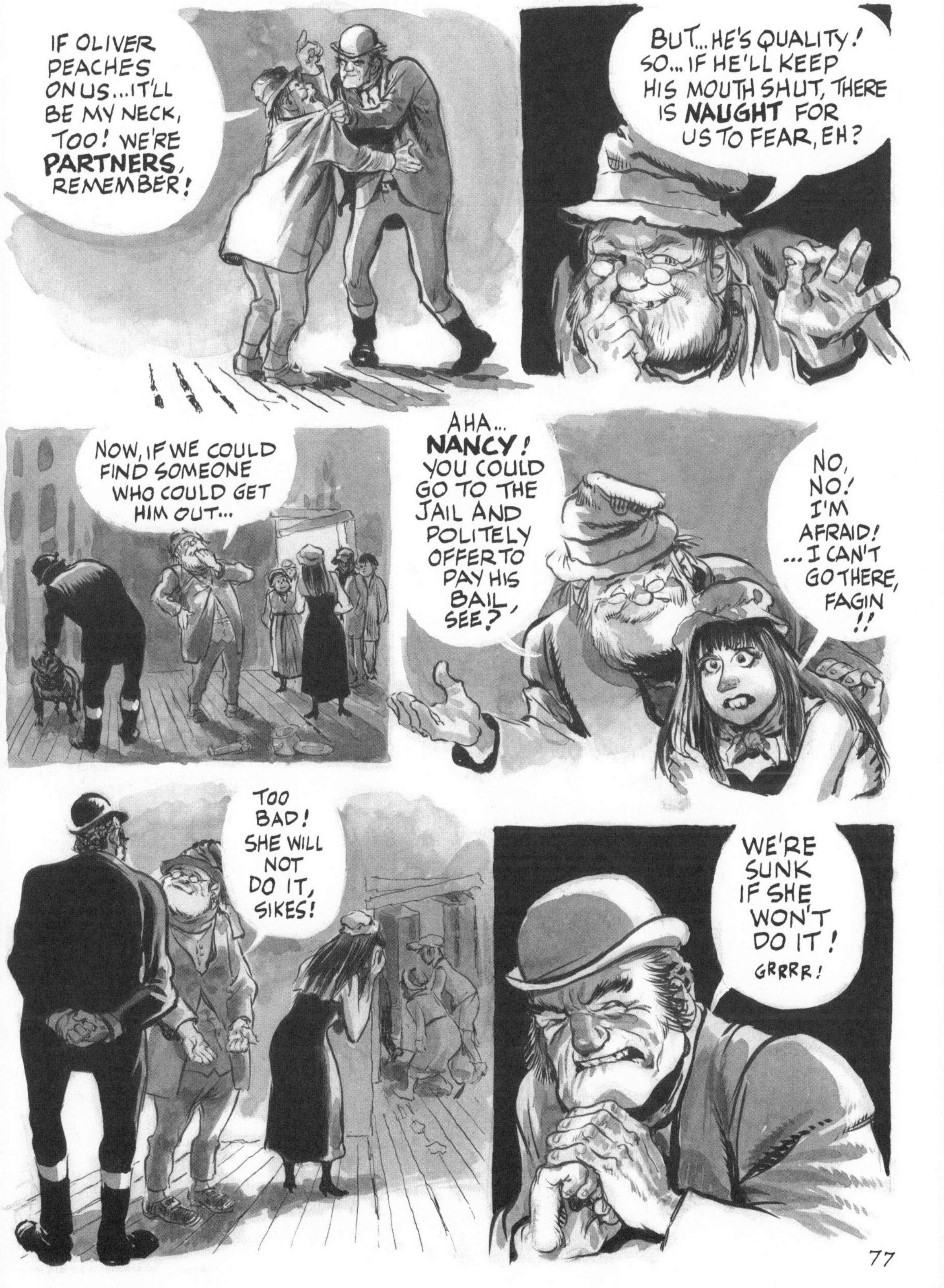
IF OLIVER PEACHES ON US...IT'LL BE MY NECK, TOO! WE'RE **PARTNERS**, REMEMBER!
BUT... HE'S QUALITY! SO... IF HE'LL KEEP HIS MOUTH SHUT, THERE IS **NAUGHT** FOR US TO FEAR, EH?
NOW, IF WE COULD FIND SOMEONE WHO COULD GET HIM OUT...
AHA... **NANCY**! YOU COULD GO TO THE JAIL AND POLITELY OFFER TO PAY HIS BAIL, SEE?
NO, NO! I'M AFRAID! ...I CAN'T GO THERE, FAGIN!!
TOO BAD! SHE WILL NOT DO IT, SIKES!
WE'RE SUNK IF SHE WON'T DO IT!
GRRRR!

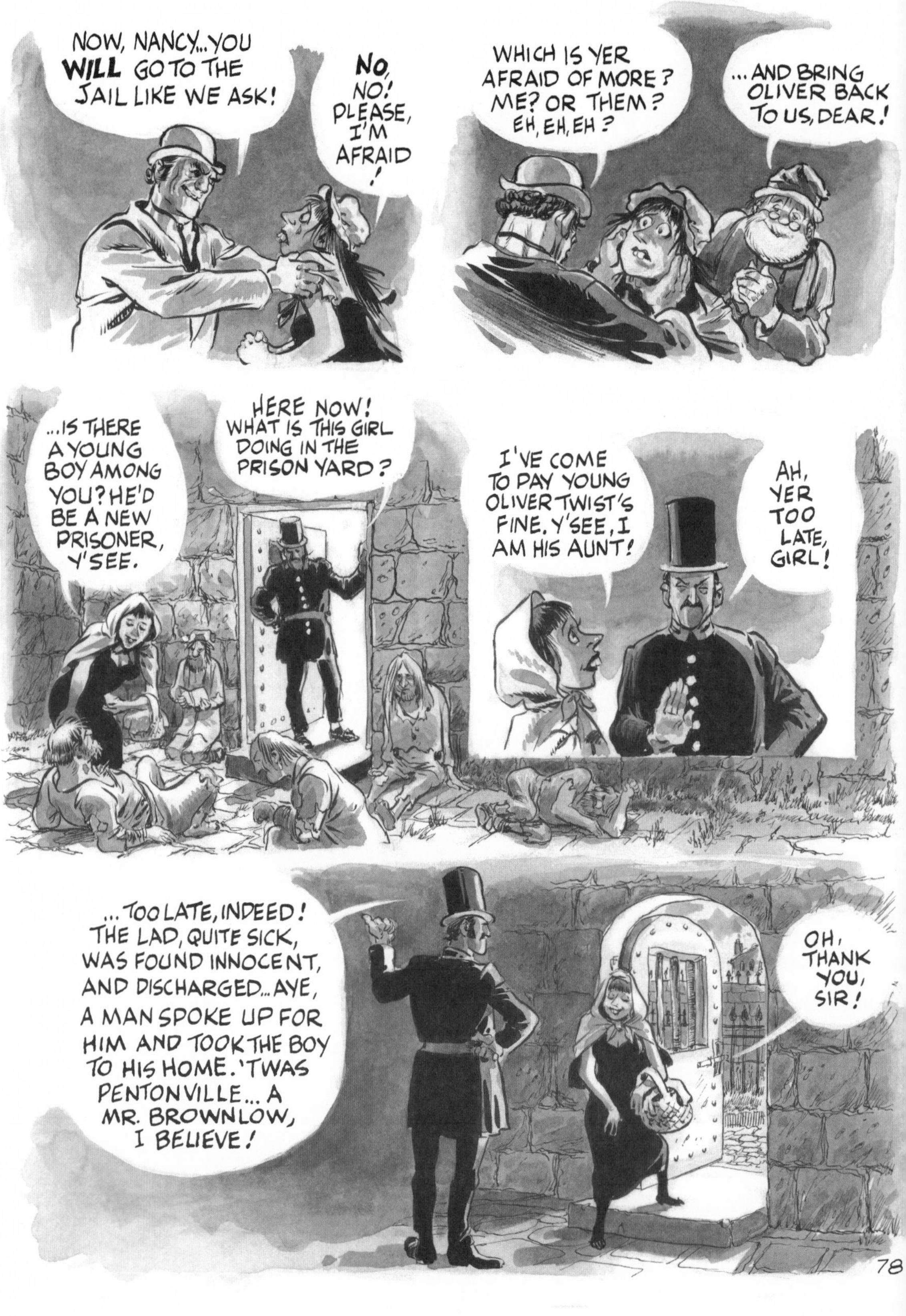
NOW, NANCY... YOU WILL GO TO THE JAIL LIKE WE ASK!
NO, NO! PLEASE, I'M AFRAID!
WHICH IS YER AFRAID OF MORE? ME? OR THEM? EH, EH, EH?
...AND BRING OLIVER BACK TO US, DEAR!
...IS THERE A YOUNG BOY AMONG YOU? HE'D BE A NEW PRISONER, Y'SEE.
HERE NOW! WHAT IS THIS GIRL DOING IN THE PRISON YARD?
I'VE COME TO PAY YOUNG OLIVER TWIST'S FINE. Y'SEE, I AM HIS AUNT!
AH, YER TOO LATE, GIRL!
...TOO LATE, INDEED! THE LAD, QUITE SICK, WAS FOUND INNOCENT, AND DISCHARGED... AYE, A MAN SPOKE UP FOR HIM AND TOOK THE BOY TO HIS HOME. 'TWAS PENTONVILLE... A MR. BROWNLOW, I BELIEVE!
OH, THANK YOU, SIR!

But Nancy had bad news for us.

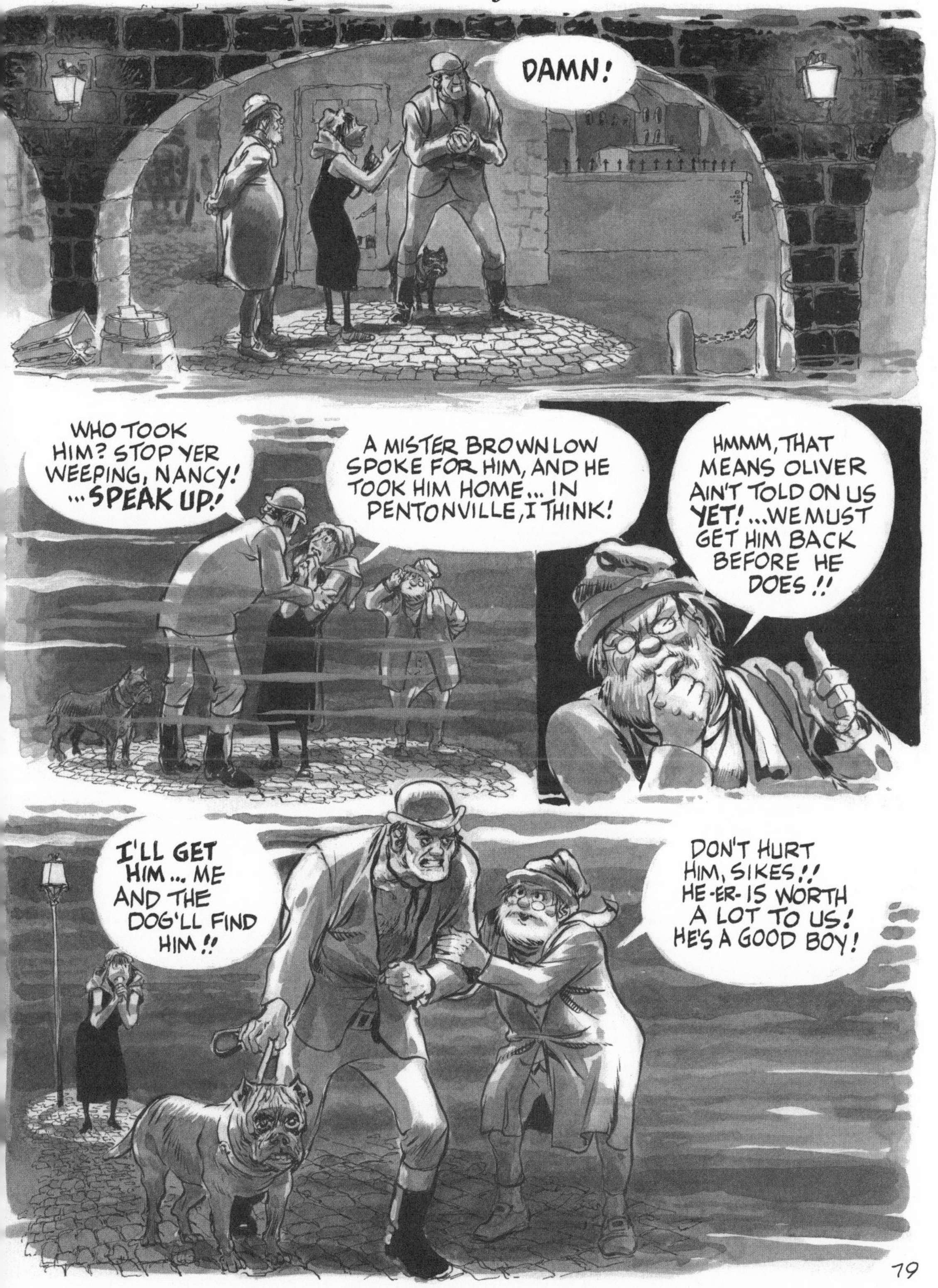
DAMN!
WHO TOOK HIM? STOP YER WEEPING, NANCY! ...SPEAK UP!
A MISTER BROWNLOW SPOKE FOR HIM, AND HE TOOK HIM HOME... IN PENTONVILLE, I THINK!
HMMM, THAT MEANS OLIVER AIN'T TOLD ON US YET! ...WE MUST GET HIM BACK BEFORE HE DOES!!
I'LL GET HIM... ME AND THE DOG'LL FIND HIM!!
DON'T HURT HIM, SIKES!! HE-ER-IS WORTH A LOT TO US! HE'S A GOOD BOY!

At the Brownlows' home, Oliver soon recovered from his fainting in the magistrate's office.

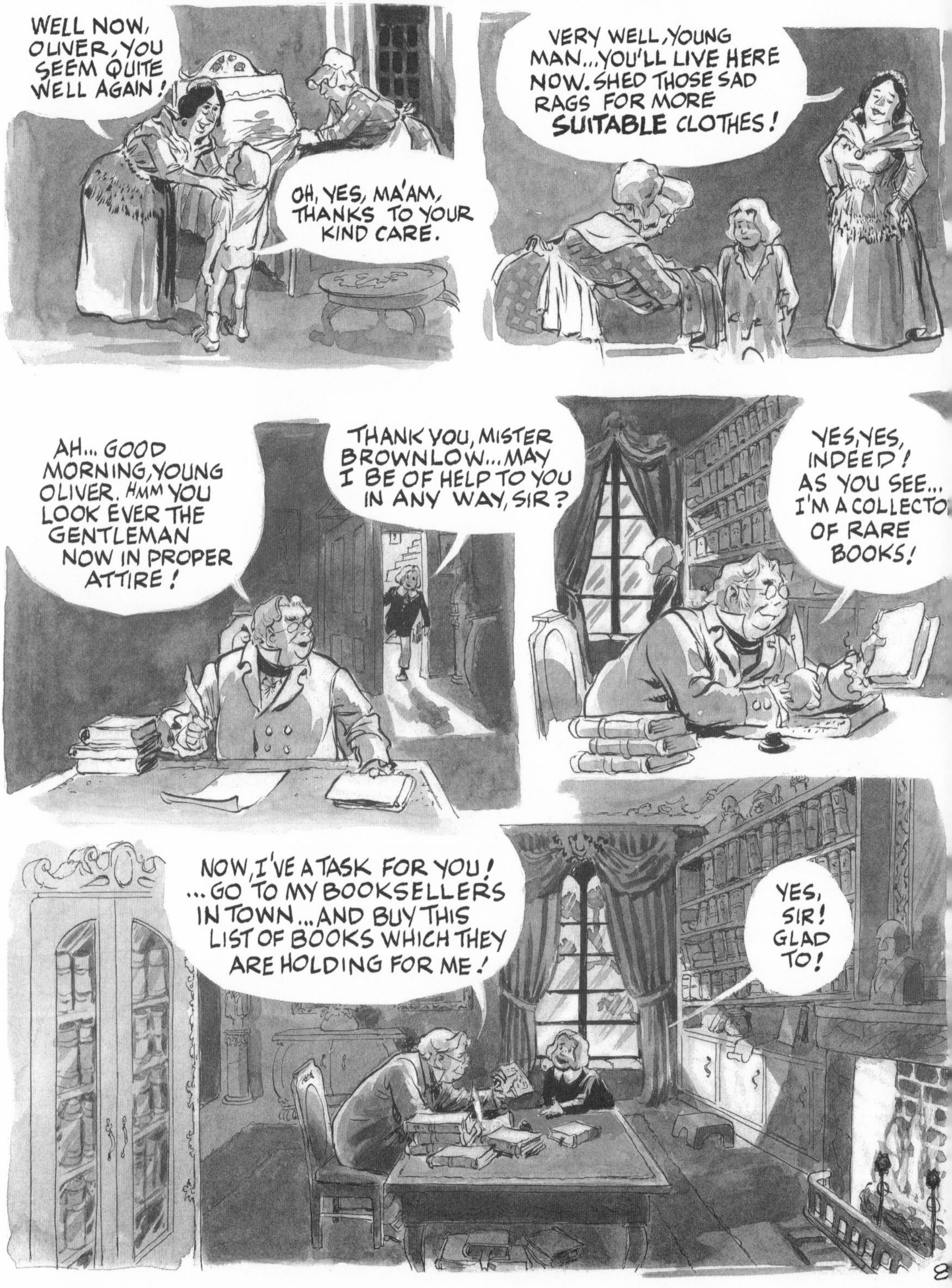
WELL NOW, OLIVER, YOU SEEM QUITE WELL AGAIN!
OH, YES, MA'AM, THANKS TO YOUR KIND CARE.
VERY WELL, YOUNG MAN... YOU'LL LIVE HERE NOW. SHED THOSE SAD RAGS FOR MORE SUITABLE CLOTHES!
AH... GOOD MORNING, YOUNG OLIVER. HMM YOU LOOK EVER THE GENTLEMAN NOW IN PROPER ATTIRE!
THANK YOU, MISTER BROWNLOW... MAY I BE OF HELP TO YOU IN ANY WAY, SIR?
YES, YES, INDEED! AS YOU SEE... I'M A COLLECTO OF RARE BOOKS!
NOW, I'VE A TASK FOR YOU! ...GO TO MY BOOKSELLERS IN TOWN... AND BUY THIS LIST OF BOOKS WHICH THEY ARE HOLDING FOR ME!
YES, SIR! GLAD TO!

In London's streets, Sikes and my boys were persistently searching for Oliver.

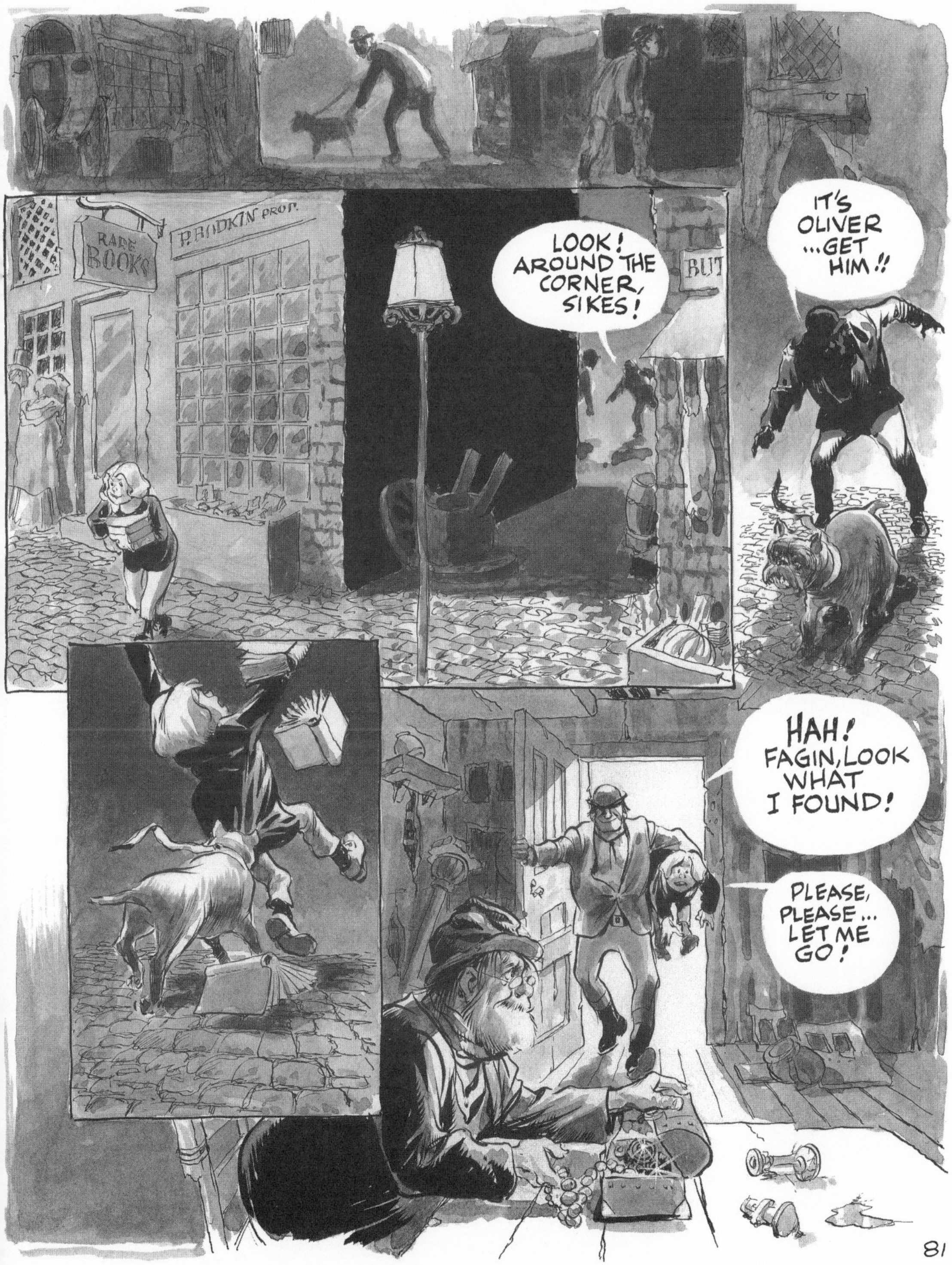
RARE BOOKS
P. BODKIN PROP.
BUT
LOOK! AROUND THE CORNER, SIKES!
IT'S OLIVER ...GET HIM!!
HAH! FAGIN, LOOK WHAT I FOUND!
PLEASE, PLEASE... LET ME GO!

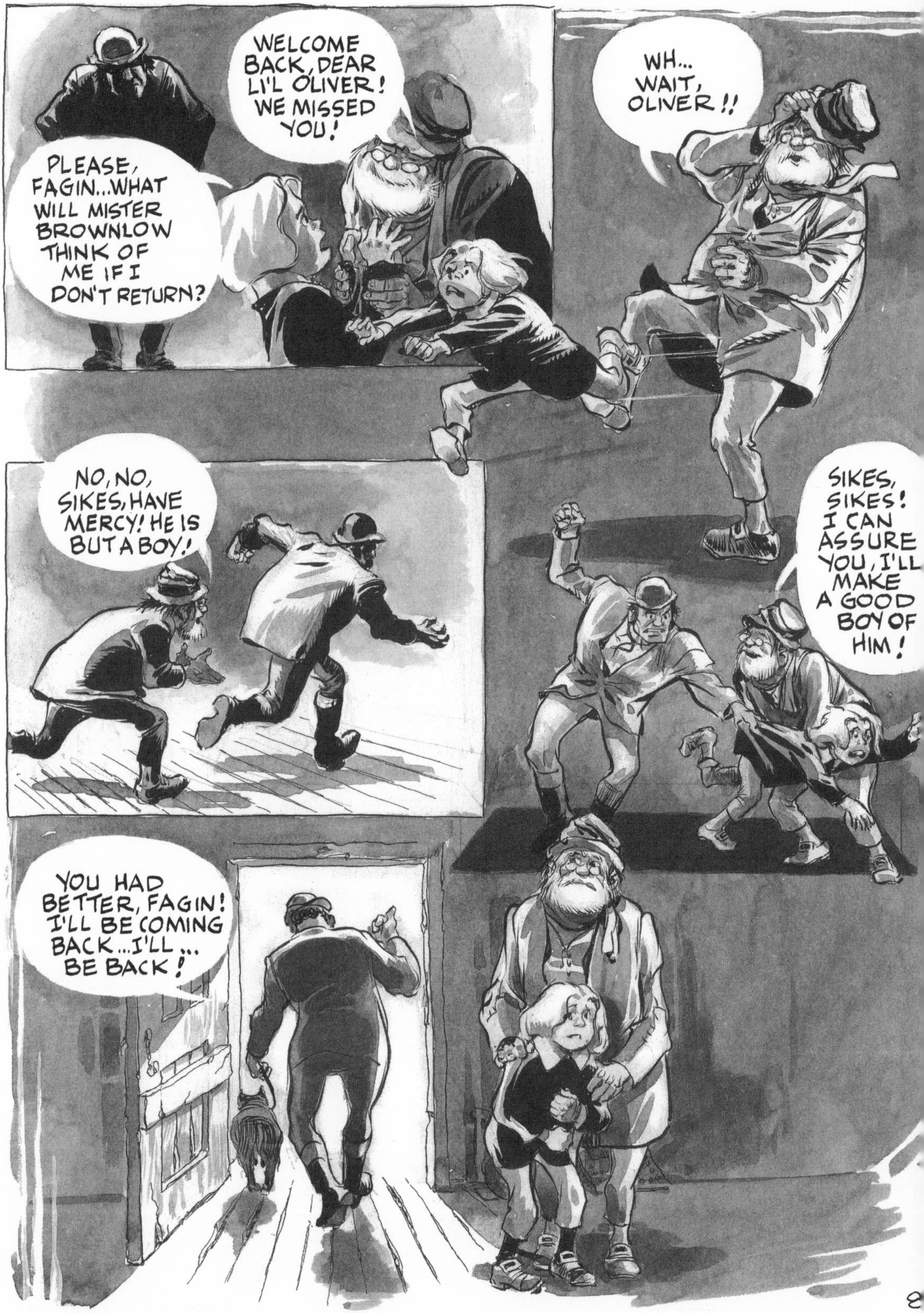
WELCOME BACK, DEAR LI'L OLIVER! WE MISSED YOU!
PLEASE, FAGIN...WHAT WILL MISTER BROWNLOW THINK OF ME IF I DON'T RETURN?
WH... WAIT, OLIVER!!
NO, NO, SIKES, HAVE MERCY! HE IS BUT A BOY!
SIKES, SIKES! I CAN ASSURE YOU, I'LL MAKE A GOOD BOY OF HIM!
YOU HAD BETTER, FAGIN! I'LL BE COMING BACK...I'LL... BE BACK!

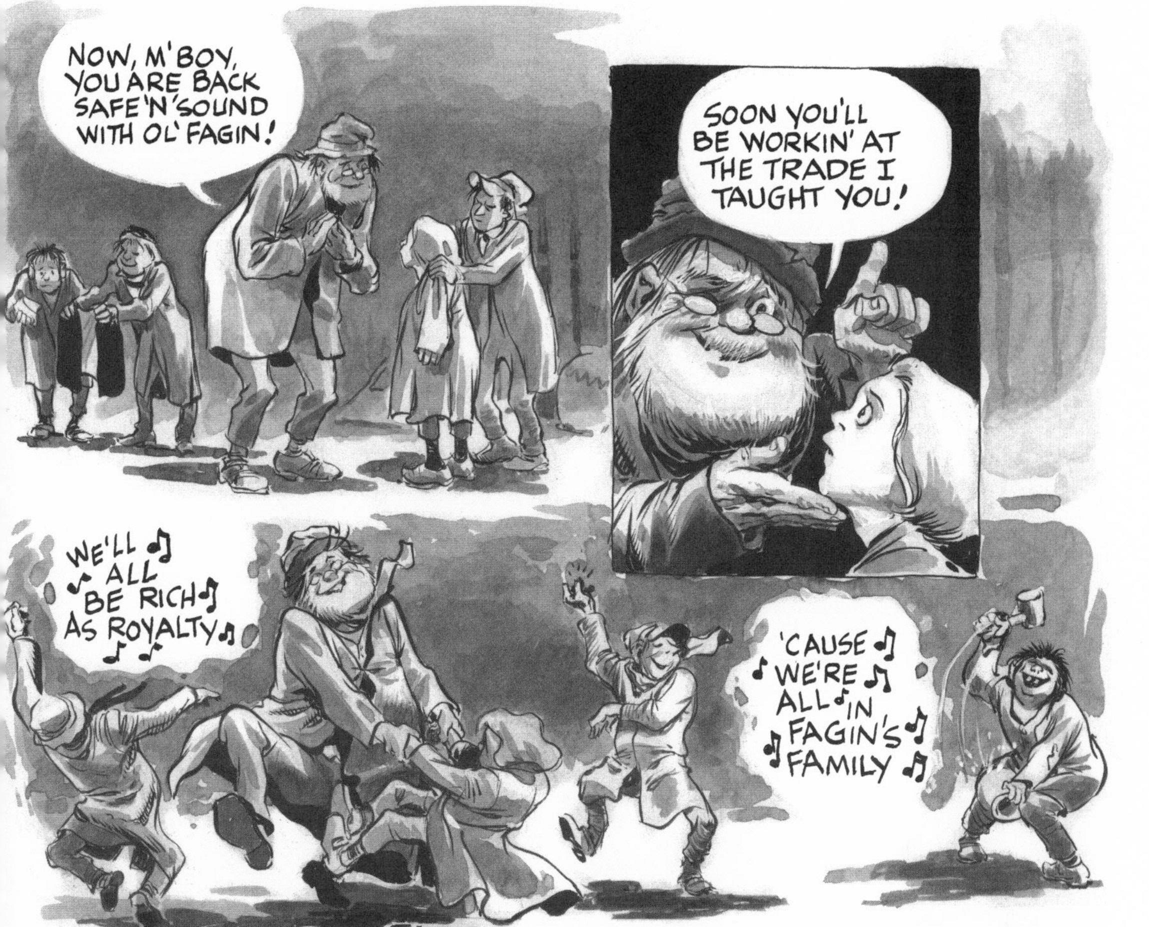
NOW, M'BOY, YOU ARE BACK SAFE 'N' SOUND WITH OL' FAGIN!
SOON YOU'LL BE WORKIN' AT THE TRADE I TAUGHT YOU!
WE'LL ♫ ♪ ALL BE RICH ♫ AS ROYALTY ♫ ♪ ♪
'CAUSE ♫ ♪ WE'RE ♫ ALL ♪ IN FAGIN'S ♫ ♫ FAMILY ♫

So, once more we had our Oliver back on the streets.

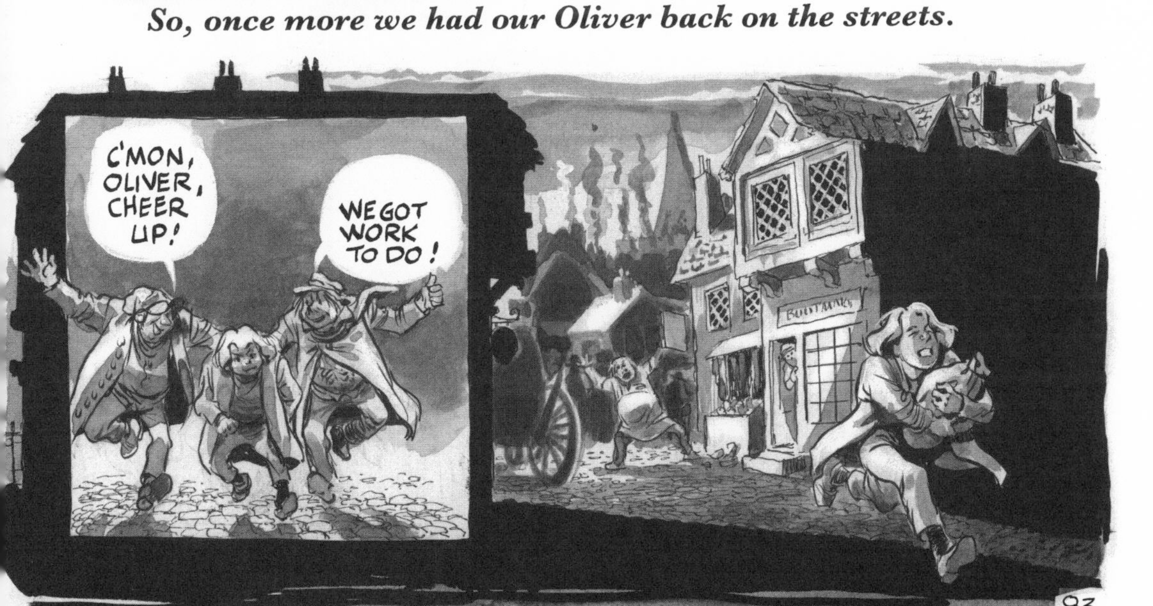
C'MON, OLIVER, CHEER UP!
WE GOT WORK TO DO!

Things were going very well again for me... until Sikes showed up.

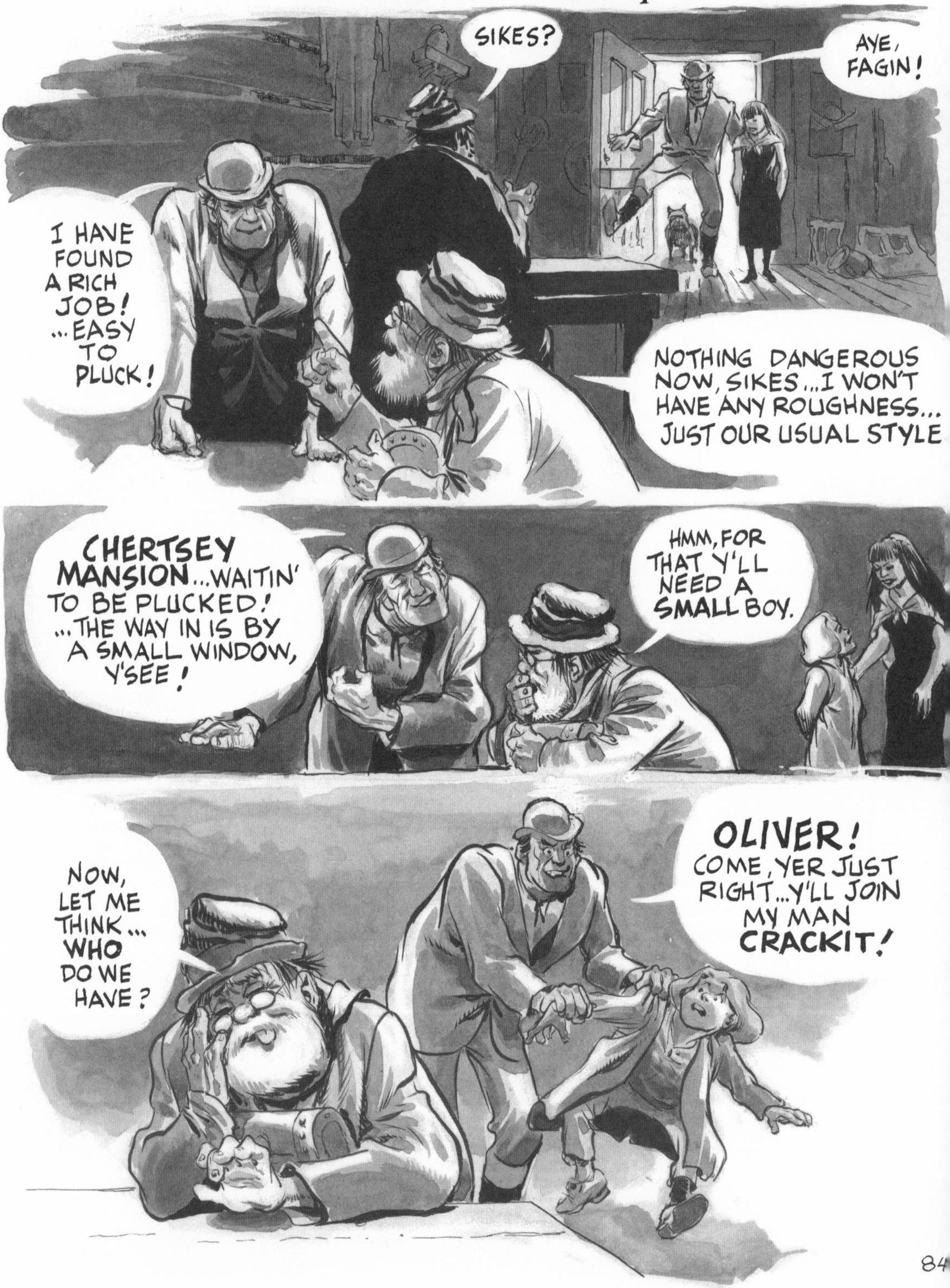
SIKES?
AYE, FAGIN!
I HAVE FOUND A RICH JOB! ...EASY TO PLUCK!
NOTHING DANGEROUS NOW, SIKES... I WON'T HAVE ANY ROUGHNESS... JUST OUR USUAL STYLE
CHERTSEY MANSION...WAITIN' TO BE PLUCKED! ...THE WAY IN IS BY A SMALL WINDOW, Y'SEE!
HMM, FOR THAT Y'LL NEED A SMALL BOY.
NOW, LET ME THINK... WHO DO WE HAVE?
OLIVER! COME, YER JUST RIGHT...Y'LL JOIN MY MAN CRACKIT!

That night, outside the Chertsey mansion...

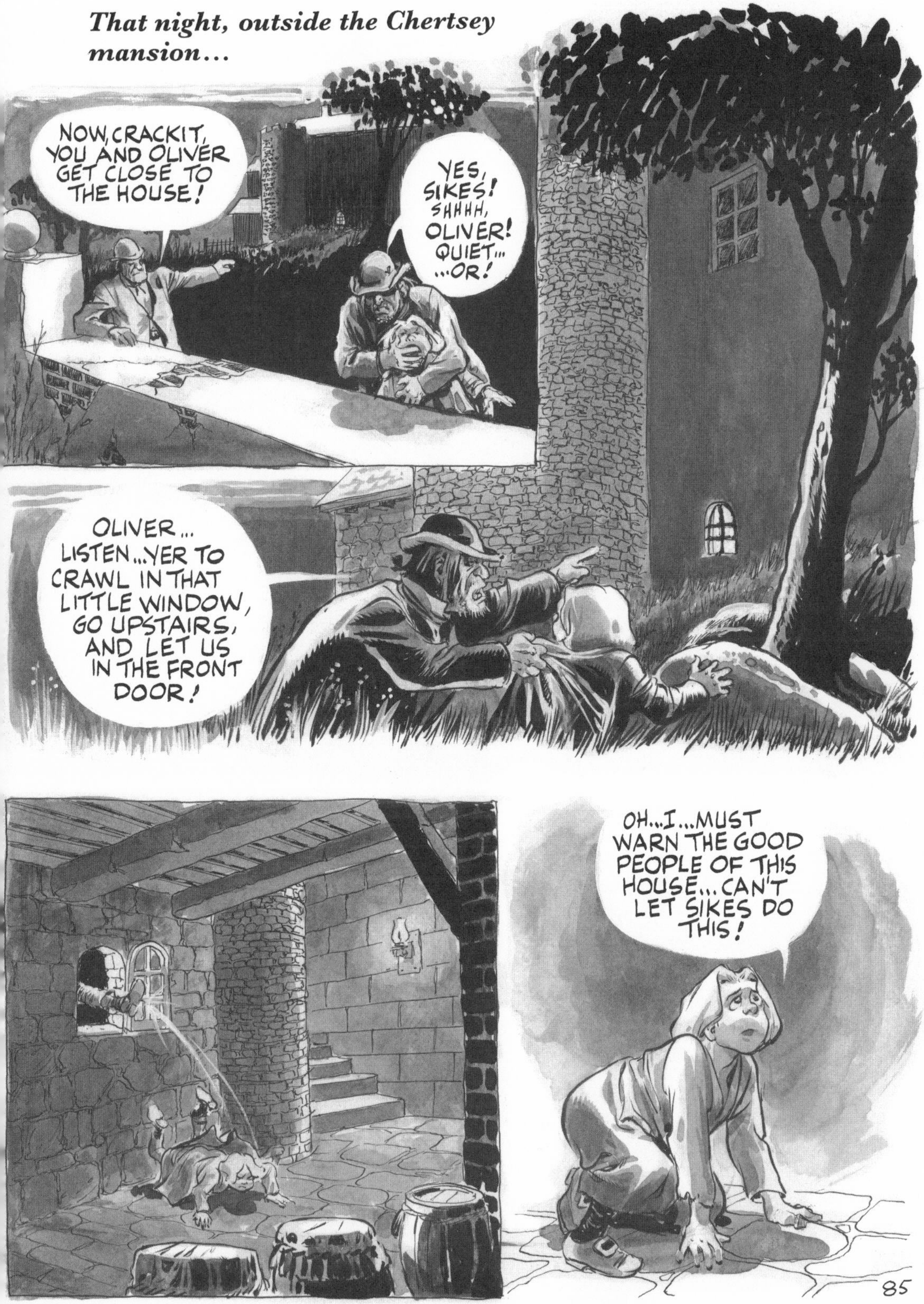
NOW, CRACKIT, YOU AND OLIVER GET CLOSE TO THE HOUSE!
YES, SIKES! SHHHH, OLIVER! QUIET... ...OR!
OLIVER... LISTEN...YER TO CRAWL IN THAT LITTLE WINDOW, GO UPSTAIRS, AND LET US IN THE FRONT DOOR!
OH...I...MUST WARN THE GOOD PEOPLE OF THIS HOUSE...CAN'T LET SIKES DO THIS!

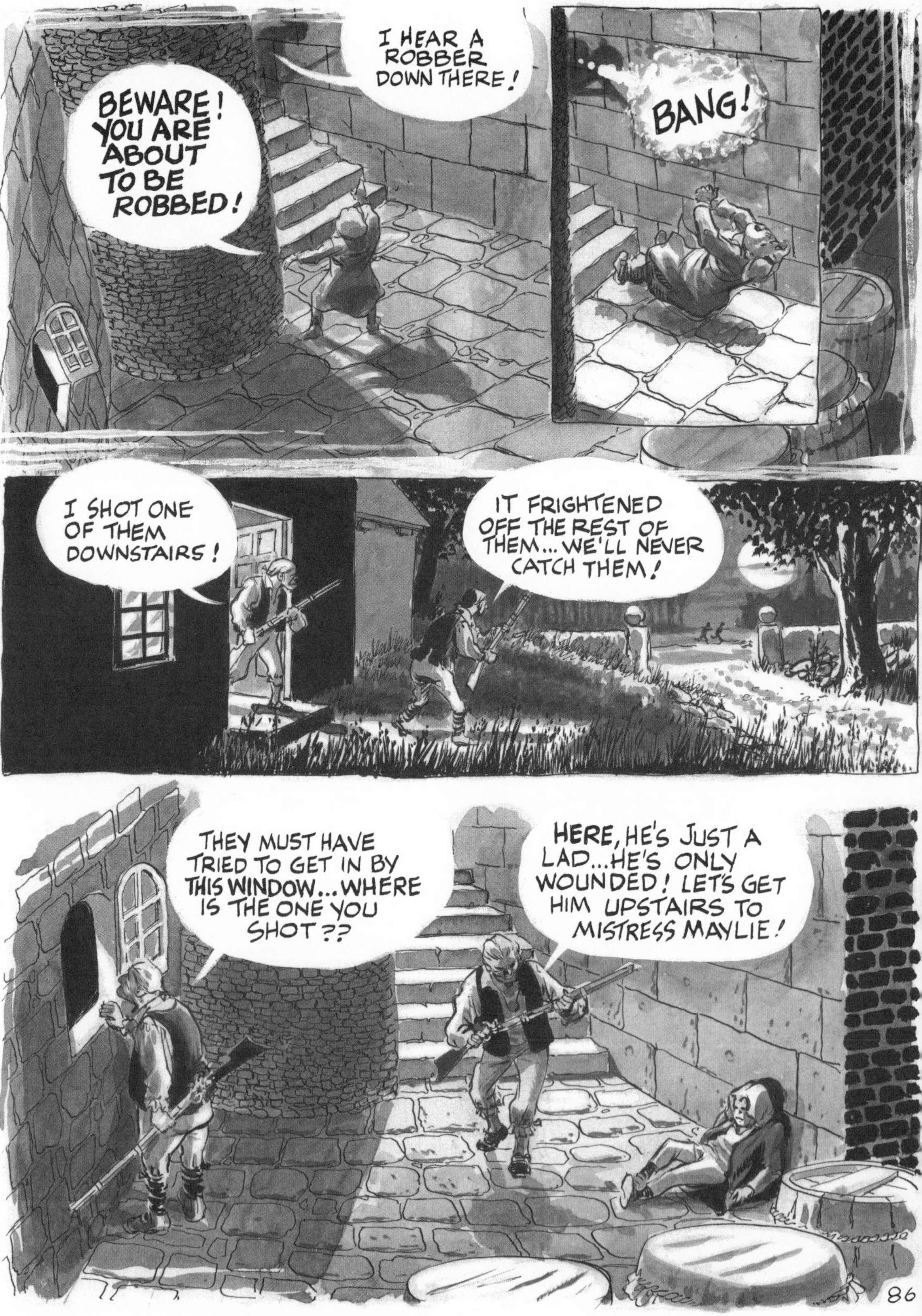
I HEAR A ROBBER DOWN THERE!
BEWARE! YOU ARE ABOUT TO BE ROBBED!
BANG!
I SHOT ONE OF THEM DOWNSTAIRS!
IT FRIGHTENED OFF THE REST OF THEM... WE'LL NEVER CATCH THEM!
THEY MUST HAVE TRIED TO GET IN BY THIS WINDOW... WHERE IS THE ONE YOU SHOT??
HERE, HE'S JUST A LAD... HE'S ONLY WOUNDED! LET'S GET HIM UPSTAIRS TO MISTRESS MAYLIE!

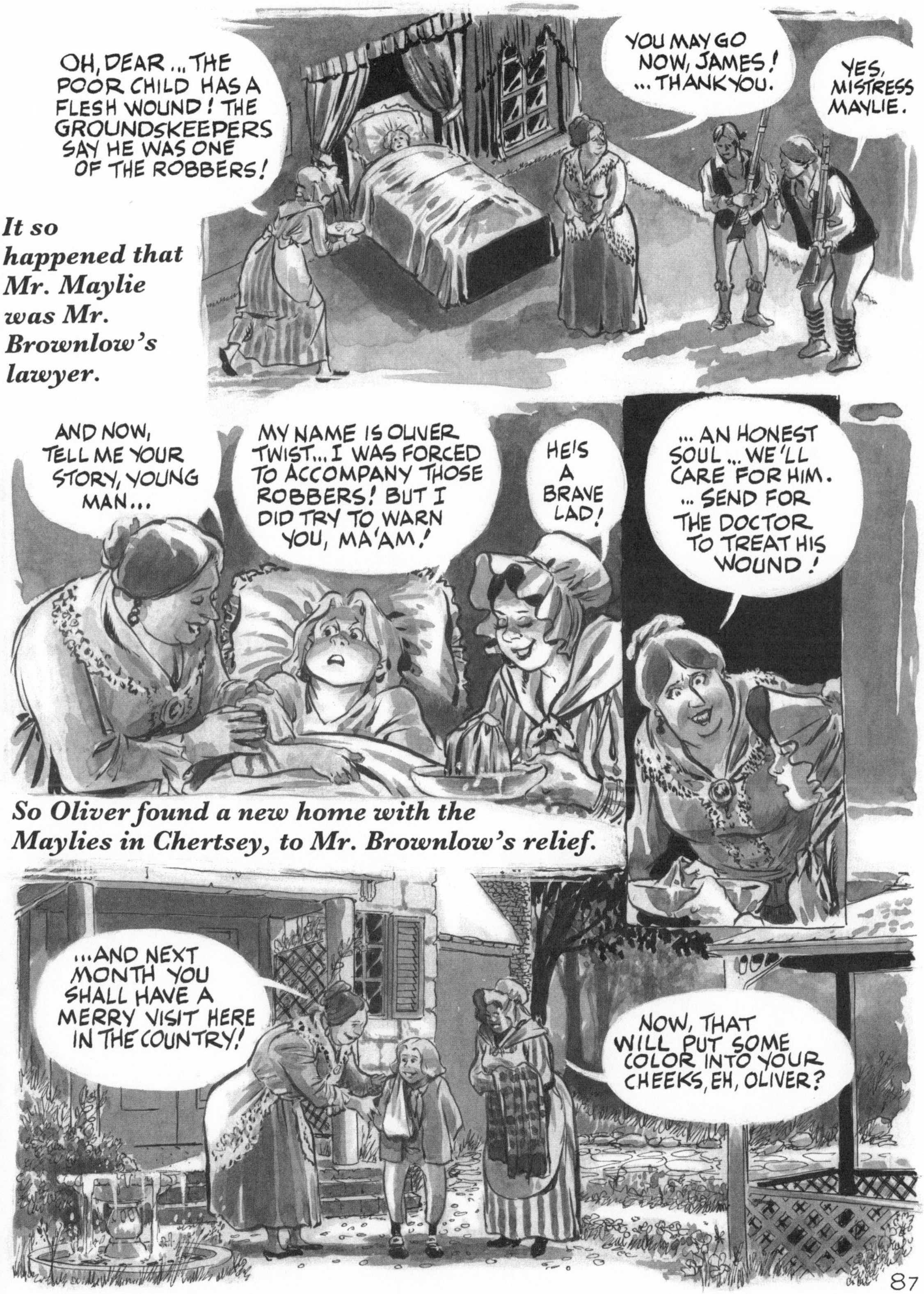
OH, DEAR ... THE POOR CHILD HAS A FLESH WOUND! THE GROUNDSKEEPERS SAY HE WAS ONE OF THE ROBBERS!
YOU MAY GO NOW, JAMES! ... THANK YOU.
YES, MISTRESS MAYLIE.
It so happened that Mr. Maylie was Mr. Brownlow's lawyer.
AND NOW, TELL ME YOUR STORY, YOUNG MAN...
MY NAME IS OLIVER TWIST... I WAS FORCED TO ACCOMPANY THOSE ROBBERS! BUT I DID TRY TO WARN YOU, MA'AM!
HE'S A BRAVE LAD!
... AN HONEST SOUL ... WE'LL CARE FOR HIM. ... SEND FOR THE DOCTOR TO TREAT HIS WOUND!
So Oliver found a new home with the Maylies in Chertsey, to Mr. Brownlow's relief.
...AND NEXT MONTH YOU SHALL HAVE A MERRY VISIT HERE IN THE COUNTRY!
NOW, THAT WILL PUT SOME COLOR INTO YOUR CHEEKS, EH, OLIVER?

I lost track of Oliver… try as I might, I could not find him. One evening an evil-looking stranger visited me…

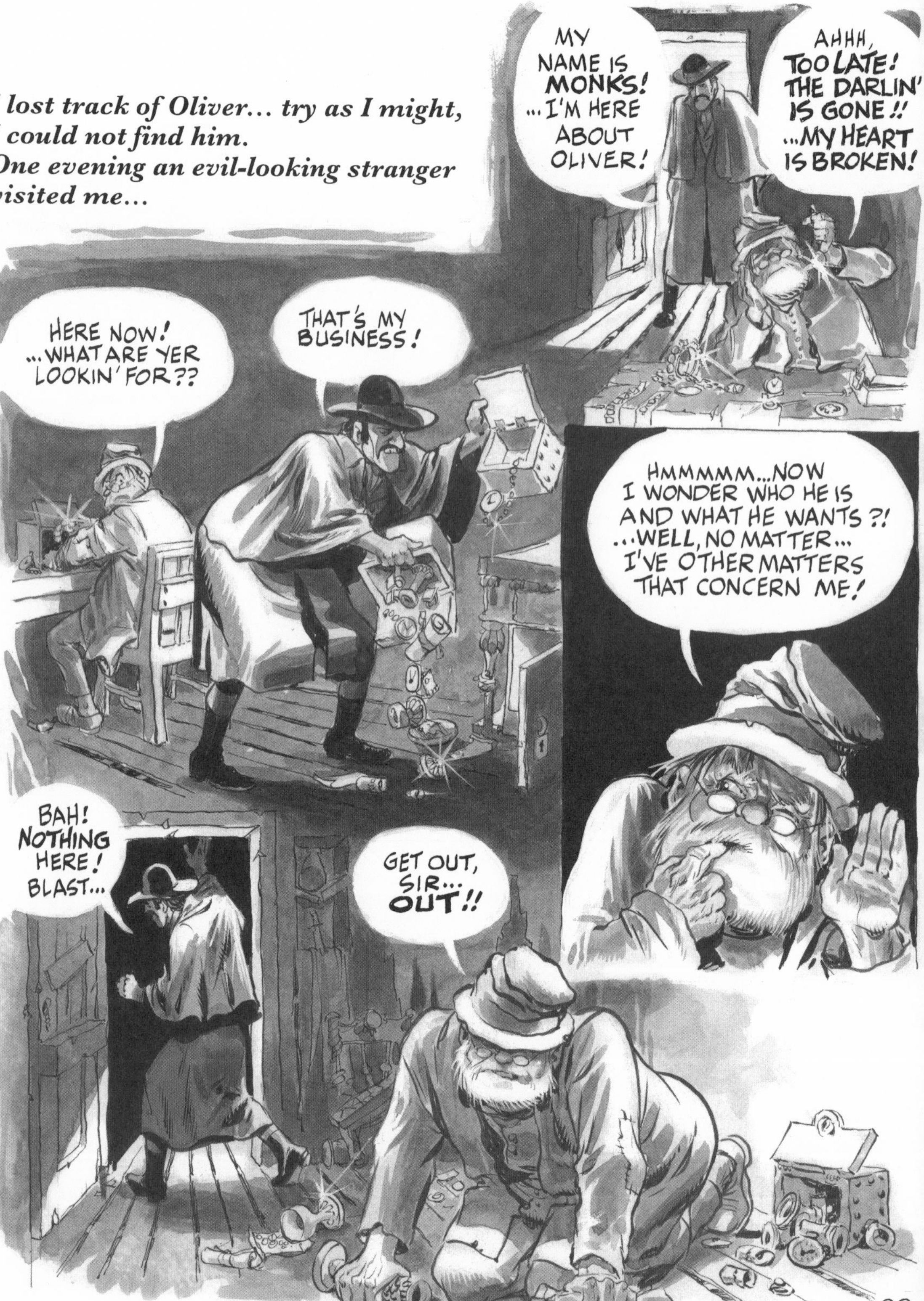
MY NAME IS MONKS! ...I'M HERE ABOUT OLIVER!
AHHH, TOO LATE! THE DARLIN' IS GONE!! ...MY HEART IS BROKEN!
HERE NOW! ...WHAT ARE YER LOOKIN' FOR??
THAT'S MY BUSINESS!
HMMMMM...NOW I WONDER WHO HE IS AND WHAT HE WANTS?! ...WELL, NO MATTER... I'VE OTHER MATTERS THAT CONCERN ME!
BAH! NOTHING HERE! BLAST...
GET OUT, SIR... OUT!!

Later I learned that Monks made his way to a tavern frequented by the beadle who was at the workhouse where Oliver was born.

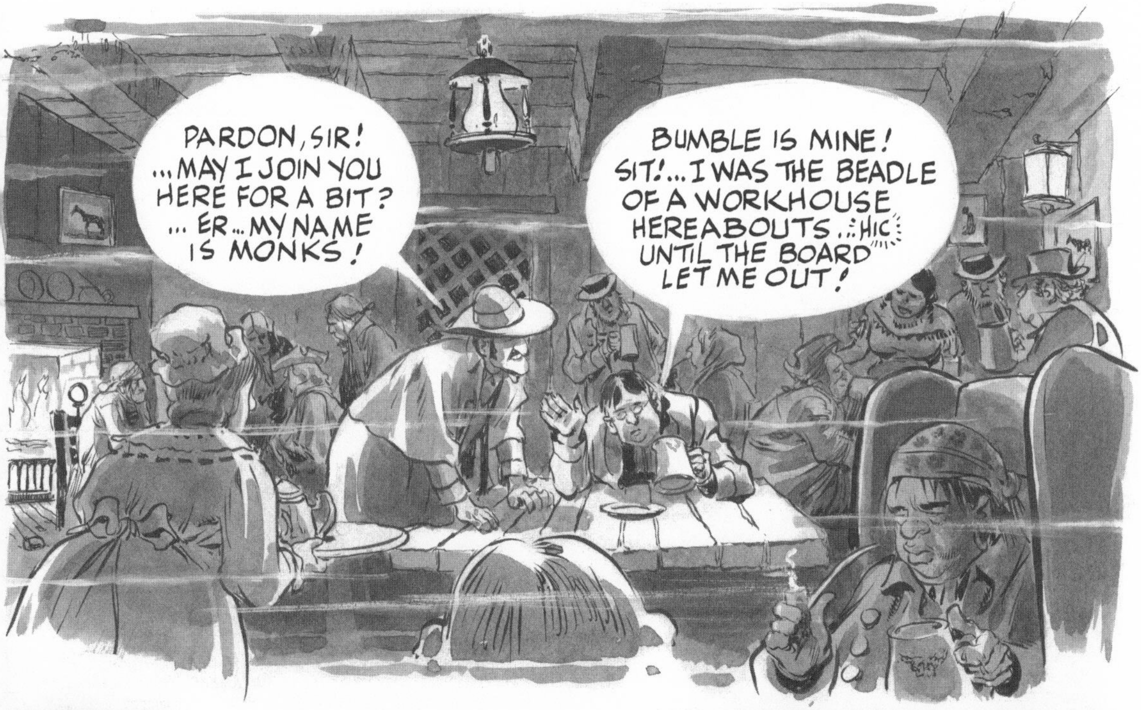
PARDON, SIR! ...MAY I JOIN YOU HERE FOR A BIT? ... ER... MY NAME IS MONKS!
BUMBLE IS MINE! SIT!... I WAS THE BEADLE OF A WORKHOUSE HEREABOUTS... HIC UNTIL THE BOARD LET ME OUT!

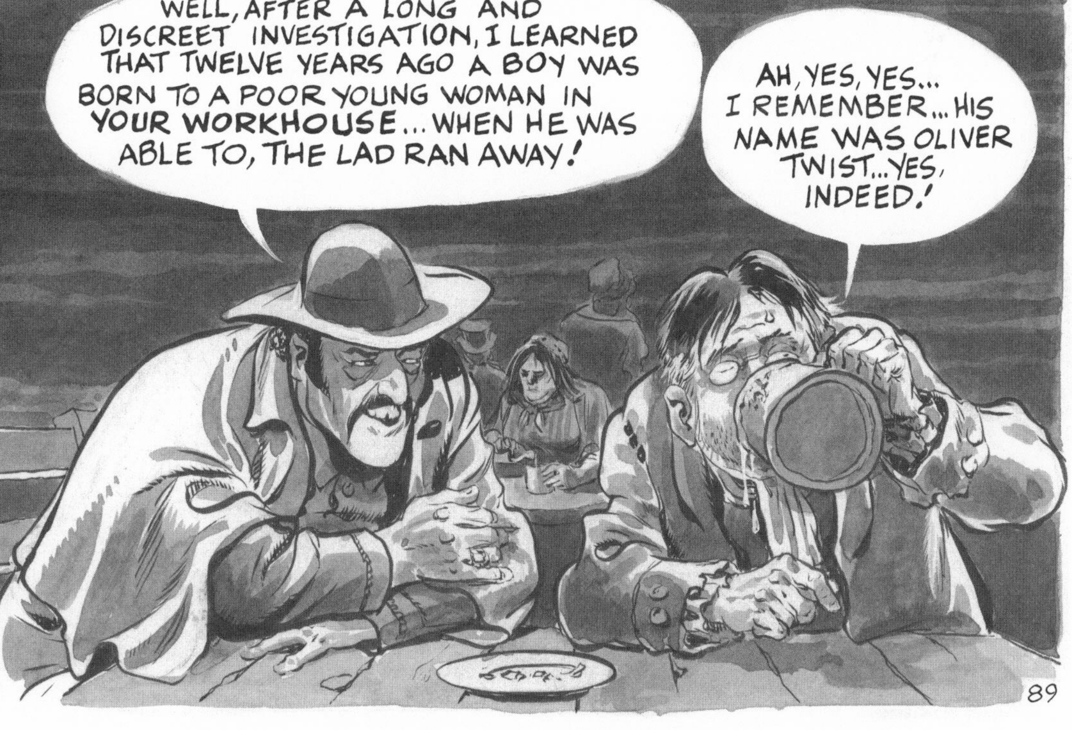
WELL, AFTER A LONG AND DISCREET INVESTIGATION, I LEARNED THAT TWELVE YEARS AGO A BOY WAS BORN TO A POOR YOUNG WOMAN IN YOUR WORKHOUSE... WHEN HE WAS ABLE TO, THE LAD RAN AWAY!
AH, YES, YES... I REMEMBER... HIS NAME WAS OLIVER TWIST... YES, INDEED!

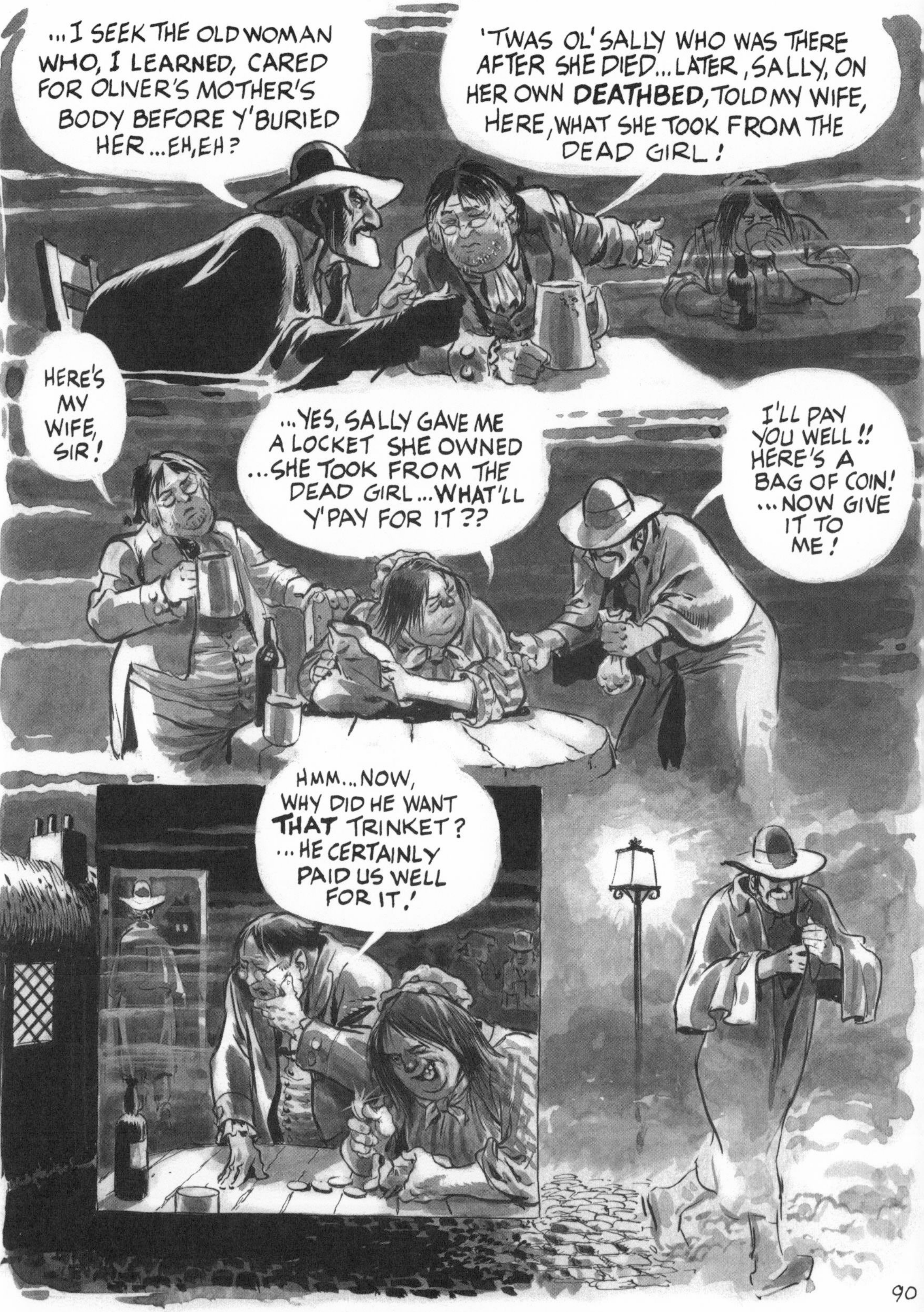
...I SEEK THE OLD WOMAN WHO, I LEARNED, CARED FOR OLIVER'S MOTHER'S BODY BEFORE Y'BURIED HER...EH,EH?
'TWAS OL' SALLY WHO WAS THERE AFTER SHE DIED... LATER, SALLY, ON HER OWN DEATHBED, TOLD MY WIFE, HERE, WHAT SHE TOOK FROM THE DEAD GIRL!
HERE'S MY WIFE, SIR!
...YES, SALLY GAVE ME A LOCKET SHE OWNED ...SHE TOOK FROM THE DEAD GIRL...WHAT'LL Y'PAY FOR IT??
I'LL PAY YOU WELL!! HERE'S A BAG OF COIN! ...NOW GIVE IT TO ME!
HMM...NOW, WHY DID HE WANT THAT TRINKET? ...HE CERTAINLY PAID US WELL FOR IT!

The next day I had another visit from Monks.

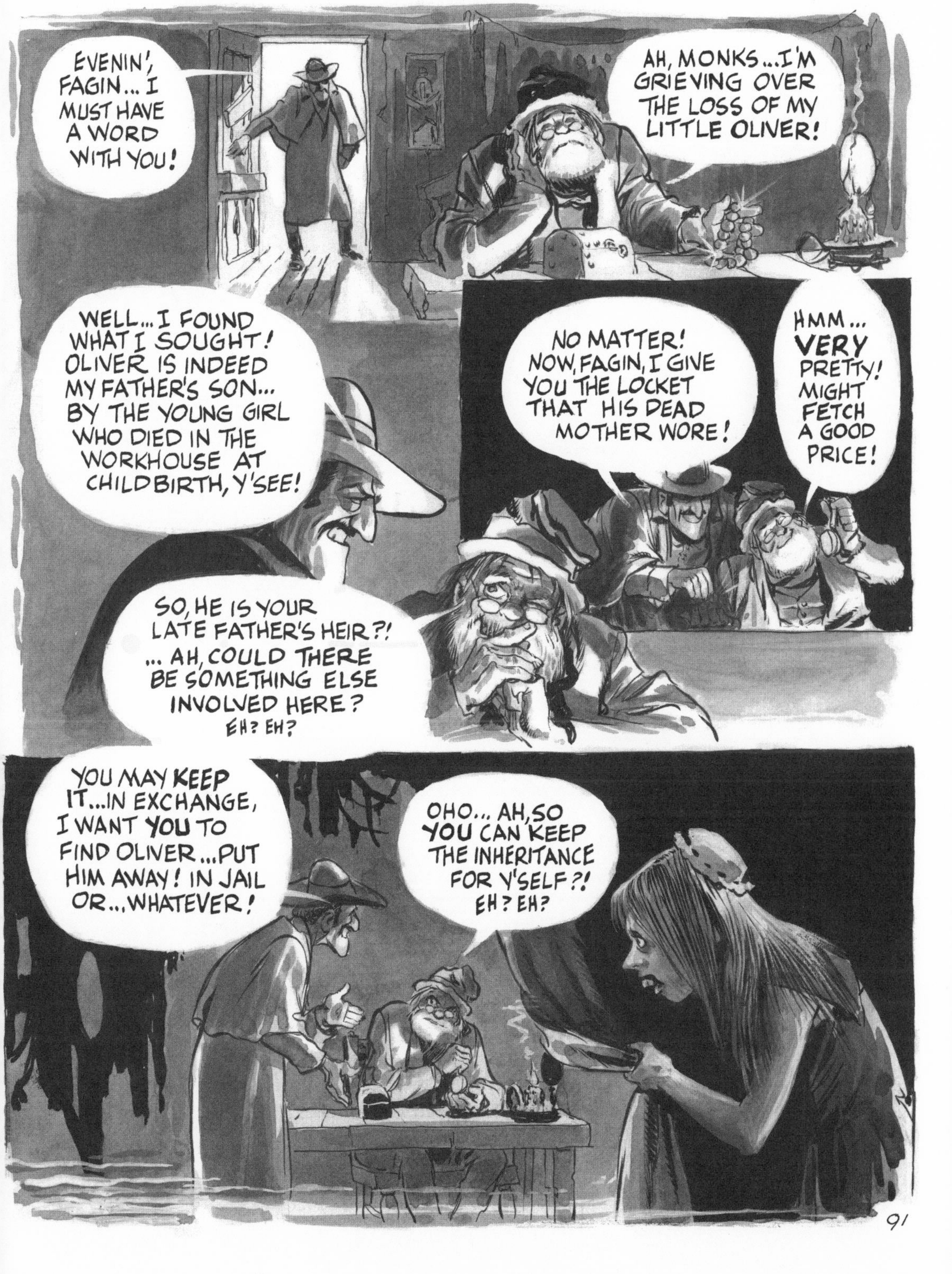
EVENIN', FAGIN... I MUST HAVE A WORD WITH YOU!
AH, MONKS...I'M GRIEVING OVER THE LOSS OF MY LITTLE OLIVER!
WELL... I FOUND WHAT I SOUGHT! OLIVER IS INDEED MY FATHER'S SON... BY THE YOUNG GIRL WHO DIED IN THE WORKHOUSE AT CHILDBIRTH, Y'SEE!
SO, HE IS YOUR LATE FATHER'S HEIR?! ... AH, COULD THERE BE SOMETHING ELSE INVOLVED HERE? EH? EH?
NO MATTER! NOW, FAGIN, I GIVE YOU THE LOCKET THAT HIS DEAD MOTHER WORE!
HMM... VERY PRETTY! MIGHT FETCH A GOOD PRICE!
YOU MAY KEEP IT...IN EXCHANGE, I WANT YOU TO FIND OLIVER...PUT HIM AWAY! IN JAIL OR...WHATEVER!
OHO... AH, SO YOU CAN KEEP THE INHERITANCE FOR Y'SELF?! EH? EH?

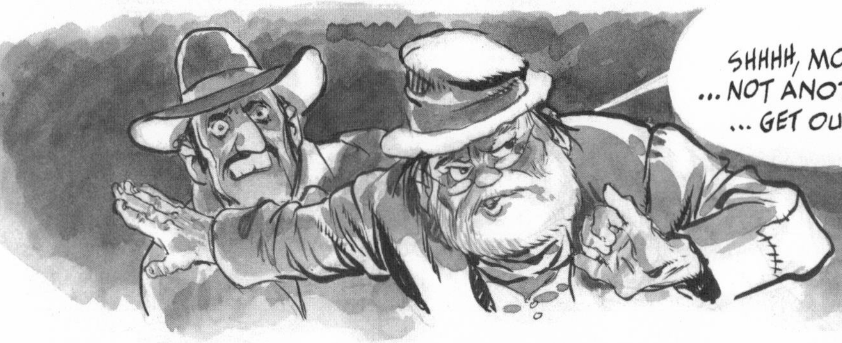
SHHHH, MONKS! ... NOT ANOTHER WORD! ... GET OUT... GO!!

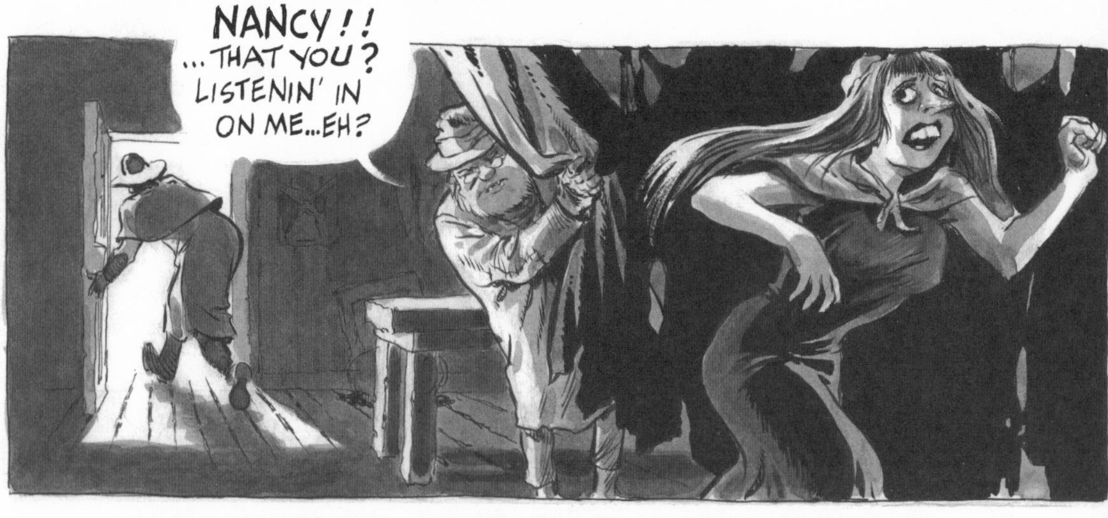
NANCY!! ... THAT YOU? LISTENIN' IN ON ME...EH?

Nancy ran off to the Maylie family. I reckon that she'd learned from Sikes's boasting where they were sheltering Oliver.

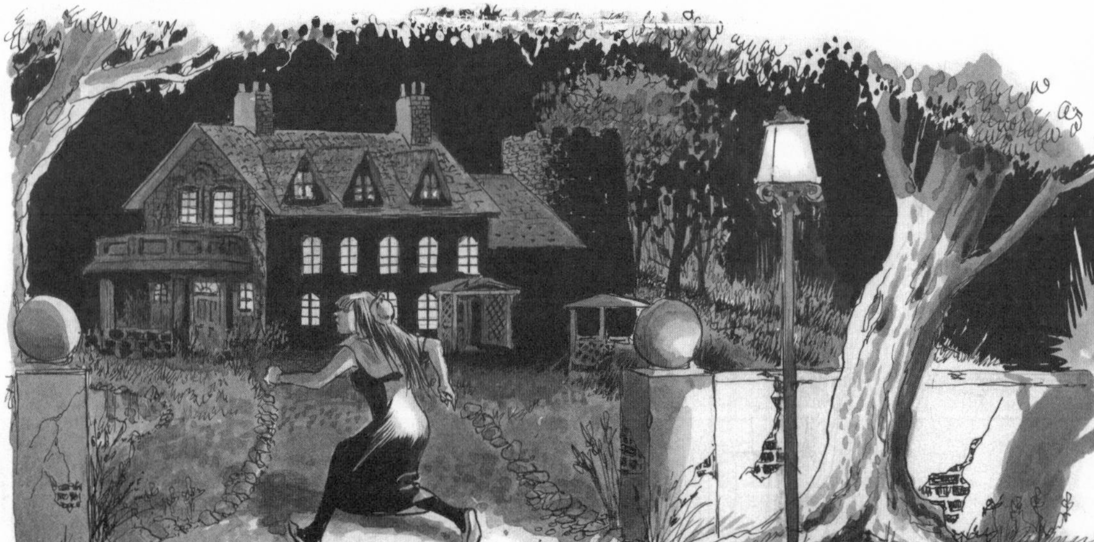

It was not hard to guess that Nancy told the Maylies what she had overheard.

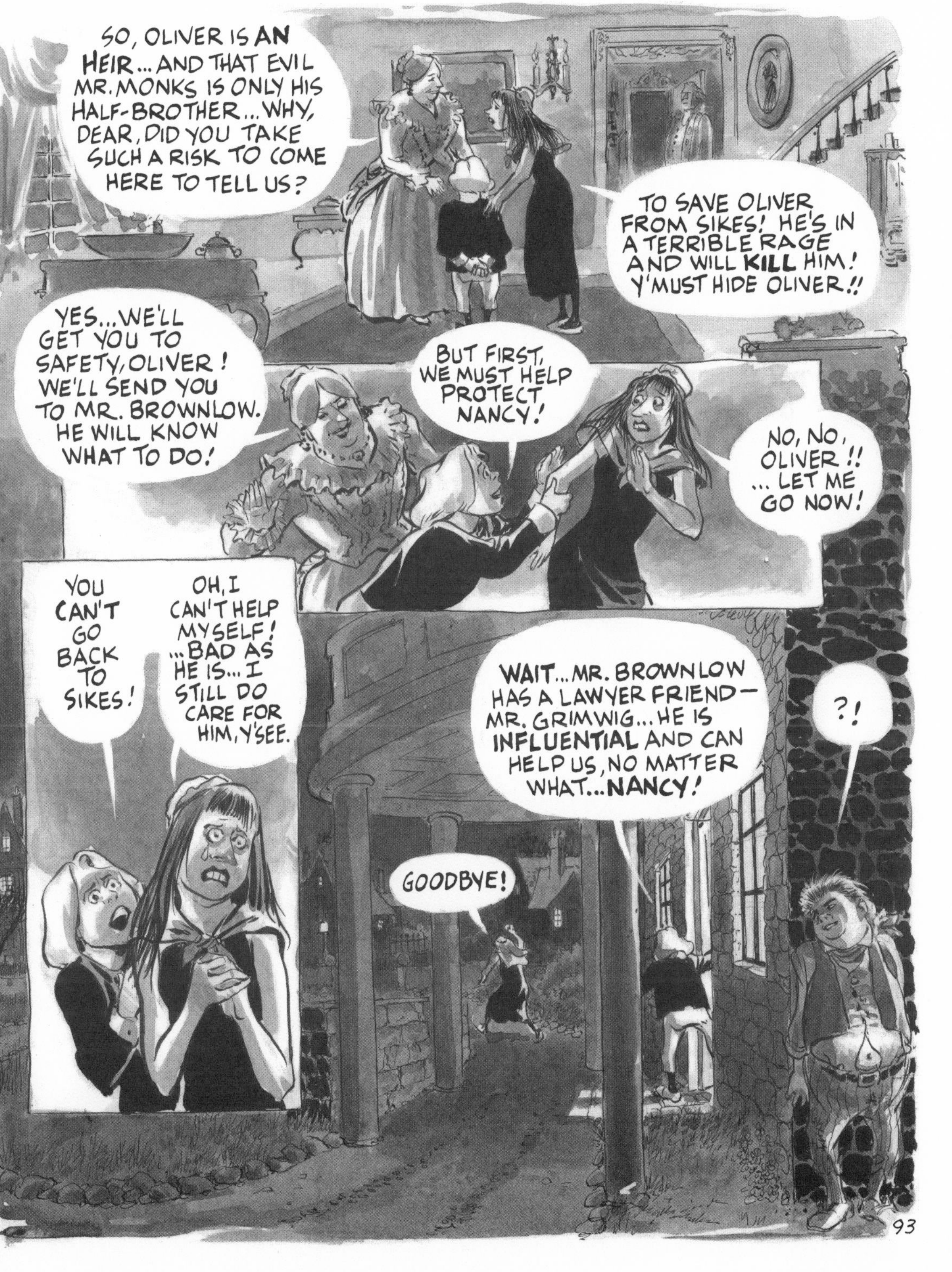

SO, OLIVER IS **AN HEIR**... AND THAT EVIL MR. MONKS IS ONLY HIS HALF-BROTHER... WHY, DEAR, DID YOU TAKE SUCH A RISK TO COME HERE TO TELL US?
TO SAVE OLIVER FROM SIKES! HE'S IN A TERRIBLE RAGE AND WILL **KILL** HIM! Y'MUST HIDE OLIVER!!
YES... WE'LL GET YOU TO SAFETY, OLIVER! WE'LL SEND YOU TO MR. BROWNLOW. HE WILL KNOW WHAT TO DO!
BUT FIRST, WE MUST HELP PROTECT NANCY!
NO, NO, OLIVER!! ... LET ME GO NOW!
YOU **CAN'T** GO BACK TO SIKES!
OH, I CAN'T HELP MYSELF! ... BAD AS HE IS... I STILL DO CARE FOR HIM, Y'SEE.
WAIT... MR. BROWNLOW HAS A LAWYER FRIEND — MR. GRIMWIG... HE IS **INFLUENTIAL** AND CAN HELP US, NO MATTER WHAT... **NANCY**!
?!
GOODBYE!

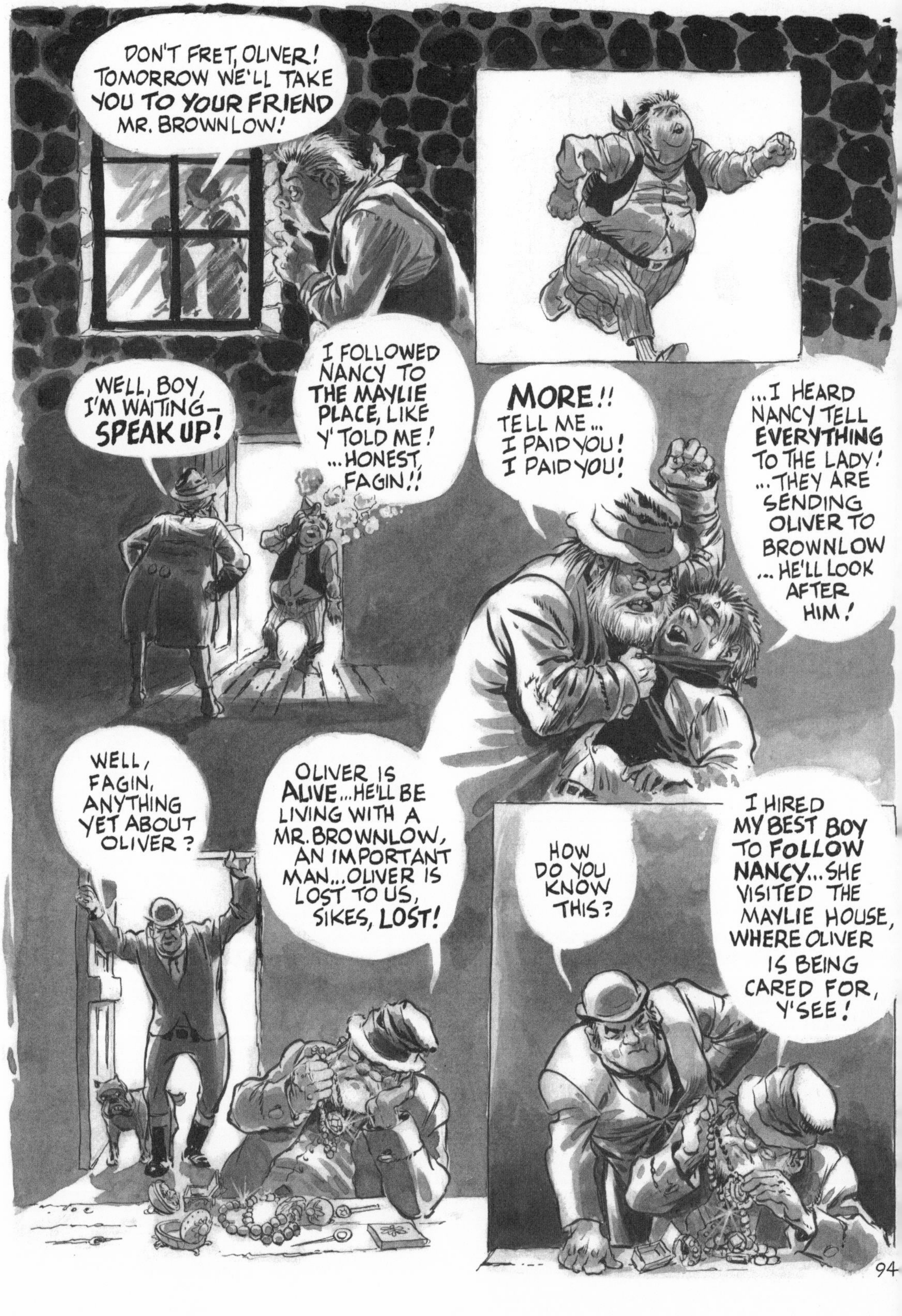
DON'T FRET, OLIVER! TOMORROW WE'LL TAKE YOU TO YOUR FRIEND MR. BROWNLOW!
WELL, BOY, I'M WAITING— SPEAK UP!
I FOLLOWED NANCY TO THE MAYLIE PLACE, LIKE Y' TOLD ME! ...HONEST, FAGIN!!
MORE!! TELL ME... I PAID YOU! I PAID YOU!
...I HEARD NANCY TELL EVERYTHING TO THE LADY! ...THEY ARE SENDING OLIVER TO BROWNLOW ... HE'LL LOOK AFTER HIM!
WELL, FAGIN, ANYTHING YET ABOUT OLIVER?
OLIVER IS ALIVE...HE'LL BE LIVING WITH A MR. BROWNLOW, AN IMPORTANT MAN...OLIVER IS LOST TO US, SIKES, LOST!
HOW DO YOU KNOW THIS?
I HIRED MY BEST BOY TO FOLLOW NANCY...SHE VISITED THE MAYLIE HOUSE, WHERE OLIVER IS BEING CARED FOR, Y'SEE!

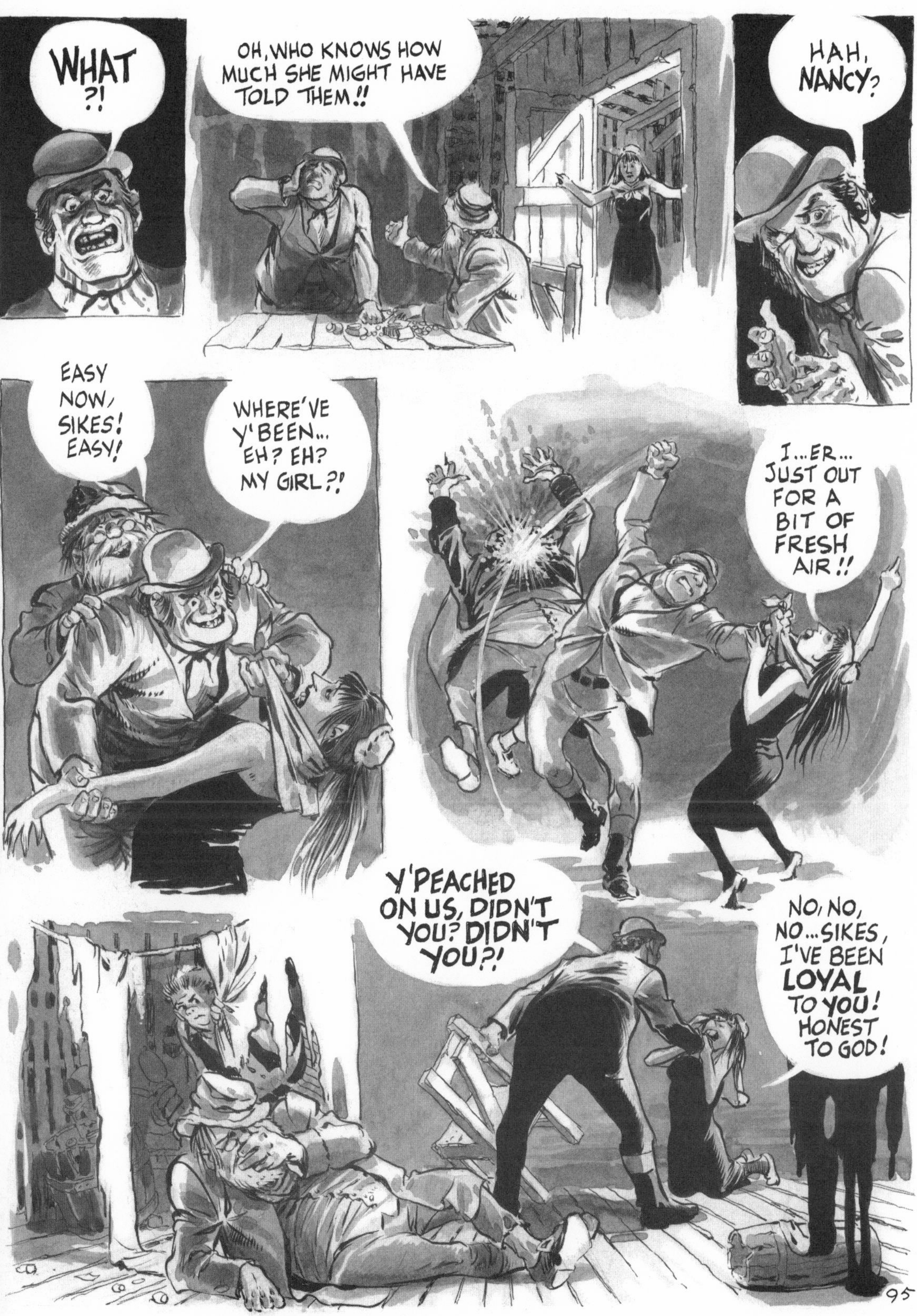
WHAT ?!
OH, WHO KNOWS HOW MUCH SHE MIGHT HAVE TOLD THEM!!
HAH, NANCY?
EASY NOW, SIKES! EASY!
WHERE'VE Y'BEEN... EH? EH? MY GIRL?!
I...ER... JUST OUT FOR A BIT OF FRESH AIR!!
Y'PEACHED ON US, DIDN'T YOU? DIDN'T YOU?!
NO, NO, NO...SIKES, I'VE BEEN LOYAL TO YOU! HONEST TO GOD!

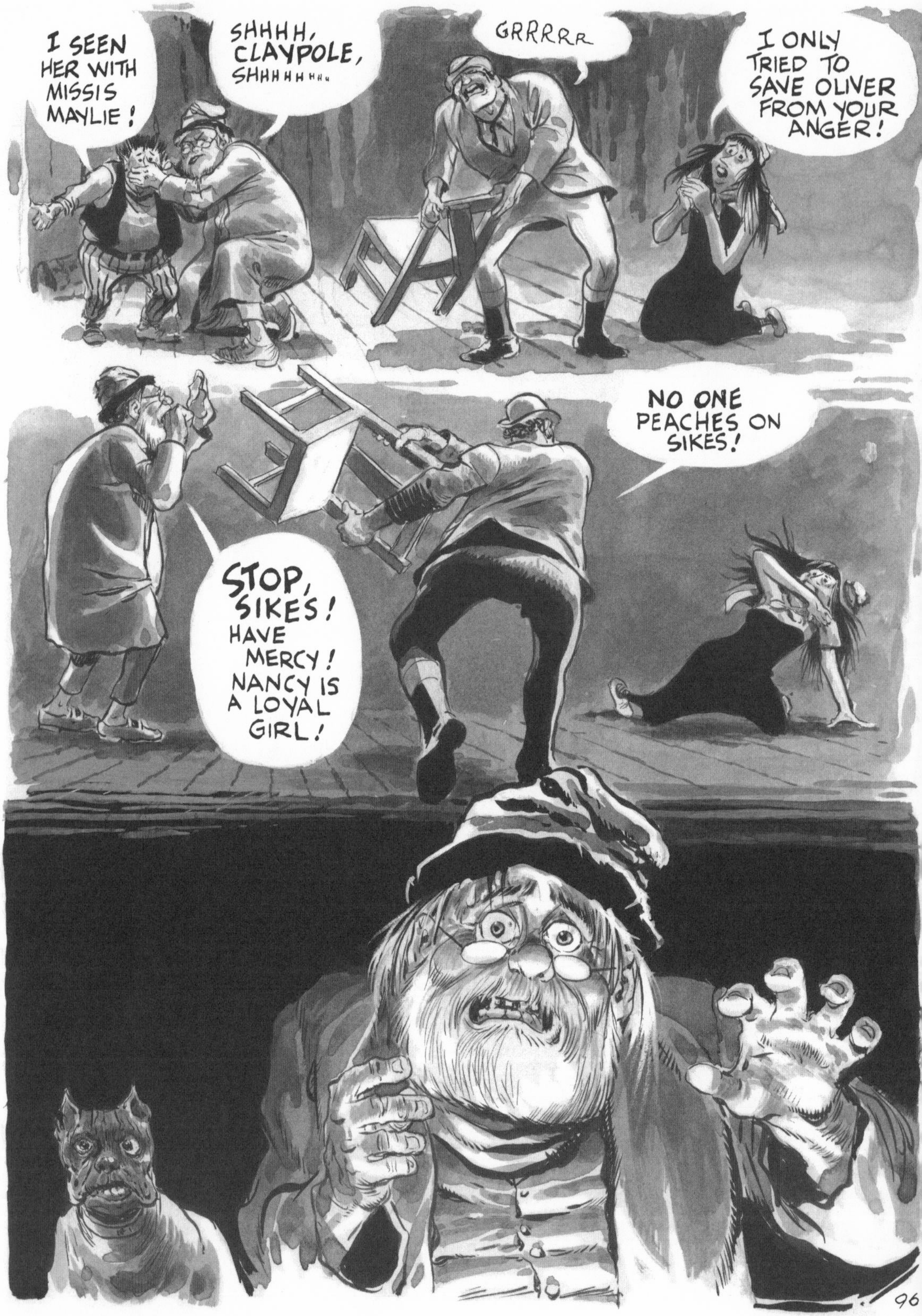
I SEEN HER WITH MISSIS MAYLIE!
SHHHH, CLAYPOLE, SHHHHHHH...
GRRRRR
I ONLY TRIED TO SAVE OLIVER FROM YOUR ANGER!
NO ONE PEACHES ON SIKES!
STOP, SIKES! HAVE MERCY! NANCY IS A LOYAL GIRL!

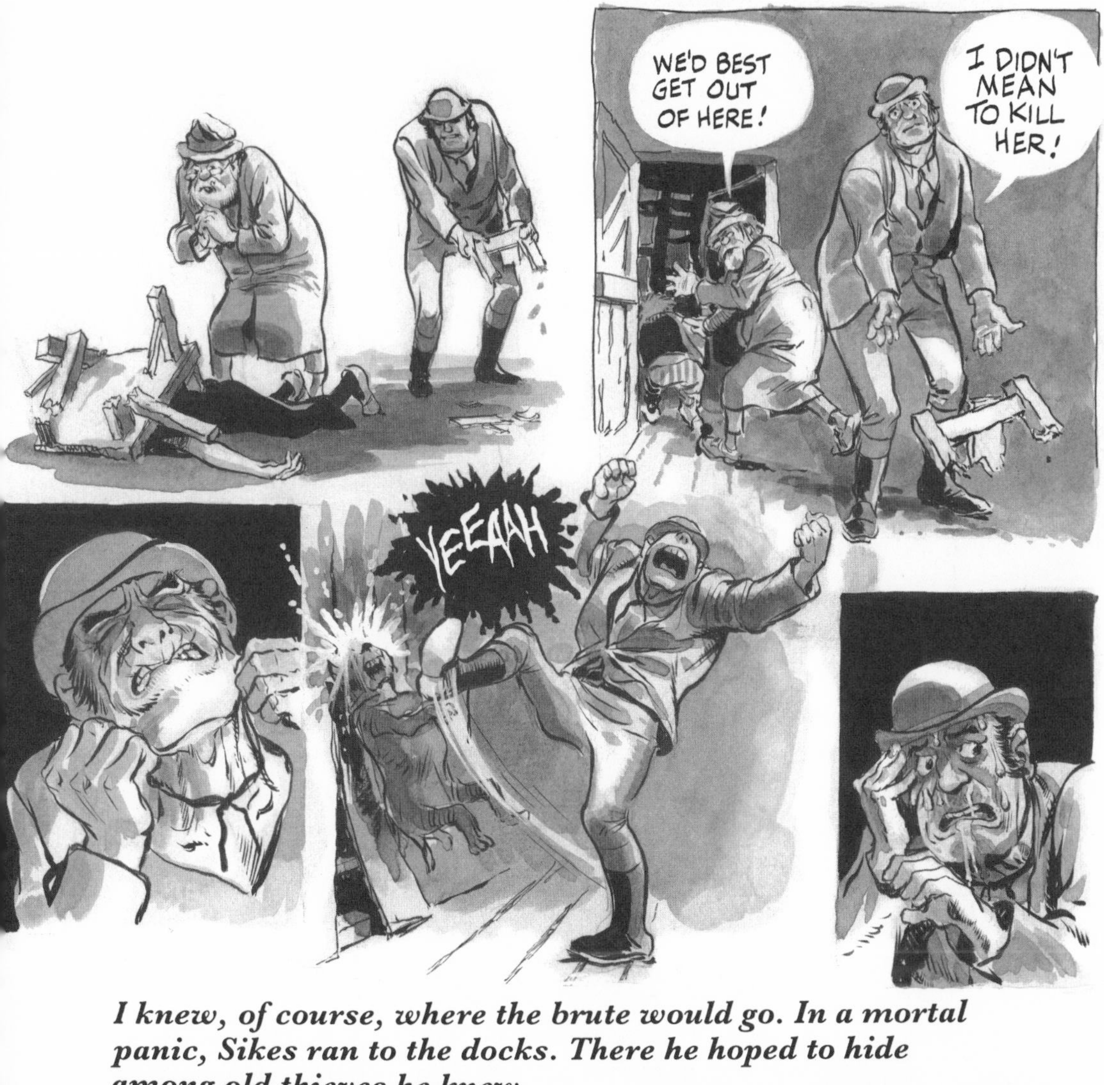
WE'D BEST GET OUT OF HERE!
I DIDN'T MEAN TO KILL HER!
YEEAAH

I knew, of course, where the brute would go. In a mortal panic, Sikes ran to the docks. There he hoped to hide among old thieves he knew.

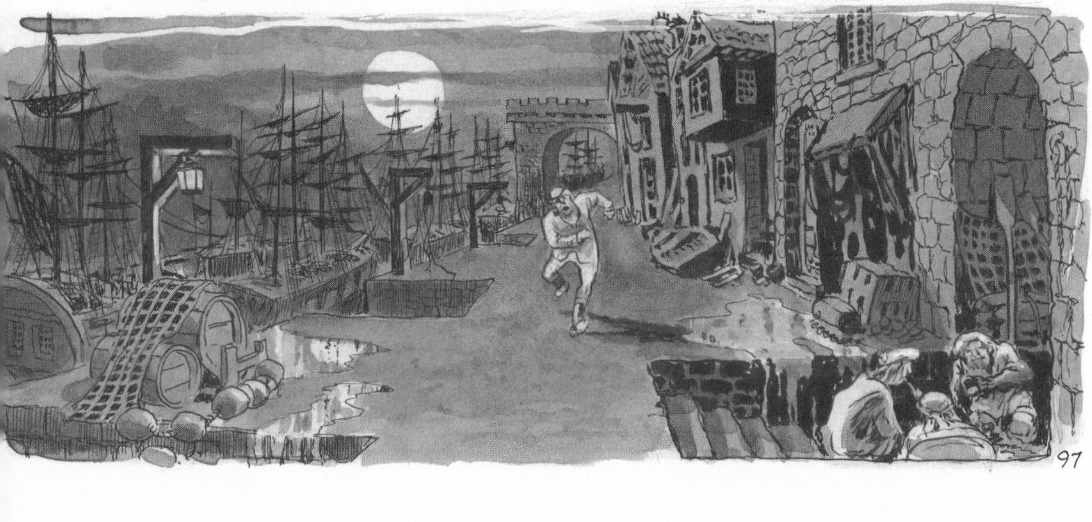

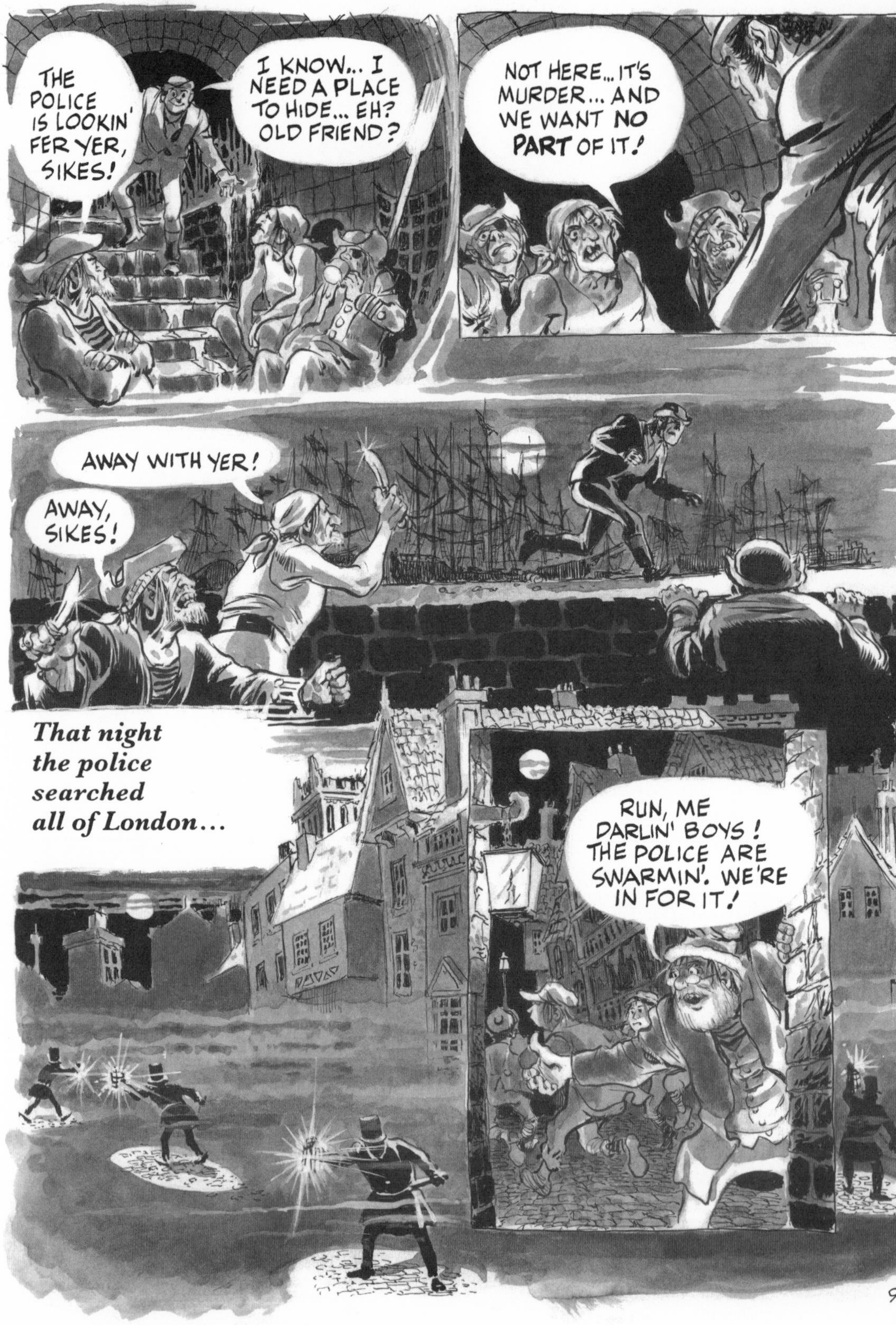
THE POLICE IS LOOKIN' FER YER, SIKES!
I KNOW... I NEED A PLACE TO HIDE... EH? OLD FRIEND?
NOT HERE... IT'S MURDER... AND WE WANT NO PART OF IT!
AWAY WITH YER!
AWAY, SIKES!
That night the police searched all of London...
RUN, ME DARLIN' BOYS! THE POLICE ARE SWARMIN'. WE'RE IN FOR IT!

Oh, I ran... on tired legs... but not quick enough...

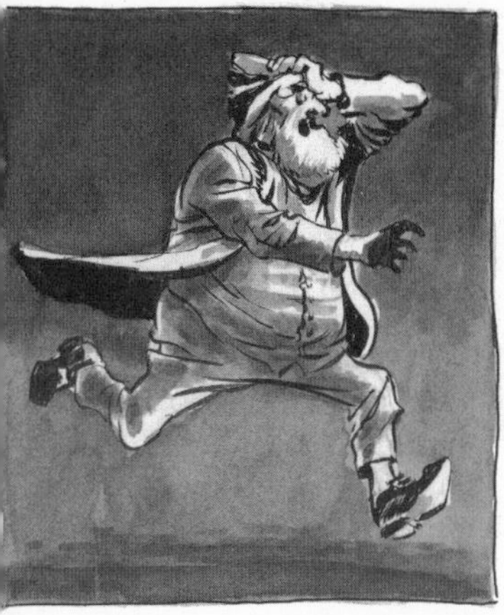

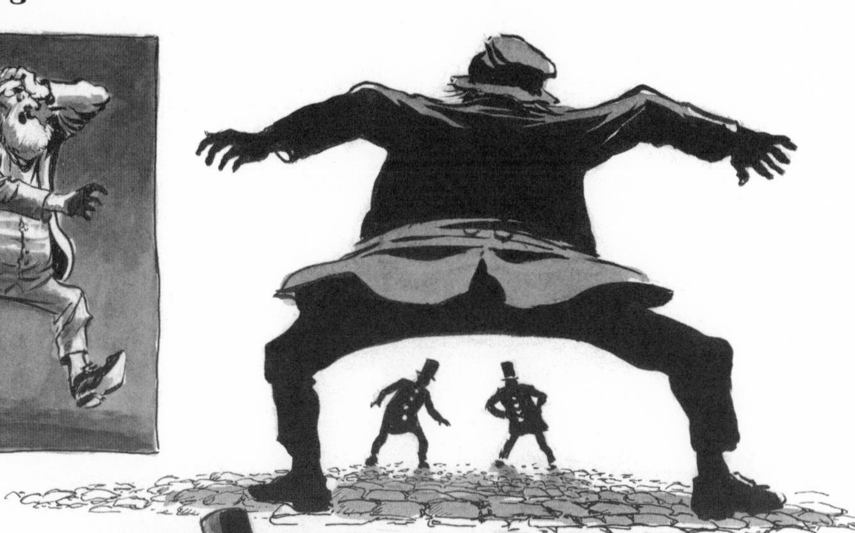

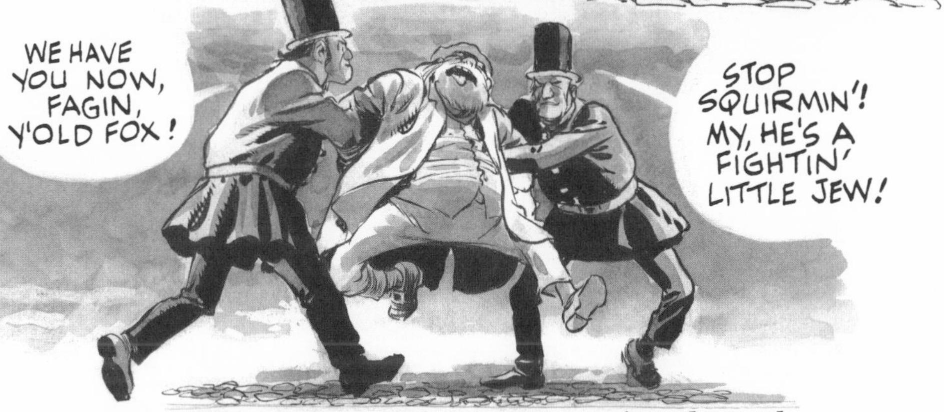
WE HAVE YOU NOW, FAGIN, Y'OLD FOX!
STOP SQUIRMIN'! MY, HE'S A FIGHTIN' LITTLE JEW!

Meanwhile, Sikes was running through the alleys... now haunted by a ghost...

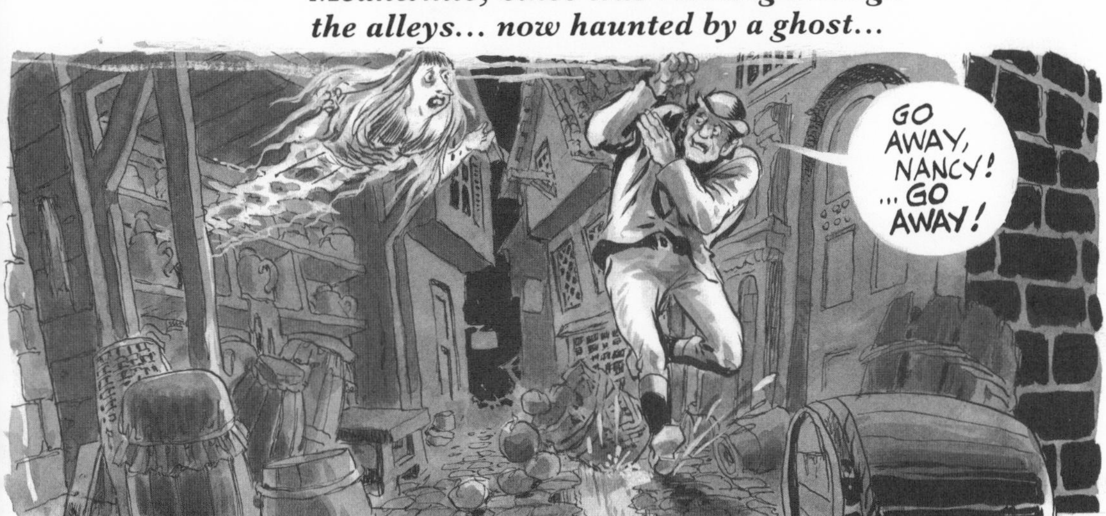
GO AWAY, NANCY! ...GO AWAY!

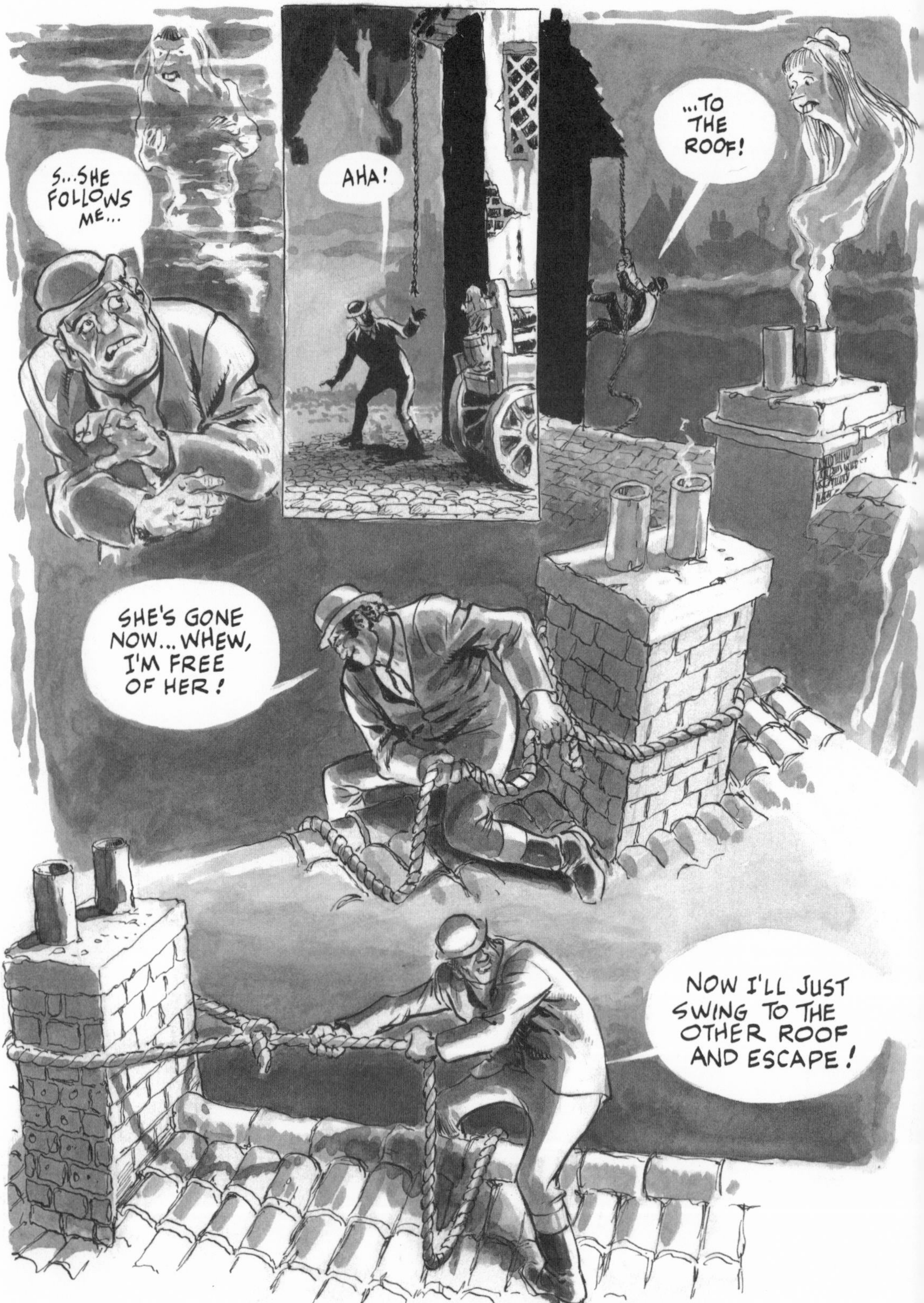
S...SHE FOLLOWS ME...
AHA!
...TO THE ROOF!
SHE'S GONE NOW... WHEW, I'M FREE OF HER!
NOW I'LL JUST SWING TO THE OTHER ROOF AND ESCAPE!

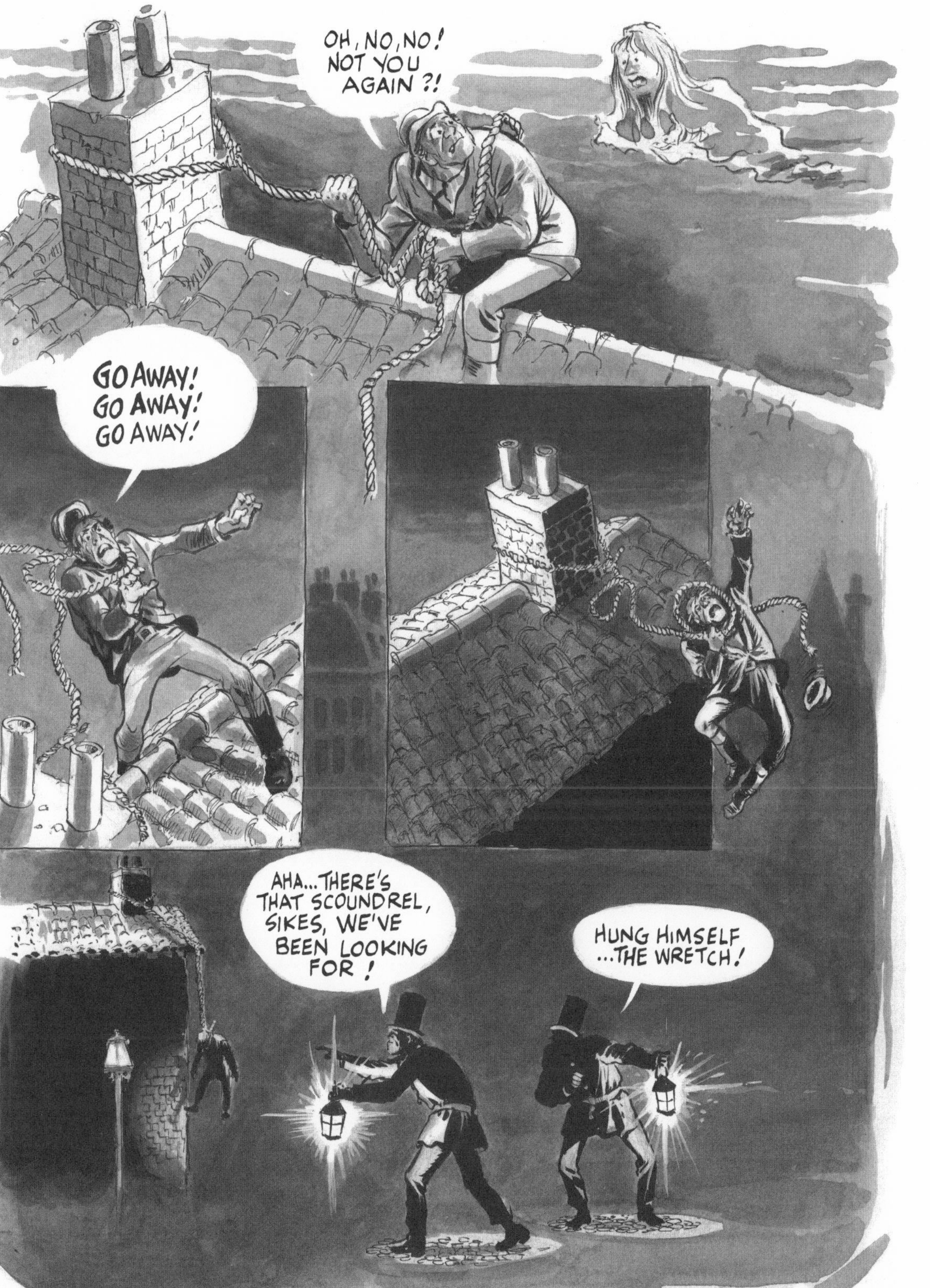
OH, NO, NO! NOT YOU AGAIN ?!
GO AWAY! GO AWAY! GO AWAY!
AHA... THERE'S THAT SCOUNDREL, SIKES, WE'VE BEEN LOOKING FOR!
HUNG HIMSELF ...THE WRETCH!

With Sikes dead, there was no one to testify to my innocence. Well, I was locked up in Newgate Prison, where I was tried and sentenced in short order.

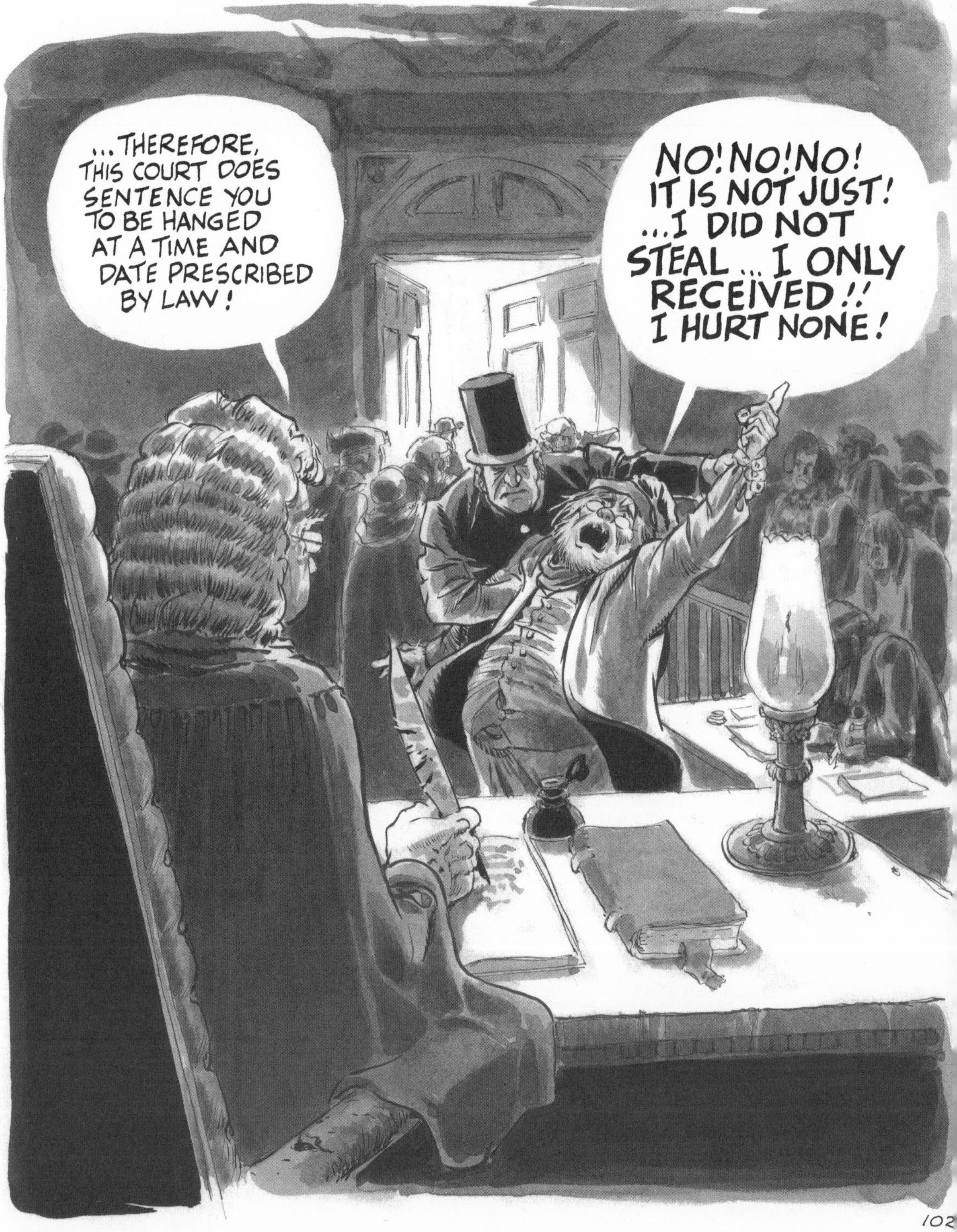
...THEREFORE, THIS COURT DOES SENTENCE YOU TO BE HANGED AT A TIME AND DATE PRESCRIBED BY LAW!
NO! NO! NO! IT IS NOT JUST! ...I DID NOT STEAL... I ONLY RECEIVED!! I HURT NONE!

I lay in my cell, exhausted from writhing and flailing against my sorry fate... Aided by his influential new benefactor and patron Mr. Brownlow, Oliver was allowed to visit me here. His visit added to my comfort and helped me endure the agony of an undeserved fate.

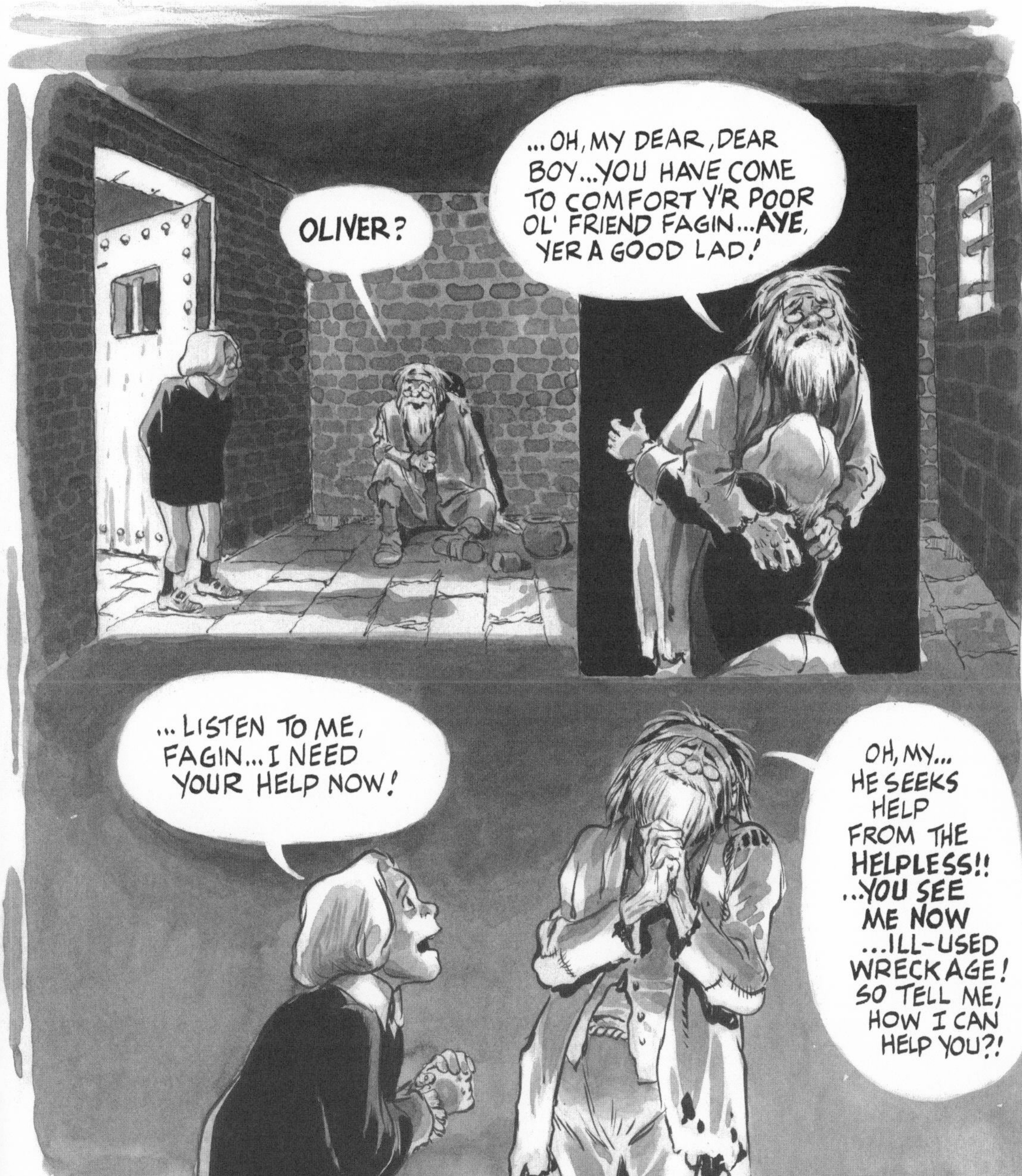
OLIVER?
...OH, MY DEAR, DEAR BOY...YOU HAVE COME TO COMFORT Y'R POOR OL' FRIEND FAGIN...AYE, YER A GOOD LAD!
...LISTEN TO ME, FAGIN...I NEED YOUR HELP NOW!
OH, MY... HE SEEKS HELP FROM THE HELPLESS!! ...YOU SEE ME NOW ...ILL-USED WRECKAGE! SO TELL ME, HOW I CAN HELP YOU?!

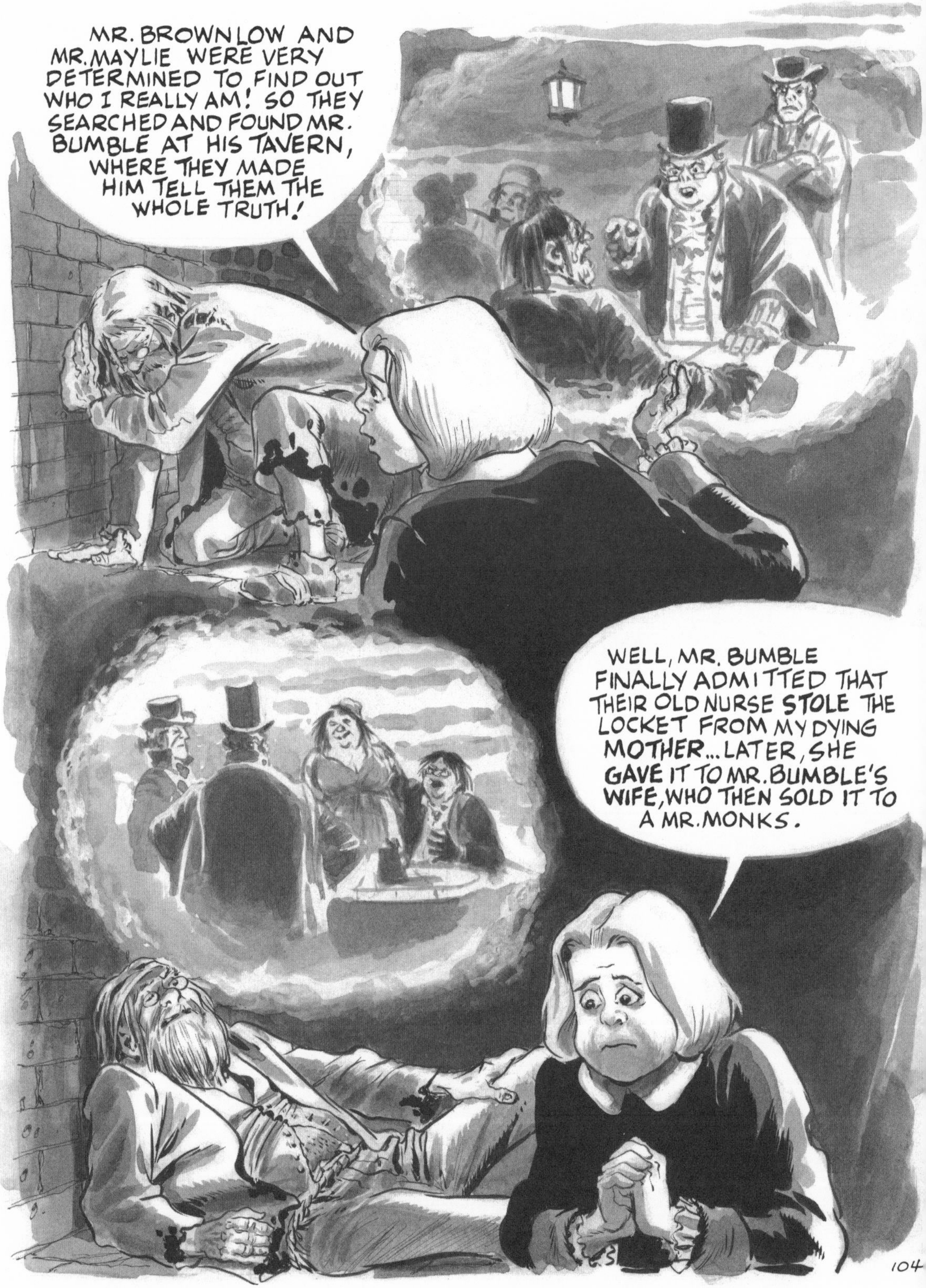
MR. BROWNLOW AND MR. MAYLIE WERE VERY DETERMINED TO FIND OUT WHO I REALLY AM! SO THEY SEARCHED AND FOUND MR. BUMBLE AT HIS TAVERN, WHERE THEY MADE HIM TELL THEM THE WHOLE TRUTH!
WELL, MR. BUMBLE FINALLY ADMITTED THAT THEIR OLD NURSE STOLE THE LOCKET FROM MY DYING MOTHER... LATER, SHE GAVE IT TO MR. BUMBLE'S WIFE, WHO THEN SOLD IT TO A MR. MONKS.

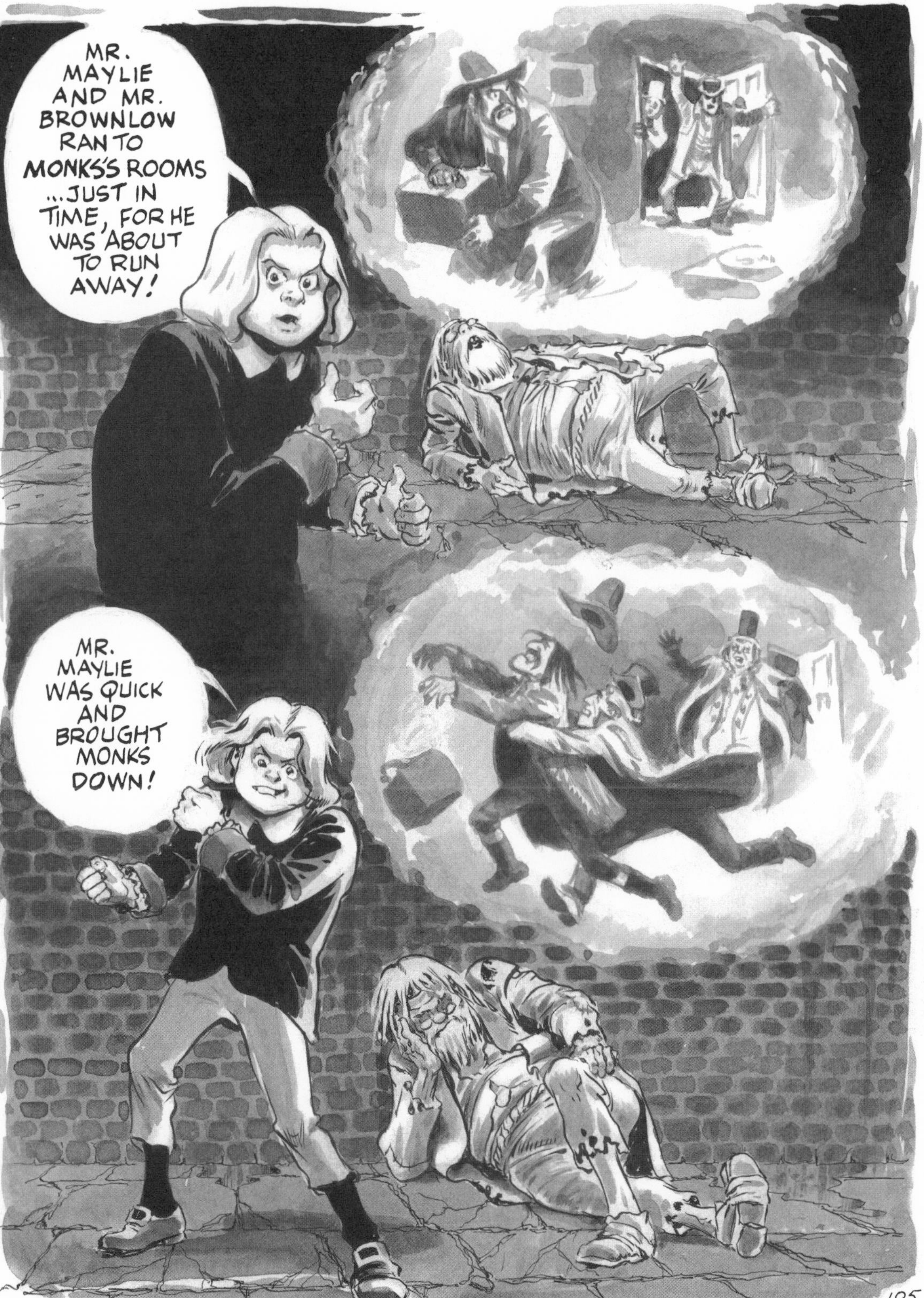
MR. MAYLIE AND MR. BROWNLOW RAN TO MONKS'S ROOMS ...JUST IN TIME, FOR HE WAS ABOUT TO RUN AWAY!
MR. MAYLIE WAS QUICK AND BROUGHT MONKS DOWN!

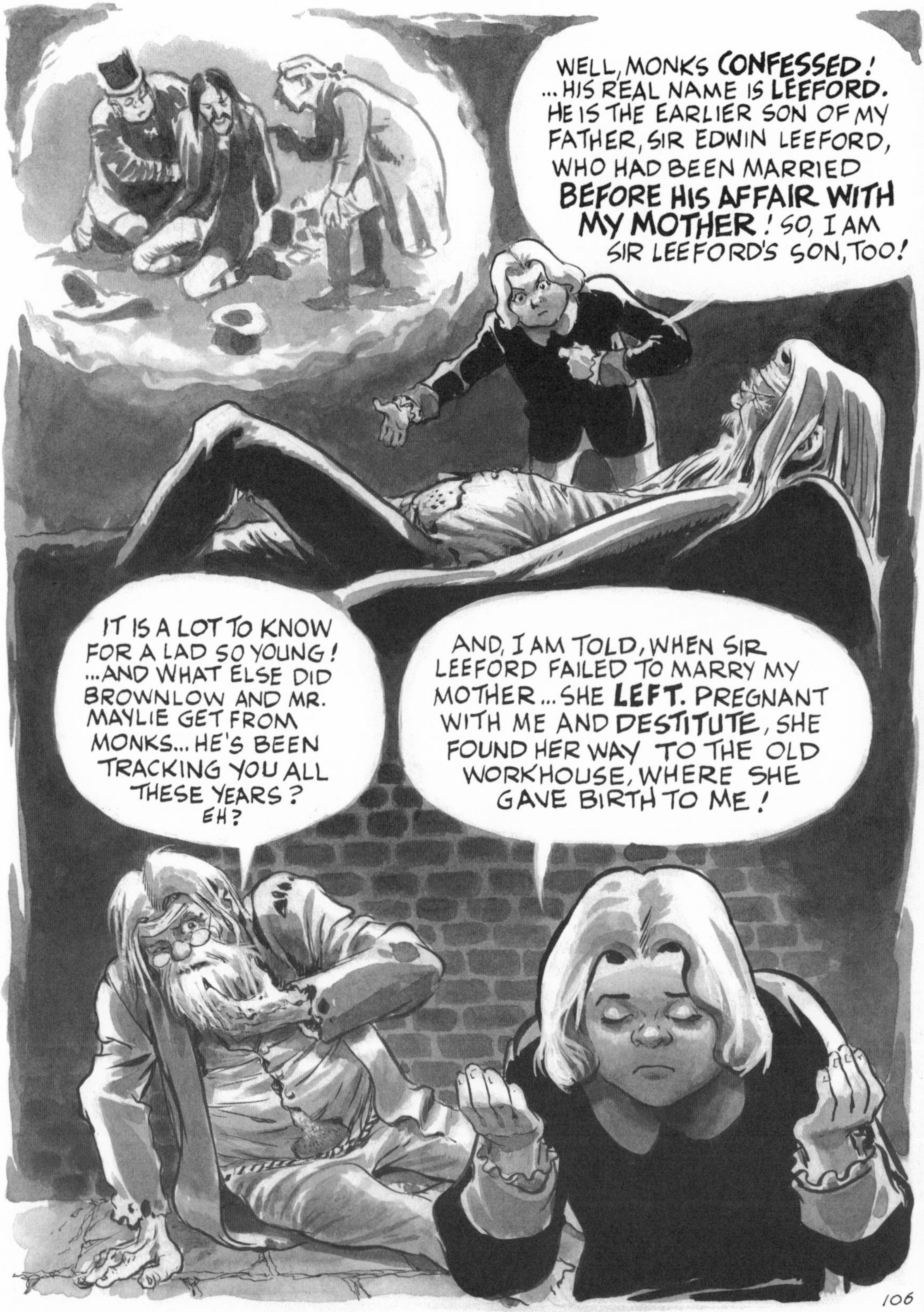
WELL, MONKS CONFESSED! ... HIS REAL NAME IS LEEFORD. HE IS THE EARLIER SON OF MY FATHER, SIR EDWIN LEEFORD, WHO HAD BEEN MARRIED BEFORE HIS AFFAIR WITH MY MOTHER! SO, I AM SIR LEEFORD'S SON, TOO!
IT IS A LOT TO KNOW FOR A LAD SO YOUNG! ...AND WHAT ELSE DID BROWNLOW AND MR. MAYLIE GET FROM MONKS... HE'S BEEN TRACKING YOU ALL THESE YEARS? EH?
AND, I AM TOLD, WHEN SIR LEEFORD FAILED TO MARRY MY MOTHER... SHE LEFT. PREGNANT WITH ME AND DESTITUTE, SHE FOUND HER WAY TO THE OLD WORKHOUSE, WHERE SHE GAVE BIRTH TO ME!

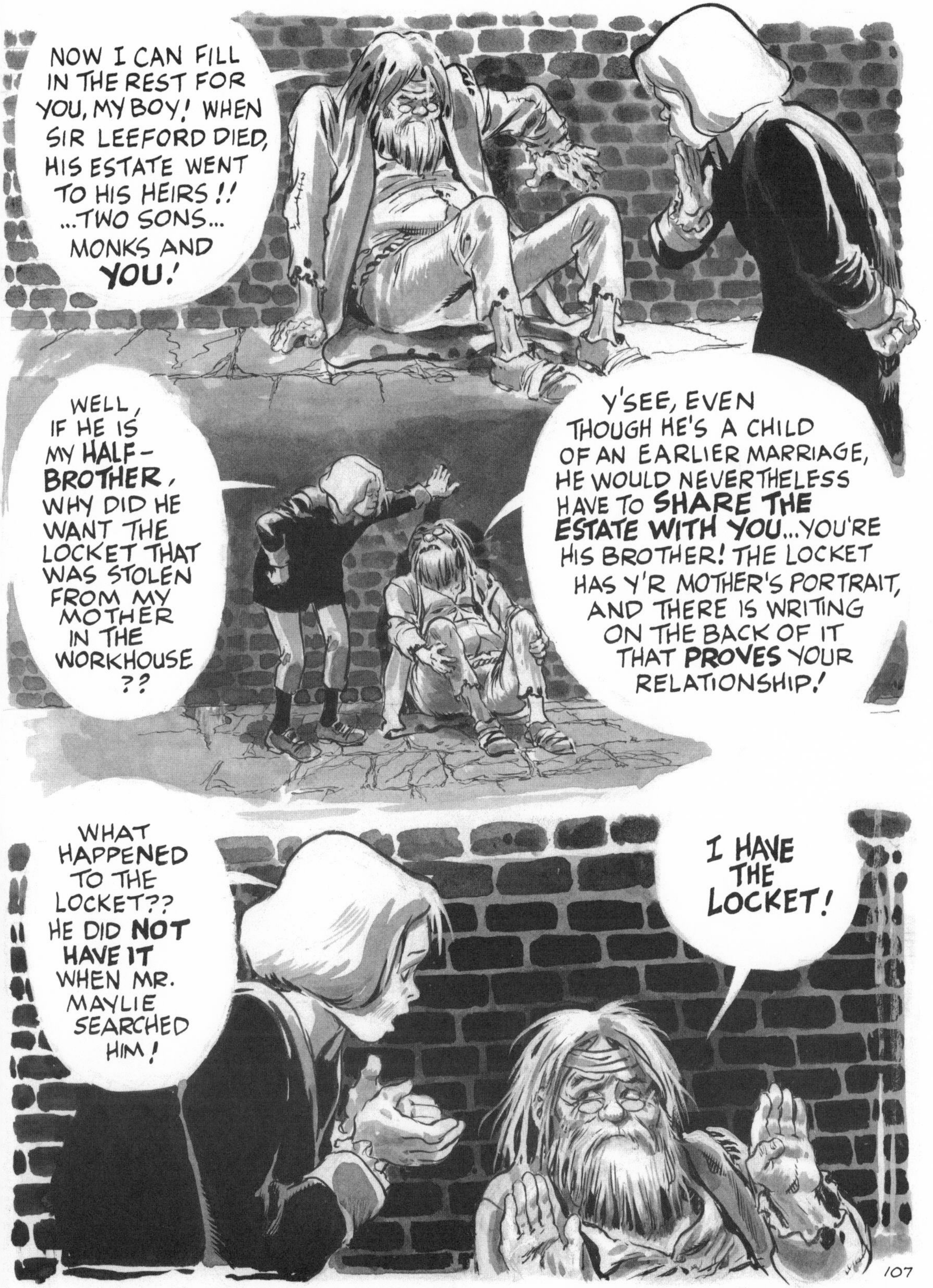
NOW I CAN FILL IN THE REST FOR YOU, MY BOY! WHEN SIR LEEFORD DIED, HIS ESTATE WENT TO HIS HEIRS!! ...TWO SONS... MONKS AND YOU!
WELL, IF HE IS MY HALF-BROTHER, WHY DID HE WANT THE LOCKET THAT WAS STOLEN FROM MY MOTHER IN THE WORKHOUSE??
Y'SEE, EVEN THOUGH HE'S A CHILD OF AN EARLIER MARRIAGE, HE WOULD NEVERTHELESS HAVE TO SHARE THE ESTATE WITH YOU...YOU'RE HIS BROTHER! THE LOCKET HAS Y'R MOTHER'S PORTRAIT, AND THERE IS WRITING ON THE BACK OF IT THAT PROVES YOUR RELATIONSHIP!
WHAT HAPPENED TO THE LOCKET?? HE DID NOT HAVE IT WHEN MR. MAYLIE SEARCHED HIM!
I HAVE THE LOCKET!

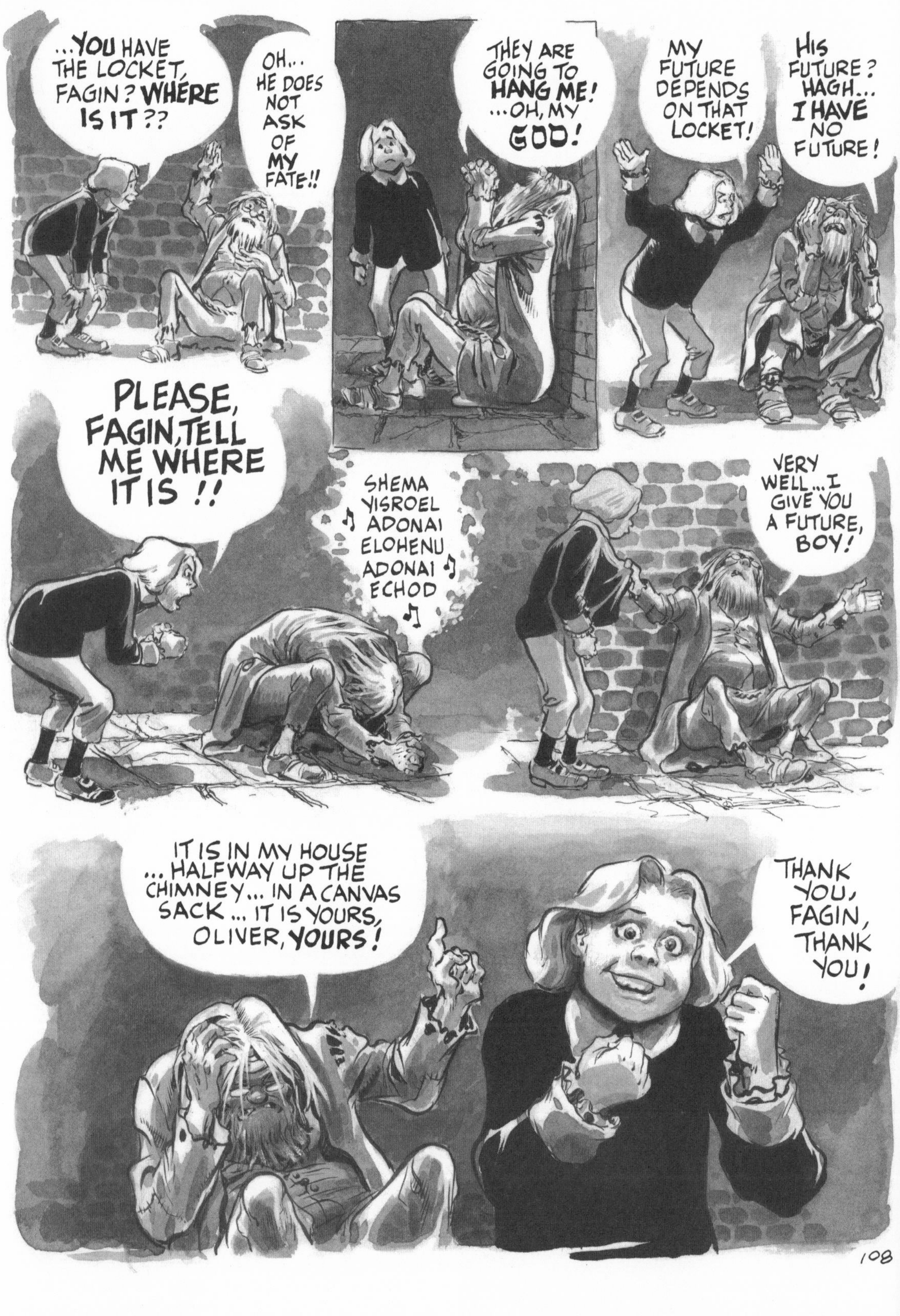
...YOU HAVE THE LOCKET, FAGIN? WHERE IS IT??
OH... HE DOES NOT ASK OF MY FATE!!
THEY ARE GOING TO HANG ME! ...OH, MY GOD!
MY FUTURE DEPENDS ON THAT LOCKET!
HIS FUTURE? HAGH... I HAVE NO FUTURE!
PLEASE, FAGIN, TELL ME WHERE IT IS!!
SHEMA YISROEL ADONAI ELOHENU ADONAI ECHOD
VERY WELL... I GIVE YOU A FUTURE, BOY!
IT IS IN MY HOUSE ... HALFWAY UP THE CHIMNEY... IN A CANVAS SACK ... IT IS YOURS, OLIVER, YOURS!
THANK YOU, FAGIN, THANK YOU!

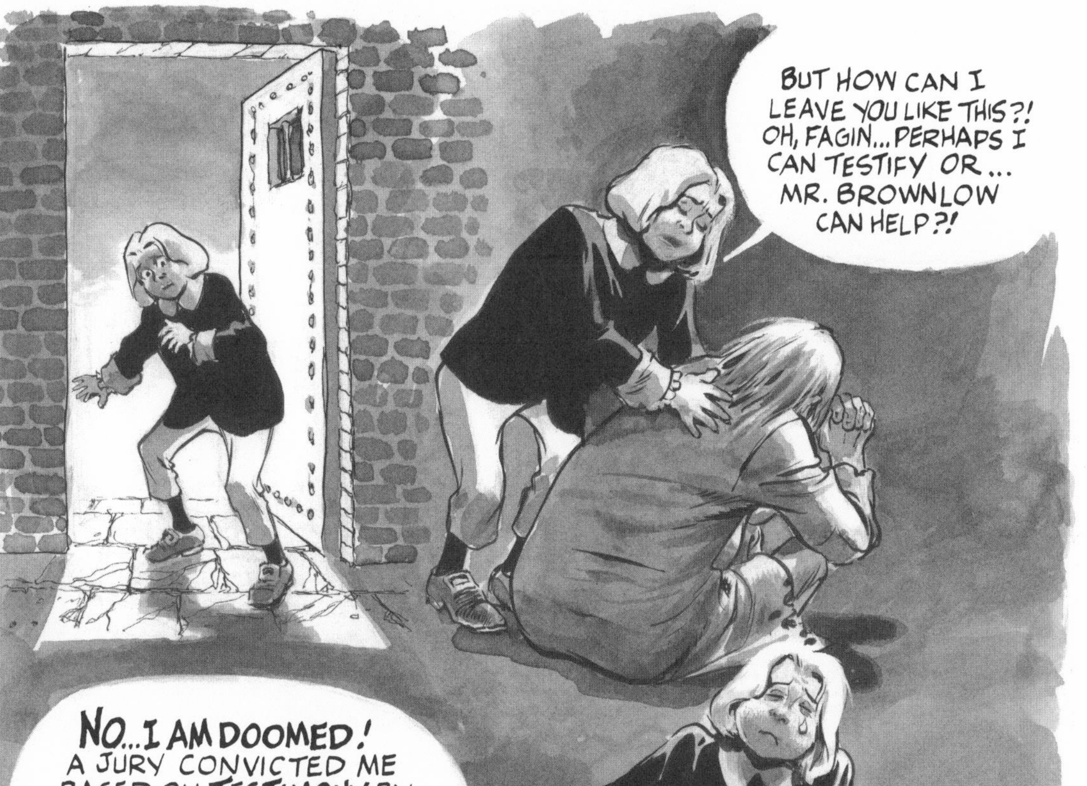
BUT HOW CAN I LEAVE YOU LIKE THIS?! OH, FAGIN... PERHAPS I CAN TESTIFY OR ... MR. BROWNLOW CAN HELP?!
NO...I AM DOOMED! A JURY CONVICTED ME BASED ON TESTIMONY BY YOUNG CLAYPOLE, AND THE JUDGE HAS PRONOUNCED SENTENCE!! I WILL BE HANGED BEFORE A CHEERING MOB!

Ah, it was a bitter departure... We clung together, I as a drowning man who holds onto a floating log, and Oliver as a mourner unable yet to separate from an attachment, the memory of which will forever remain with him. Finally the boy gathered control of his emotions enough so he could disengage.

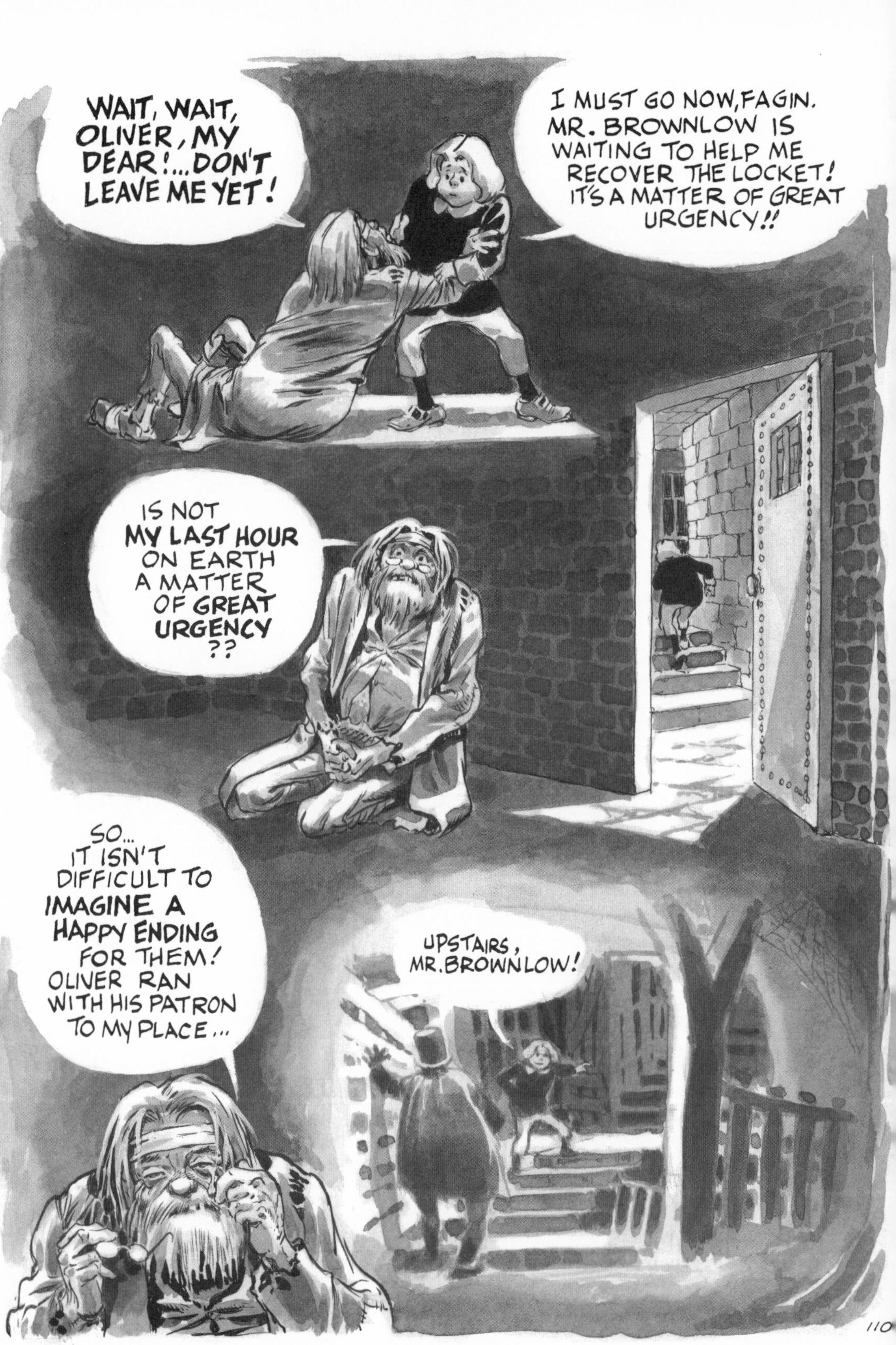
WAIT, WAIT, OLIVER, MY DEAR!...DON'T LEAVE ME YET!
I MUST GO NOW, FAGIN. MR. BROWNLOW IS WAITING TO HELP ME RECOVER THE LOCKET! IT'S A MATTER OF GREAT URGENCY!!
IS NOT MY LAST HOUR ON EARTH A MATTER OF GREAT URGENCY ??
SO... IT ISN'T DIFFICULT TO IMAGINE A HAPPY ENDING FOR THEM! OLIVER RAN WITH HIS PATRON TO MY PLACE...
UPSTAIRS, MR. BROWNLOW!

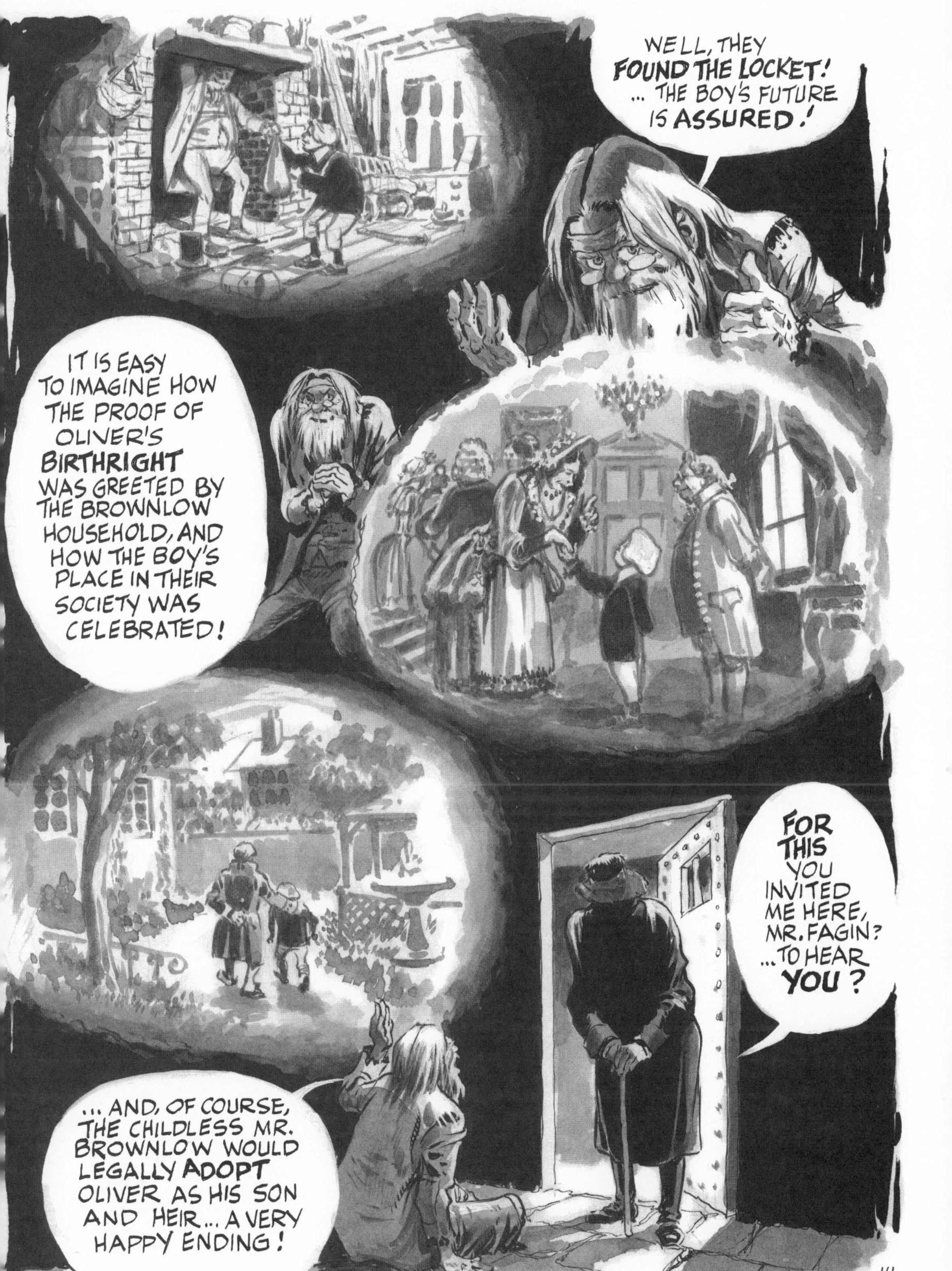
WELL, THEY FOUND THE LOCKET! ... THE BOY'S FUTURE IS ASSURED!
IT IS EASY TO IMAGINE HOW THE PROOF OF OLIVER'S BIRTHRIGHT WAS GREETED BY THE BROWNLOW HOUSEHOLD, AND HOW THE BOY'S PLACE IN THEIR SOCIETY WAS CELEBRATED!
... AND, OF COURSE, THE CHILDLESS MR. BROWNLOW WOULD LEGALLY ADOPT OLIVER AS HIS SON AND HEIR... A VERY HAPPY ENDING!
FOR THIS YOU INVITED ME HERE, MR. FAGIN? ...TO HEAR YOU?

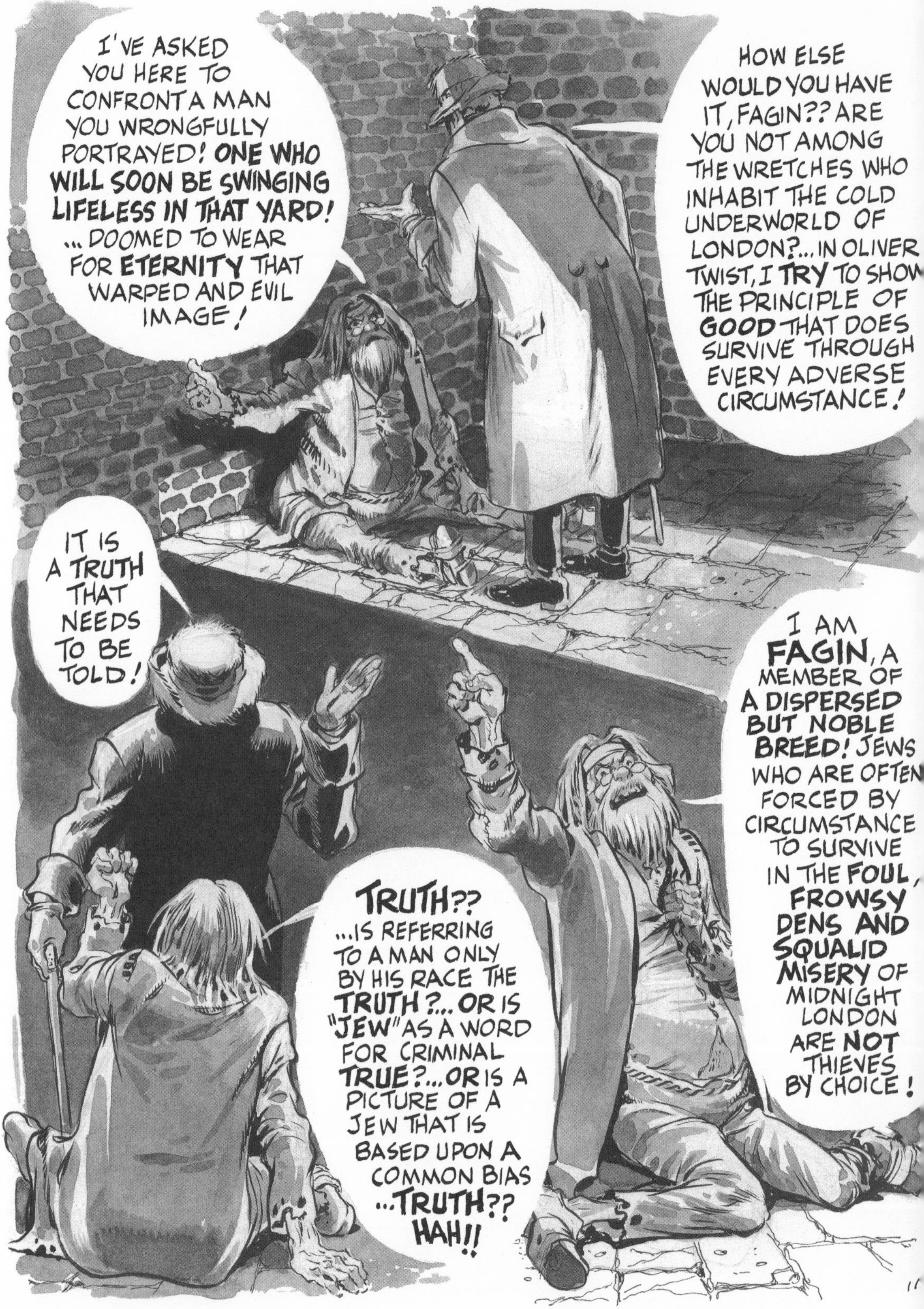
I'VE ASKED YOU HERE TO CONFRONT A MAN YOU WRONGFULLY PORTRAYED! ONE WHO WILL SOON BE SWINGING LIFELESS IN THAT YARD! ...DOOMED TO WEAR FOR ETERNITY THAT WARPED AND EVIL IMAGE!
HOW ELSE WOULD YOU HAVE IT, FAGIN?? ARE YOU NOT AMONG THE WRETCHES WHO INHABIT THE COLD UNDERWORLD OF LONDON?... IN OLIVER TWIST, I TRY TO SHOW THE PRINCIPLE OF GOOD THAT DOES SURVIVE THROUGH EVERY ADVERSE CIRCUMSTANCE!
IT IS A TRUTH THAT NEEDS TO BE TOLD!
I AM FAGIN, A MEMBER OF A DISPERSED BUT NOBLE BREED! JEWS WHO ARE OFTEN FORCED BY CIRCUMSTANCE TO SURVIVE IN THE FOUL, FROWSY DENS AND SQUALID MISERY OF MIDNIGHT LONDON ARE NOT THIEVES BY CHOICE!
TRUTH?? ...IS REFERRING TO A MAN ONLY BY HIS RACE THE TRUTH?... OR IS "JEW" AS A WORD FOR CRIMINAL TRUE?... OR IS A PICTURE OF A JEW THAT IS BASED UPON A COMMON BIAS ...TRUTH?? HAH!!
11

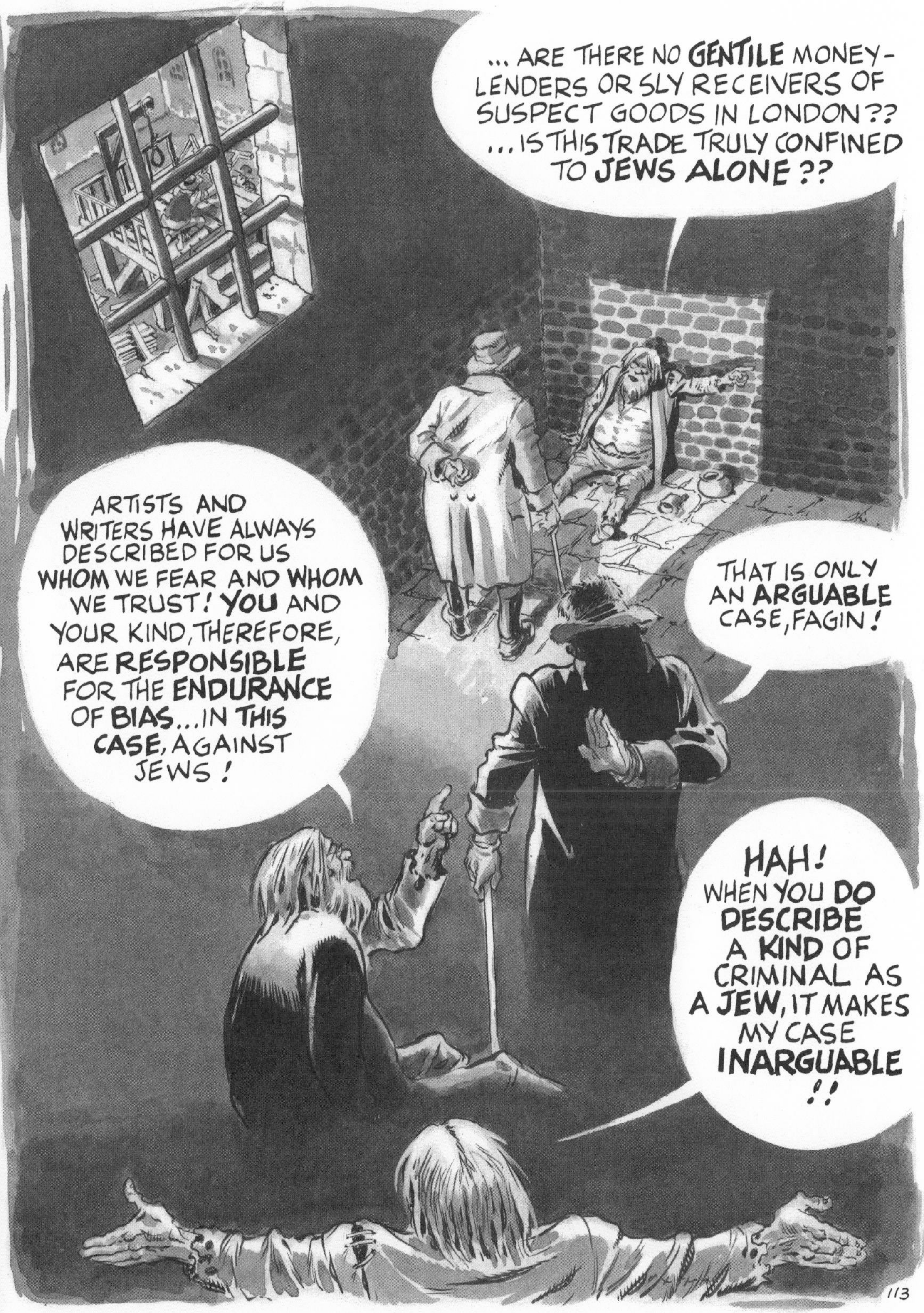
... ARE THERE NO GENTILE MONEY-LENDERS OR SLY RECEIVERS OF SUSPECT GOODS IN LONDON?? ... IS THIS TRADE TRULY CONFINED TO JEWS ALONE??
ARTISTS AND WRITERS HAVE ALWAYS DESCRIBED FOR US WHOM WE FEAR AND WHOM WE TRUST! YOU AND YOUR KIND, THEREFORE, ARE RESPONSIBLE FOR THE ENDURANCE OF BIAS... IN THIS CASE, AGAINST JEWS!
THAT IS ONLY AN ARGUABLE CASE, FAGIN!
HAH! WHEN YOU DO DESCRIBE A KIND OF CRIMINAL AS A JEW, IT MAKES MY CASE INARGUABLE !!

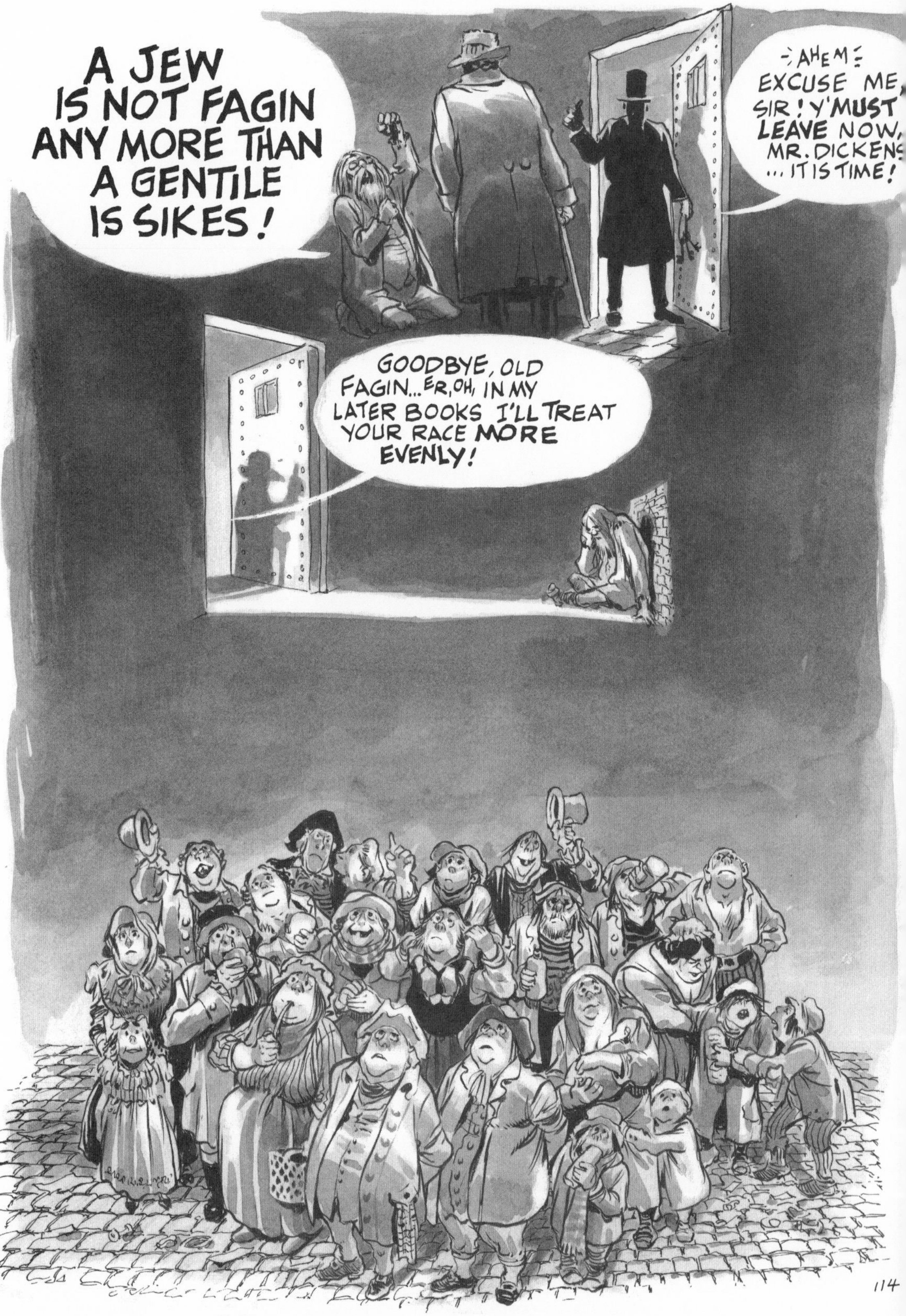
A JEW IS NOT FAGIN ANY MORE THAN A GENTILE IS SIKES!
AHEM EXCUSE ME, SIR! Y'MUST LEAVE NOW, MR. DICKENS ... IT IS TIME!
GOODBYE, OLD FAGIN... ER, OH, IN MY LATER BOOKS I'LL TREAT YOUR RACE MORE EVENLY!

EPILOGUE

Fagin was hanged and buried ignominiously, in a pauper's grave, together with others whom fate had demeaned.

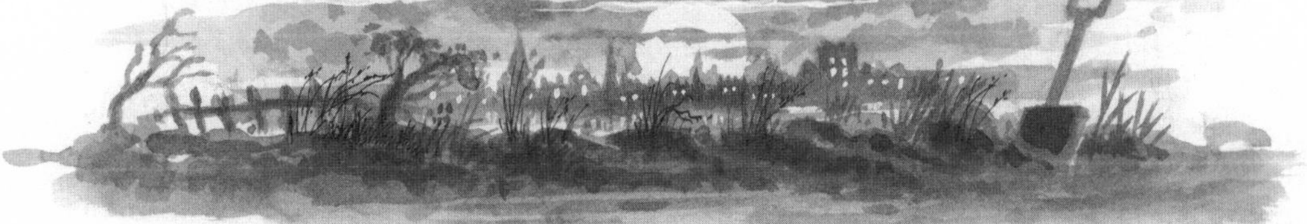

The young lad Oliver was adopted by Mr. Brownlow. He became a successful barrister who at last found out about a turning point in Fagin's life and his legacy.

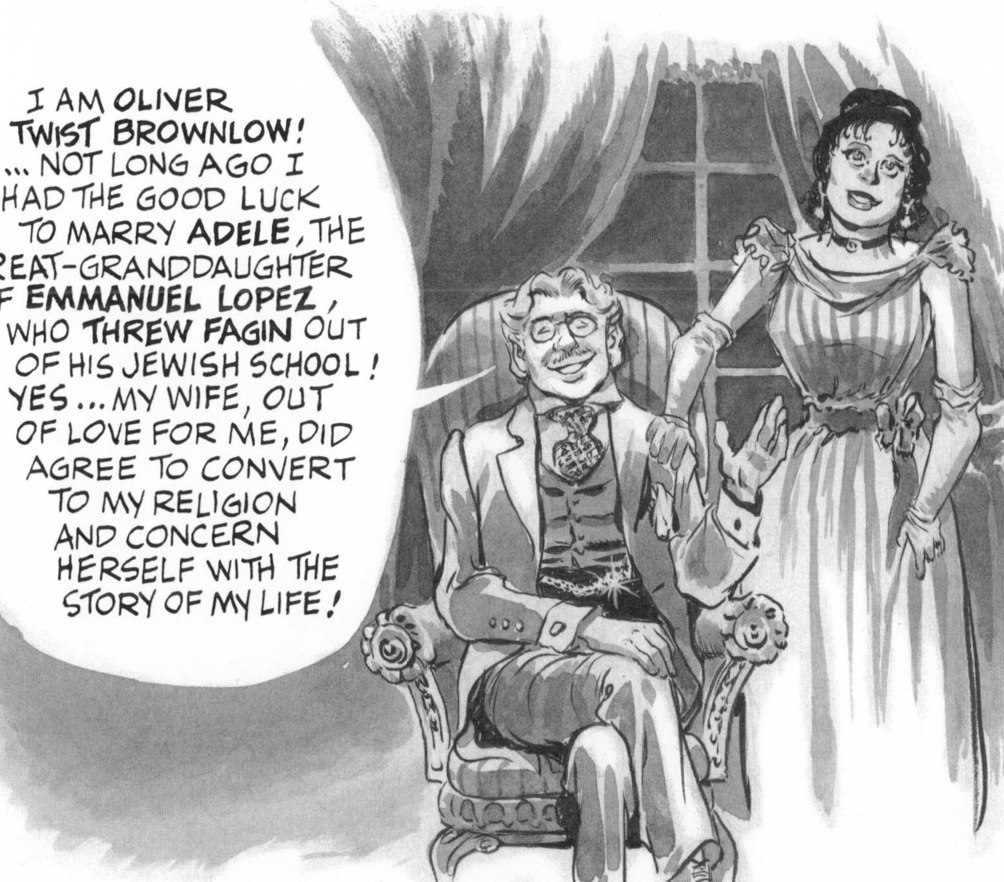
I AM OLIVER TWIST BROWNLOW! ... NOT LONG AGO I HAD THE GOOD LUCK TO MARRY ADELE, THE GREAT-GRANDDAUGHTER OF EMMANUEL LOPEZ, WHO THREW FAGIN OUT OF HIS JEWISH SCHOOL! YES ... MY WIFE, OUT OF LOVE FOR ME, DID AGREE TO CONVERT TO MY RELIGION AND CONCERN HERSELF WITH THE STORY OF MY LIFE!

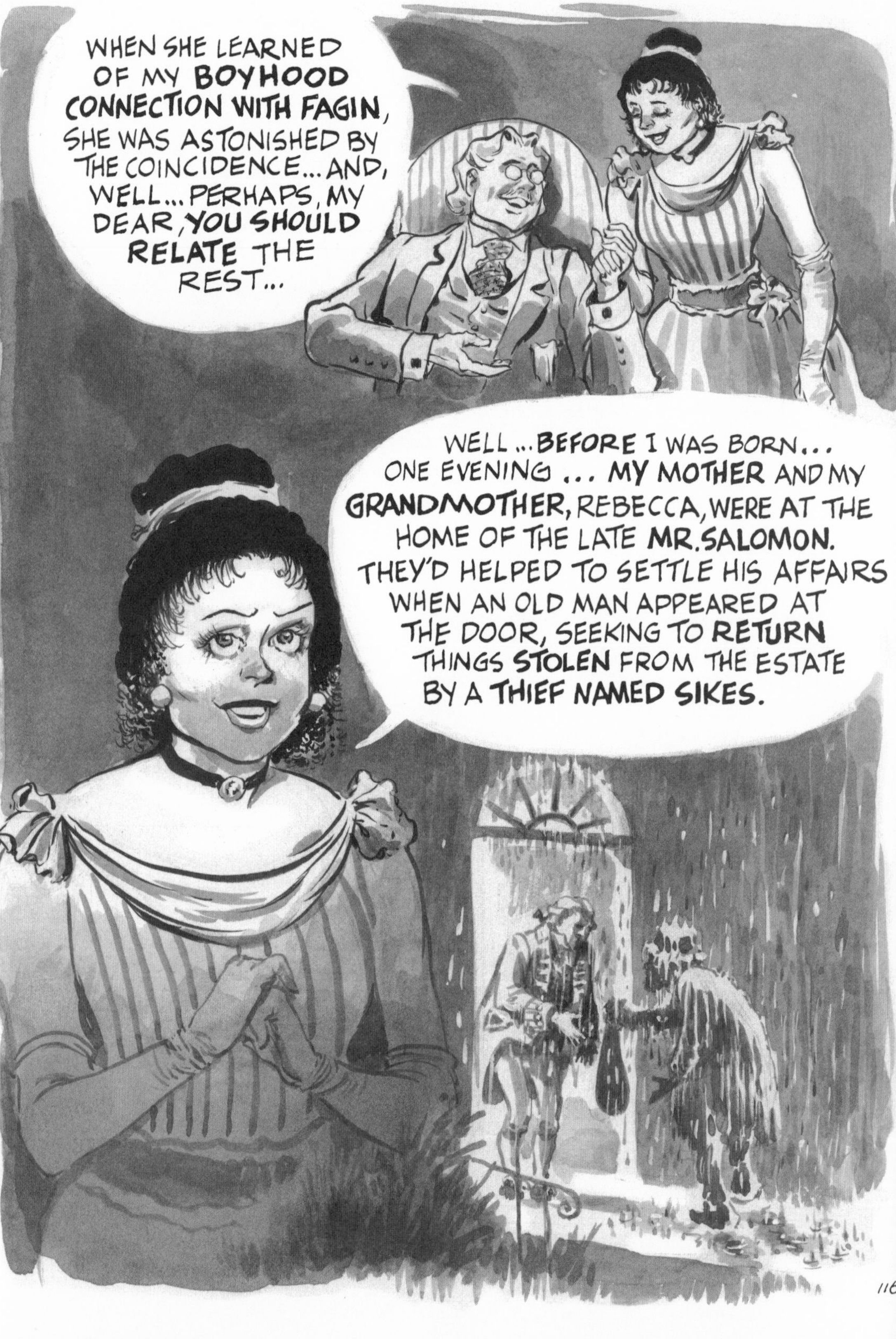
WHEN SHE LEARNED OF MY BOYHOOD CONNECTION WITH FAGIN, SHE WAS ASTONISHED BY THE COINCIDENCE... AND, WELL... PERHAPS, MY DEAR, YOU SHOULD RELATE THE REST...
WELL ... BEFORE I WAS BORN... ONE EVENING ... MY MOTHER AND MY GRANDMOTHER, REBECCA, WERE AT THE HOME OF THE LATE MR. SALOMON. THEY'D HELPED TO SETTLE HIS AFFAIRS WHEN AN OLD MAN APPEARED AT THE DOOR, SEEKING TO RETURN THINGS STOLEN FROM THE ESTATE BY A THIEF NAMED SIKES.

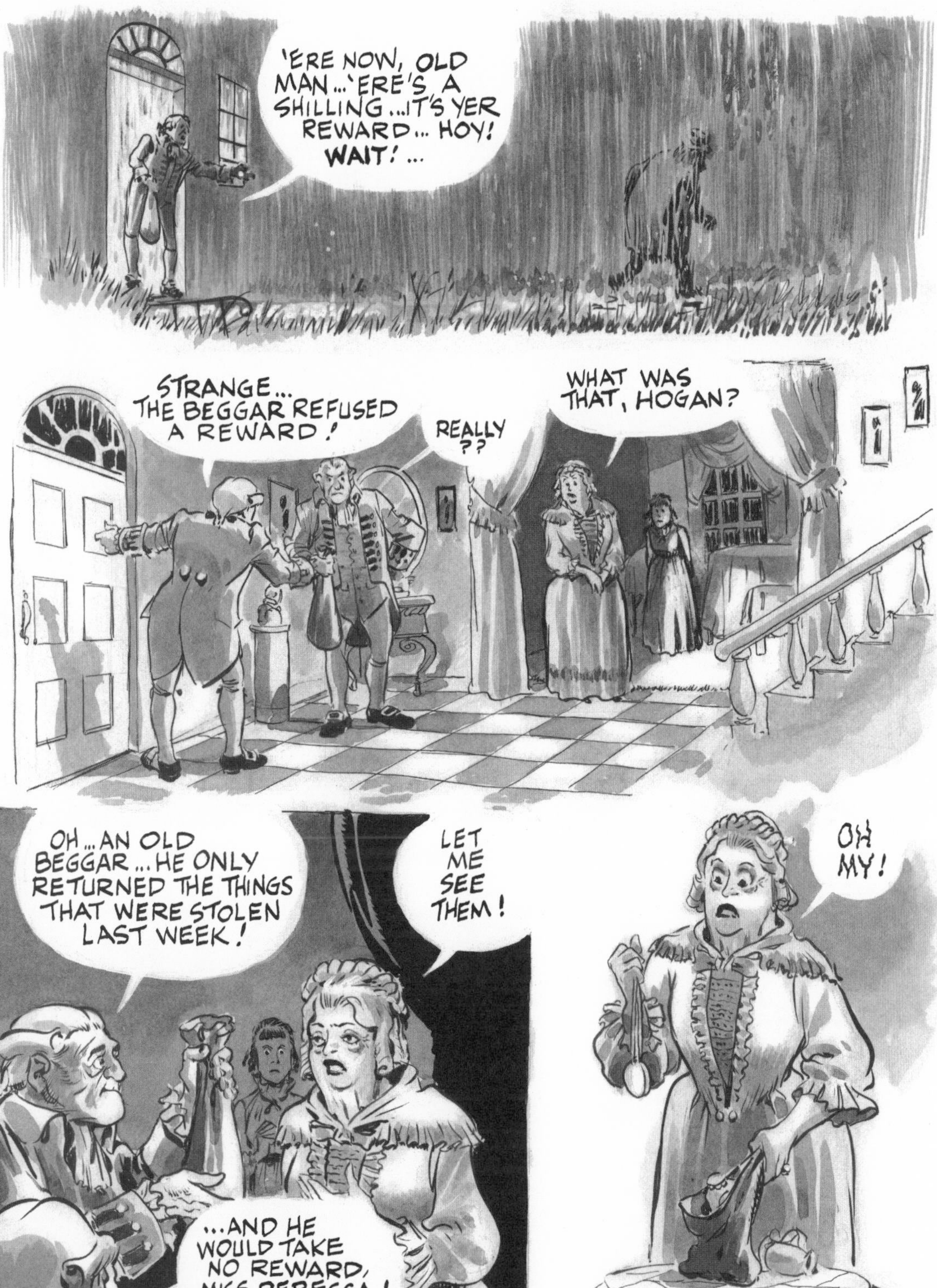
'ERE NOW, OLD MAN...'ERE'S A SHILLING...IT'S YER REWARD... HOY! WAIT! ...
STRANGE... THE BEGGAR REFUSED A REWARD!
REALLY ??
WHAT WAS THAT, HOGAN?
OH...AN OLD BEGGAR...HE ONLY RETURNED THE THINGS THAT WERE STOLEN LAST WEEK!
LET ME SEE THEM!
...AND HE WOULD TAKE NO REWARD, MISS REBECCA!
OH MY!

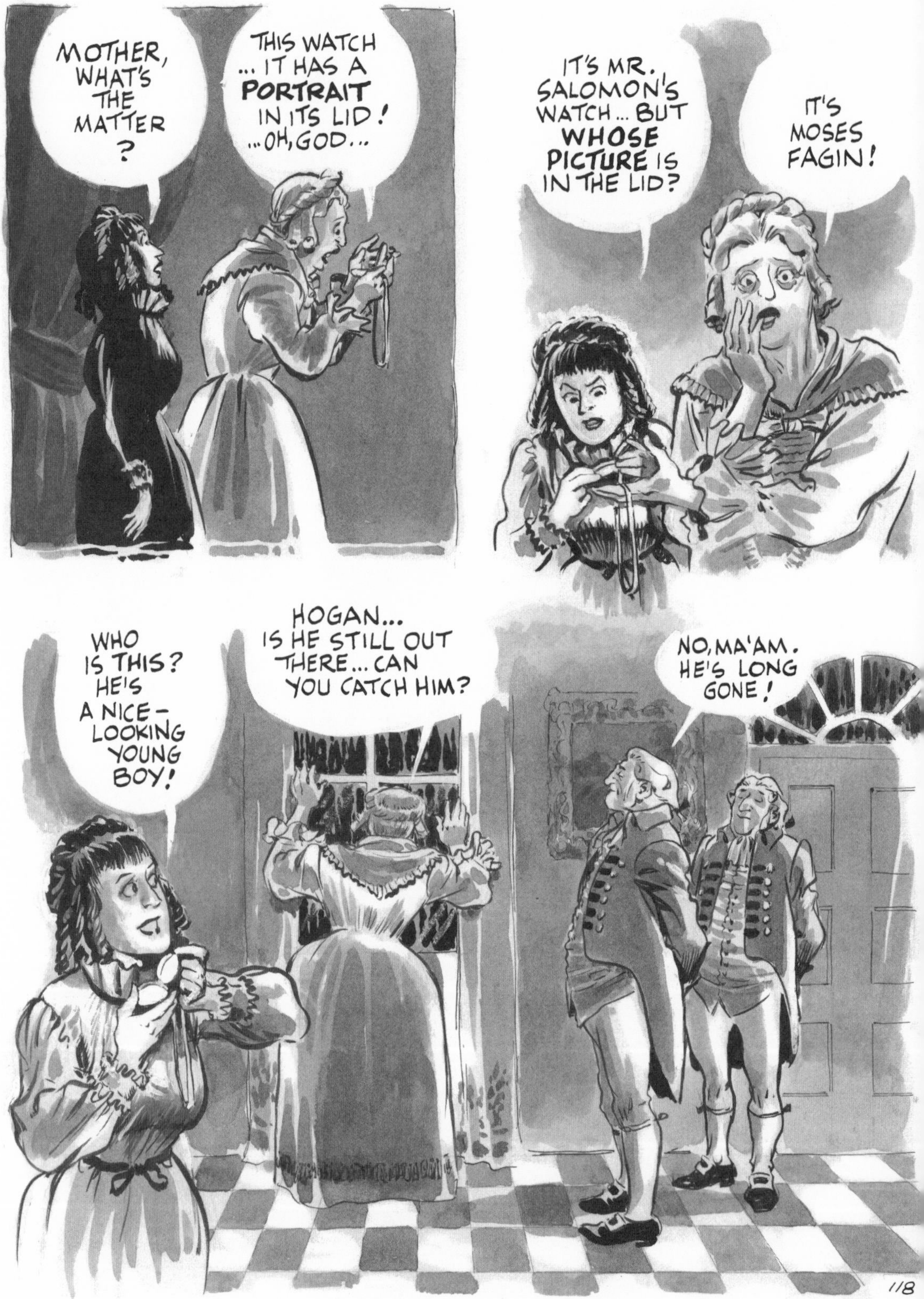
MOTHER, WHAT'S THE MATTER ?
THIS WATCH ... IT HAS A **PORTRAIT** IN ITS LID! ...OH, GOD...
IT'S MR. SALOMON'S WATCH... BUT **WHOSE PICTURE** IS IN THE LID?
IT'S MOSES FAGIN!
WHO IS **THIS**? HE'S A NICE-LOOKING YOUNG BOY!
HOGAN... IS HE STILL OUT THERE... CAN YOU CATCH HIM?
NO, MA'AM. HE'S LONG GONE!

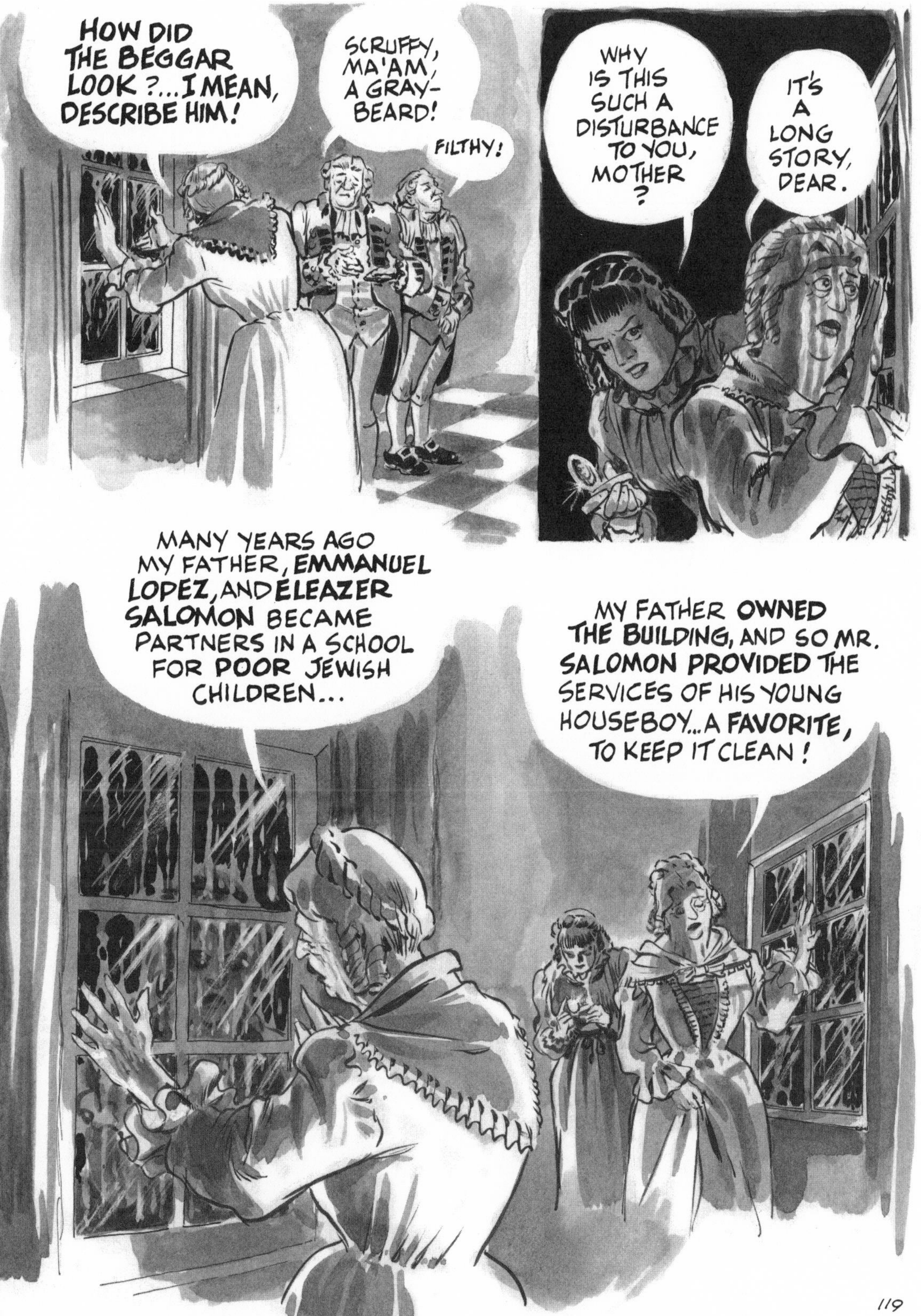
HOW DID THE BEGGAR LOOK ?... I MEAN, DESCRIBE HIM!
SCRUFFY, MA'AM, A GRAY-BEARD!
FILTHY!
WHY IS THIS SUCH A DISTURBANCE TO YOU, MOTHER ?
IT'S A LONG STORY, DEAR.
MANY YEARS AGO MY FATHER, EMMANUEL LOPEZ, AND ELEAZER SALOMON BECAME PARTNERS IN A SCHOOL FOR POOR JEWISH CHILDREN...
MY FATHER OWNED THE BUILDING, AND SO MR. SALOMON PROVIDED THE SERVICES OF HIS YOUNG HOUSEBOY... A FAVORITE, TO KEEP IT CLEAN!

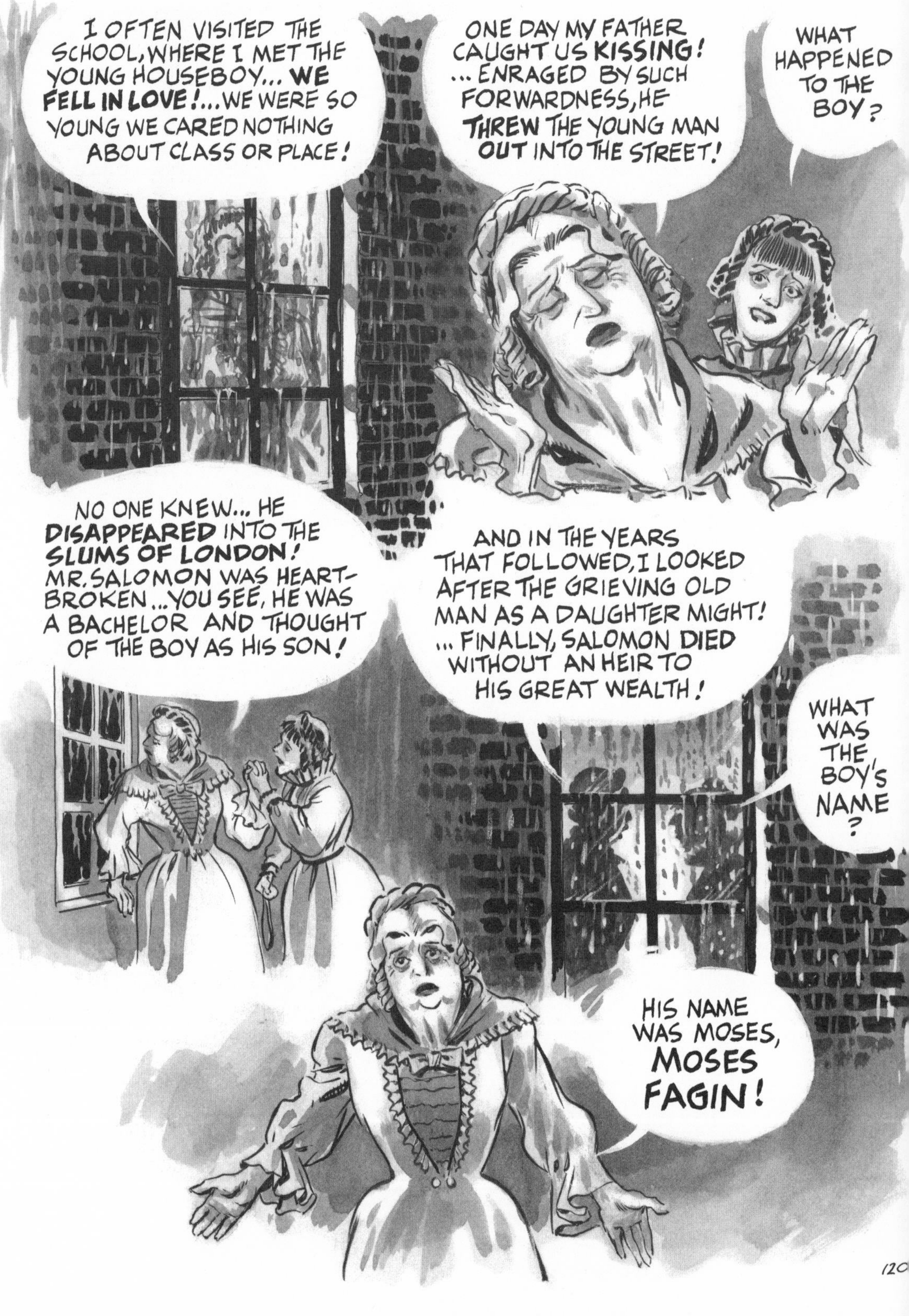
I OFTEN VISITED THE SCHOOL, WHERE I MET THE YOUNG HOUSEBOY... WE FELL IN LOVE!... WE WERE SO YOUNG WE CARED NOTHING ABOUT CLASS OR PLACE!
ONE DAY MY FATHER CAUGHT US KISSING! ... ENRAGED BY SUCH FORWARDNESS, HE THREW THE YOUNG MAN OUT INTO THE STREET!
WHAT HAPPENED TO THE BOY?
NO ONE KNEW... HE DISAPPEARED INTO THE SLUMS OF LONDON! MR. SALOMON WAS HEART-BROKEN... YOU SEE, HE WAS A BACHELOR AND THOUGHT OF THE BOY AS HIS SON!
AND IN THE YEARS THAT FOLLOWED, I LOOKED AFTER THE GRIEVING OLD MAN AS A DAUGHTER MIGHT! ... FINALLY, SALOMON DIED WITHOUT AN HEIR TO HIS GREAT WEALTH!
WHAT WAS THE BOY'S NAME?
HIS NAME WAS MOSES, MOSES FAGIN!

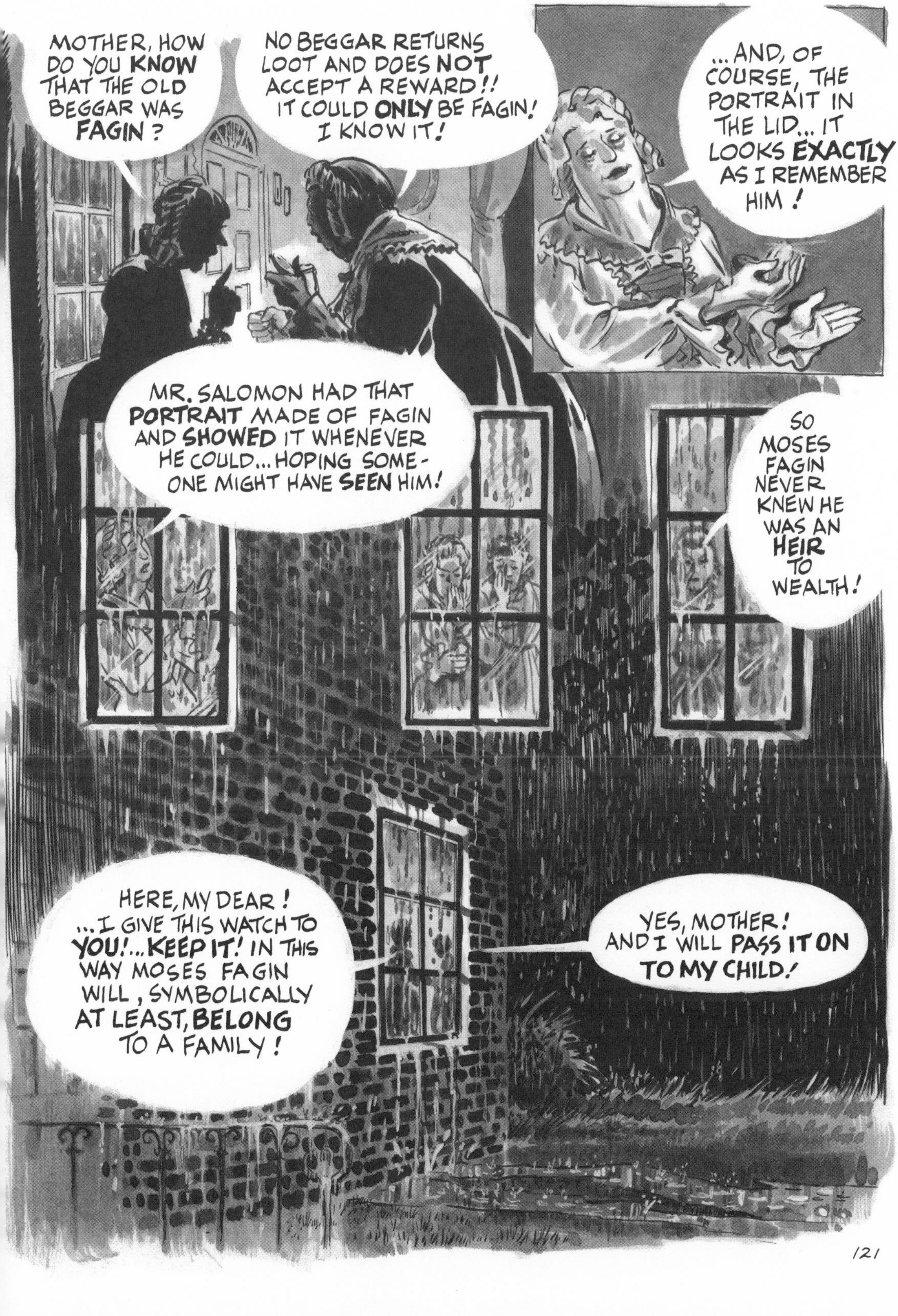
MOTHER, HOW DO YOU KNOW THAT THE OLD BEGGAR WAS FAGIN?
NO BEGGAR RETURNS LOOT AND DOES NOT ACCEPT A REWARD!! IT COULD ONLY BE FAGIN! I KNOW IT!
...AND, OF COURSE, THE PORTRAIT IN THE LID... IT LOOKS EXACTLY AS I REMEMBER HIM!
MR. SALOMON HAD THAT PORTRAIT MADE OF FAGIN AND SHOWED IT WHENEVER HE COULD... HOPING SOME-ONE MIGHT HAVE SEEN HIM!
SO MOSES FAGIN NEVER KNEW HE WAS AN HEIR TO WEALTH!
HERE, MY DEAR! ...I GIVE THIS WATCH TO YOU!...KEEP IT! IN THIS WAY MOSES FAGIN WILL, SYMBOLICALLY AT LEAST, BELONG TO A FAMILY!
YES, MOTHER! AND I WILL PASS IT ON TO MY CHILD!

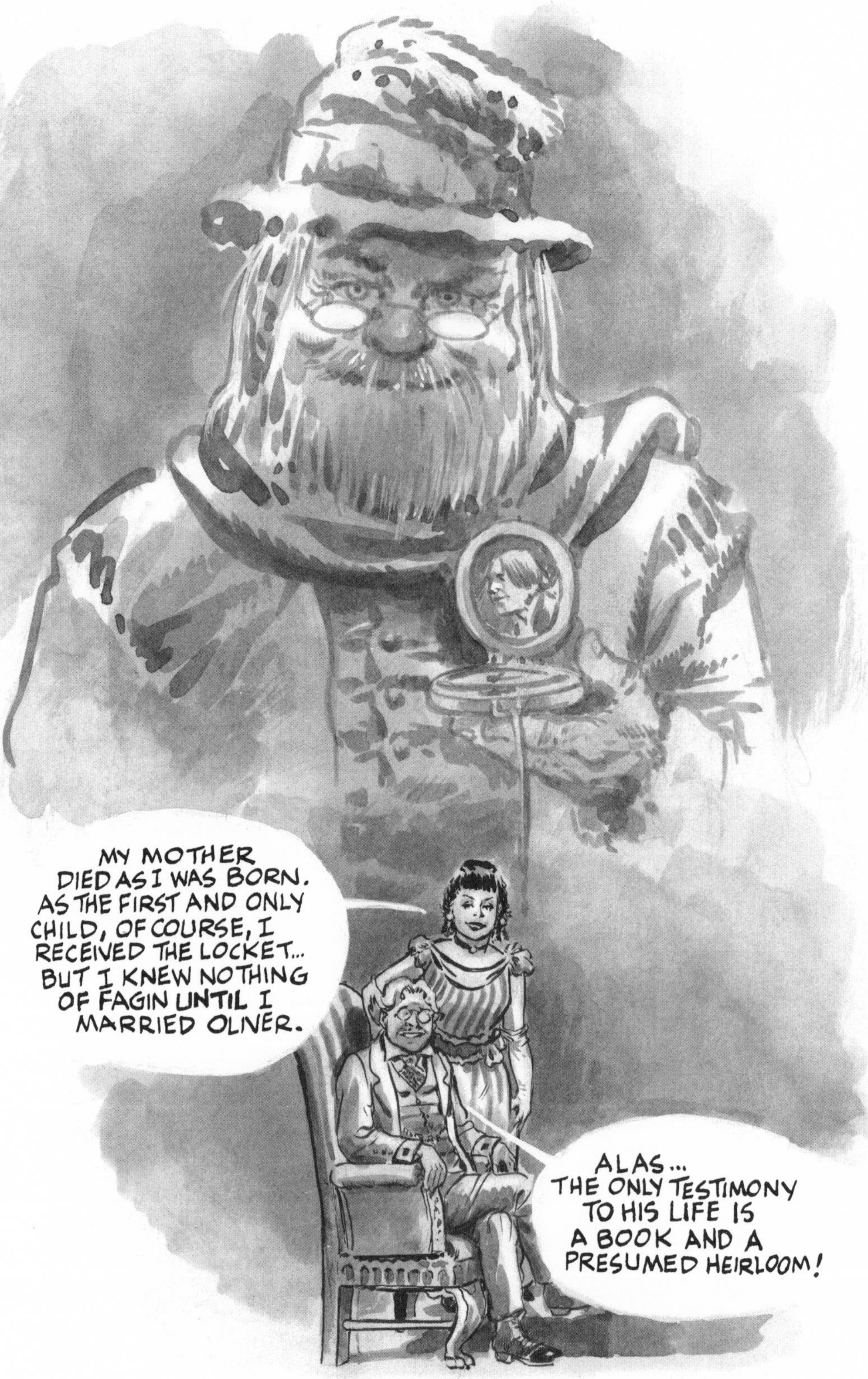
MY MOTHER DIED AS I WAS BORN. AS THE FIRST AND ONLY CHILD, OF COURSE, I RECEIVED THE LOCKET... BUT I KNEW NOTHING OF FAGIN UNTIL I MARRIED OLIVER.
ALAS... THE ONLY TESTIMONY TO HIS LIFE IS A BOOK AND A PRESUMED HEIRLOOM!

APPENDIX
by Will Eisner

THROUGHOUT HISTORY, certain fictional characters in our literature have achieved an illusion of reality due to their popularity. In the main, they became enduring stereotypes and influenced social judgment. Shylock the Jew and Sherlock Holmes the detective are classic examples.

Fagin, created by Charles Dickens in *Oliver Twist*, ultimately became one such "profile" of a Jew that embedded itself in popular culture and prejudice. In truth, the author never intended to defame the Jewish people, but by referring to Fagin as "the Jew" throughout the book, he abetted the prejudice against them. Over the years, *Oliver Twist* became a staple of juvenile literature, and the stereotype was perpetuated.

Despite his treatment of Fagin, Charles Dickens maintained that he was not an anti-Semite. He did use anti-Jewish epithets and offhand remarks in his letters and conversation, which were common to the language of the era. Dickens once referred to Richard Bentley, his (Gentile) English publisher, as "a thundering old Jew." However, in books such as *A Child's History of England*, he deemed "cruel and inexcusable" the persecution and expulsion of Jews in 1290 by Edward I. Later, he condemned Thomas Carlyle for his well-known aversion to Jews. In a letter to the Westminster Jewish Free School in 1854, Dickens claimed, "I do my part towards the assertion of [Jews'] civil and religious liberty, and . . . I have expressed a strong abhorrence of their persecution in old time."

The following segments from Dickens's 1841 preface to the third edition of *Oliver Twist* indicate his intentions, by explaining his use of Fagin for the role and, by implication, justifying his use of the label "Jew" to describe him:

The greater part of this Tale was originally published in a magazine. When I completed it and put it forth in its present form three years ago, I fully expected it would be objected to on some very high moral grounds in some very high moral quarters. The result did not fail to prove the justice of my anticipations. . . .

It is, it seems, a very coarse and shocking circumstance, that some of the characters in these pages are chosen from the most criminal and degraded of London's population; that Sikes is a thief, and Fagin a receiver of stolen goods; that the boys are pickpockets, and the girl is a prostitute. . . .

It appeared to me that to draw a knot of such associates in crime as really do exist; to paint them in all their deformity, in all their wretchedness, in all the squalid poverty of their lives; to show them as they really are, for ever skulking uneasily through the dirtiest paths of life, with the great, black, ghastly gallows closing up their prospect, turn them where they may; it appeared to me that to do this, would be to attempt a something which was greatly needed, and which would be a service to society. And therefore I did it as best I could.

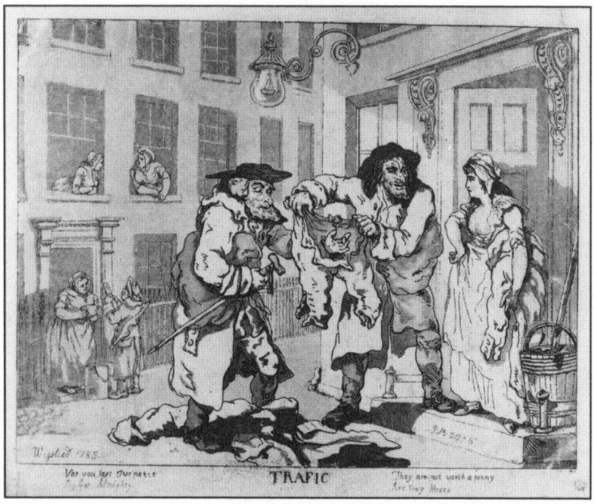
TRAFIC

An aquatint etching by Henry Wigstead (1785) showing two Jewish old-clothes dealers in London buying clothes from a domestic. The title, *Trafic*, is accompanied by dialogue.

Furthermore, about twenty years later, after having received a letter of complaint from Mrs. Eliza Davis, the wife of a Jewish banker, Dickens tried to eliminate most of the frequent references to Fagin as a Jew in an 1867 edition of *Oliver Twist*. This, however, was too late, for the earlier and well-distributed popular editions still in use today contain the original text that uses "Jew" to refer to Fagin.

Nonetheless, I believe that Dickens's stated intention to describe the conditions of the time places the burden of reportorial accuracy upon him. It has always troubled me that Fagin "the Jew" never got fair treatment, and I challenge Charles Dickens and his illustrator, George Cruikshank, for their description and delineation of Fagin as a classic stereotypical Jew. I believe this depiction was based on ill-considered evidence, imitation, and popular ignorance. Cartoonists certainly understand how easy it is to rely on a common image in the visual language to portray a character, but like the mistakes of illustrators before him, Cruikshank's misuse of a necessary staple in portraying Fagin, one that was so common to contemporary publications, is a contribution to further reprehensible stereotyping of Jews by bigots throughout history.

The Jewish community of London around 1800 consisted of two main groups, the Sephardim and the Ashkenazim. The Sephardim originally came from Portugal and Spain to settle in England after fleeing the Spanish Inquisition. Because they were mostly educated, they were able to achieve an acceptable position in the English community. England was attractive to Jews because it was then one of the more liberal societies, with some religious tolerance and an accessible legal system. The Sephardim assimilated easily and for the most part became professionals, tradesmen, and financiers. Their numbers increased over the years with the arrival of others who had also fled Spain but had sought refuge in Holland. The growth of

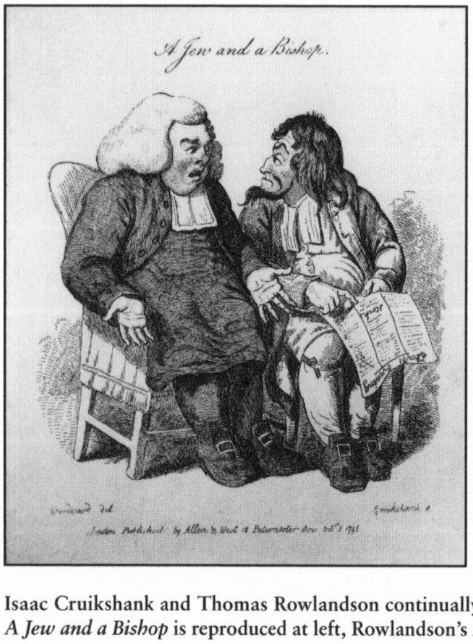
A Jew and a Bishop.

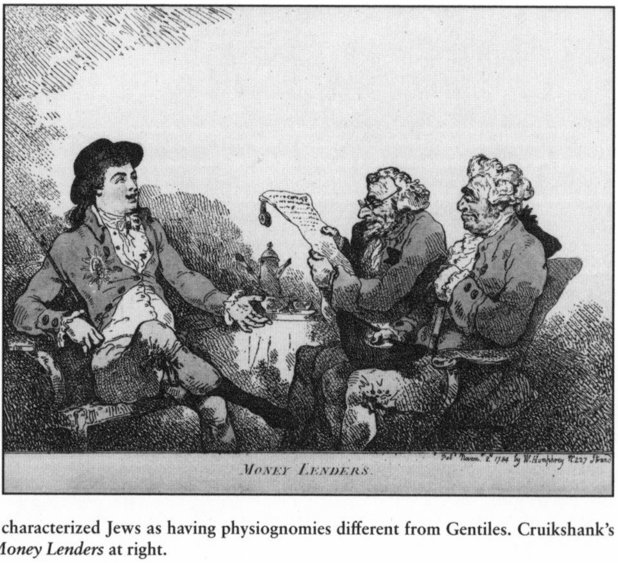
MONEY LENDERS.

Isaac Cruikshank and Thomas Rowlandson continually characterized Jews as having physiognomies different from Gentiles. Cruikshank's *A Jew and a Bishop* is reproduced at left, Rowlandson's *Money Lenders* at right.

a lively trade between London and Amsterdam led to an increase in Jewish immigration.

Until about 1700, the Sephardim were the dominant Jewish population in England, but the "lower class" Jews who arrived during the eighteenth century were mostly Ashkenazim. They came from Germany and Middle Europe, where they had lived in small villages until driven out by intolerance, repression, and pogroms. Rural life and peasant culture had rendered them less educated and more crude in their ways. As a result, when they arrived in London, they had difficulty assimilating. Like all new, poor immigrant arrivals throughout history, they clung to old ghetto habits and social behavior. Impoverished and illiterate, they took up marginal occupations in the grimier quarters of London. It is reasonable to assume that Fagin came from such origins.

In my opinion, the limning of Jews by illustrators of Dickens's time was most likely inaccurate with regard to Fagin's appearance. Because of their Eastern European origins, Ashkenazic Jews likely had features that had come to resemble the German physiognomy. There were many blond Jews, as a result of rapes that occurred during pogroms. However, the popular illustrations of Jews, including Cruikshank's, were based on the appearance of the Sephardim, whose features, when they arrived, were sharper, with dark hair and complexions, the result of their four-hundred-year sojourn among the Latin and Mediterranean peoples. The careless disregard of this demography, and its impact on cultural acceptance, made it necessary to reintroduce Fagin at long last.

The lithograph prints and etchings that were popular in England in the eighteenth century provided the public with satirical commentary on social life of the day. They were sold, sometimes even by Jewish peddlers, on the streets of English cities, in print shops, and in bookstalls. They were generally collected in albums or hung in dens, libraries, or workplaces.

In Charles Dickens's time, the most popular creators of these prints included Thomas Rowlandson, Henry Wigstead, George Woodward, Isaac Cruikshank (father of George Cruikshank, who illustrated *Oliver Twist*), and James Gilray.

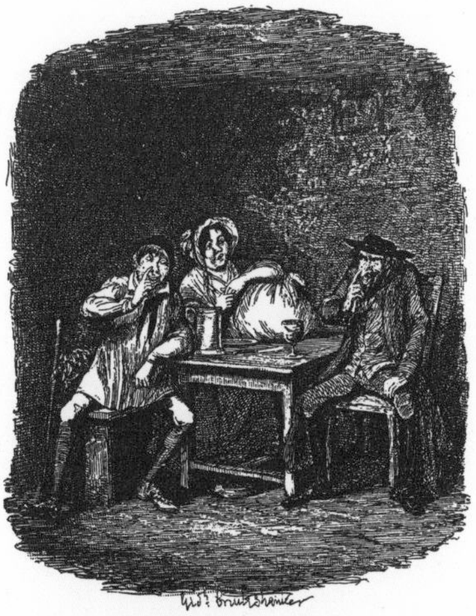

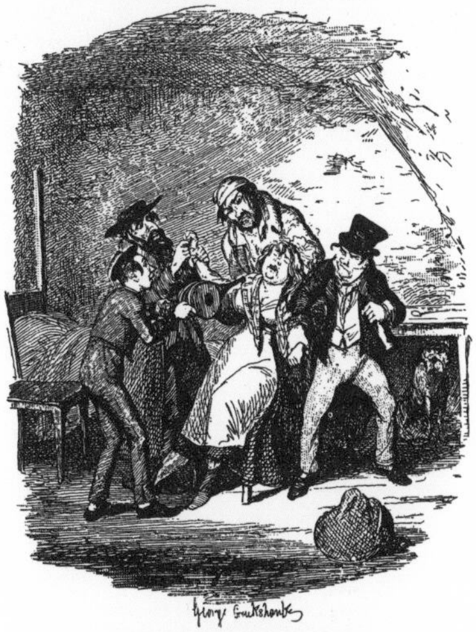

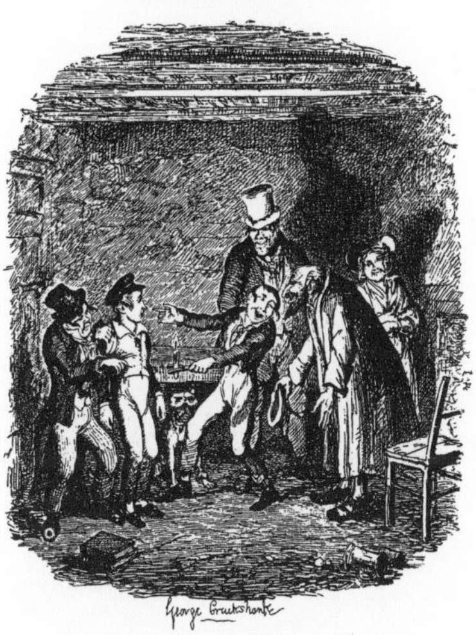

In George Cruikshank's version of Fagin, he shows a "Sephardic" physiognomy. My version of Fagin is based on the more Germanic face, which I believe is more truthful.

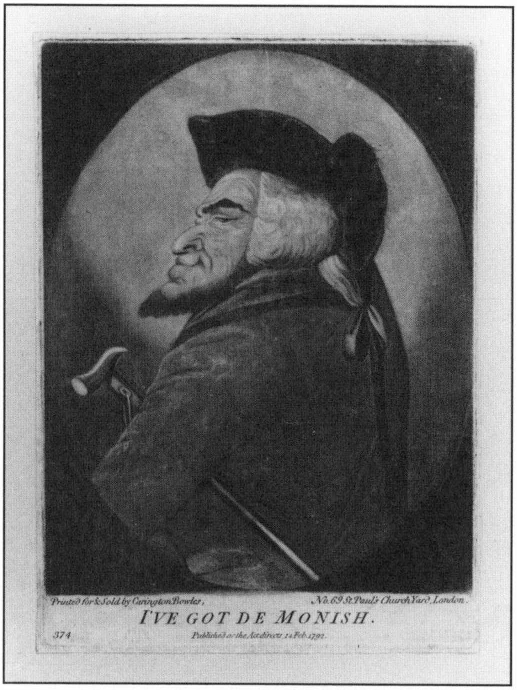
Printed for & Sold by Carington Bowles,
No. 69 St. Paul's Church Yard, London.
I'VE GOT DE MONISH.
374
Published as the Act directs 14 Feb. 1792.

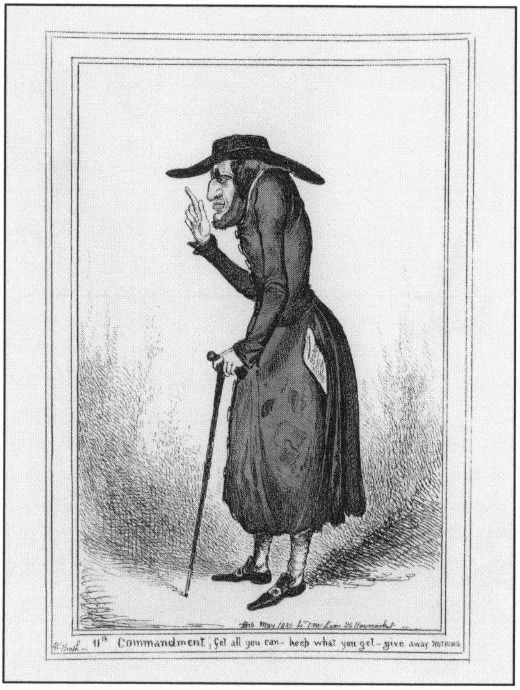
11th Commandment; Get all you can - keep what you get - give away NOTHING

These two published prints, *I've Got de Monish* (circa 1792) and *Commandment, Get all you can* (circa 1830), are examples of popular images that were widely sold in London. They helped create the accepted public stereotype of a Jew.

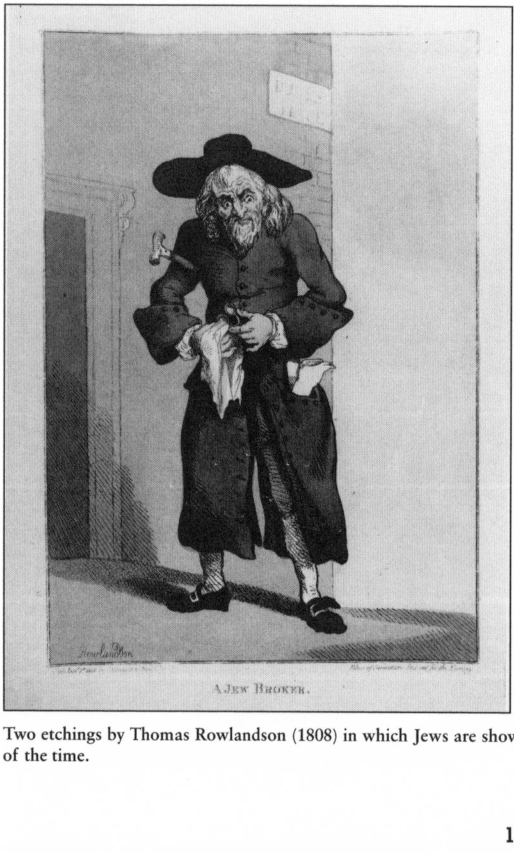
A JEW BROKER.

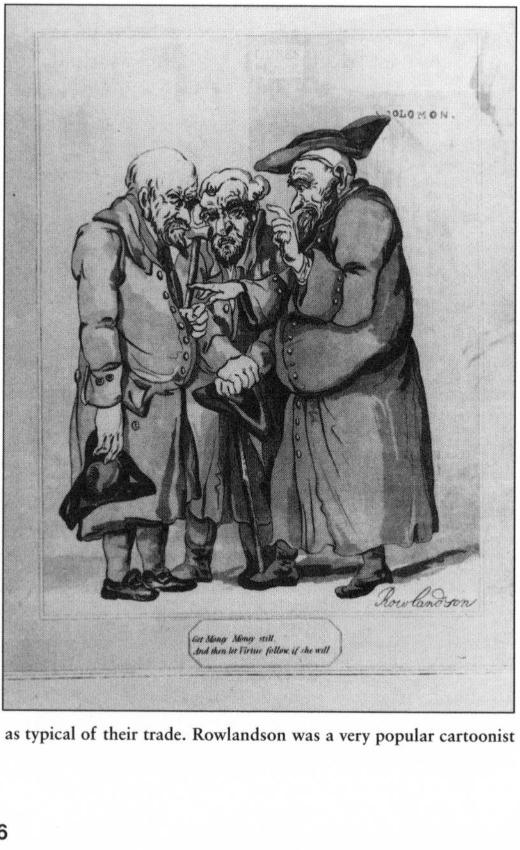
Rowlandson
Get Money Money still
And then let Virtue follow if she will

Two etchings by Thomas Rowlandson (1808) in which Jews are shown as typical of their trade. Rowlandson was a very popular cartoonist of the time.

Like the great English artist Hogarth before them, they enjoyed considerable professional stature and popular fame. It was their delineations that contributed to the perpetuation of the negative stereotype of Jews and that today provide a record of the public perceptions of that time.

In America during the twentieth century, this genre of illustration and cartoon appeared in newspapers, humor magazines, and family publications that catered to the public taste. Because of this country's large immigrant population, the ethnic caricatures were less vitriolic but persisted nevertheless. The influential political drawings by Thomas Nast and other political cartoonists dwelling on the stereotypes of corrupt politicos were successors to their English forerunners. The more social observations of Charles Dana Gibson and James Montgomery Flagg used depictions that mostly avoided exaggerated ethnic characterization.

Included herein are several examples of prints and illustrations from that period, which demonstrate the limning of Jews by the eighteenth-century illustrators who were most influential at that time.

My version of Fagin is, I believe, a more truthful stereotype.

SOURCES

Endelman, Todd M. 1999. *The Jews of Georgian England, 1714–1830: Tradition and Change in a Liberal Society.* Ann Arbor: University of Michigan Press.

Katz, David S. 1994. *The Jews in the History of England, 1485–1850.* Oxford: Clarendon Press.

The Jew as Other: A Century of English Caricature. April 6–July 31, 1995. Exhibition by the Jewish Theological Seminary of America.

Schlicke, Paul, ed. 1999. *Oxford Reader's Companion to Dickens.* Oxford: Oxford University Press.

Photo by Greg Preston | sampselpreston.com

WILL EISNER (1917–2005) is internationally recognized as a comics legend and the father of the graphic novel. One of comics' first true auteurs, Eisner was present at the birth of the industry, and his professional achievements mark every significant stage of the medium's coming-of-age as an art and literary form. Eisner broke new ground in the development of visual narrative and the language of comics, creating many memorable characters and series along the way, including *The Spirit*, which debuted in 1940 and influenced an entire generation of young cartoonists with its innovative storytelling and design. An indispensable part of comics' literary canon, *The Spirit* continues to inspire successive generations of readers.

Eisner's seminal graphic novel, *A Contract with God*, revolutionized comics with its 1978 publication, spearheading an industry shift from periodical, disposable entertainment to perennial, enduring literature. Eisner then went on to produce another twenty graphic novels during his "retirement" years, garnering many awards both in the US and abroad, and establishing the graphic novel as a literary form in its own right.

The comics industry's top annual awards, the Eisners, are named in his honor.

REWRITING DICKENS:
EISNER'S *FAGIN THE JEW*
Afterword by Jeet Heer

WILL EISNER SHARED many affinities with Charles Dickens, the Victorian novelist and creator of the infamous Fagin. Like Dickens, Eisner was a popular entertainer who elevated a previously despised art form to the level of high art. Both the cartoonist and the novelist were adept at mixing words with pictures—all of Dickens's novels were heavily illustrated, and he worked closely with artists to make sure that the images enriched the reading experience. Both men created serialized stories that appeared in periodical form before being collected into books. The big city left its mark on Dickens and Eisner alike: the sights and smells of Victorian England live on in Dickens's fiction, while Eisner was one of the great delineators of twentieth-century New York. The two authors were unabashed in borrowing the histrionic techniques of the stage in order to create vivid characters who swagger and strut off the page. In trying to describe the incomparable Dickensian gallery of memorable and often grotesque characters, critics often resort to the label *caricaturist*. Since caricature is a branch of cartooning, this tendency of Dickens to vividly etch his characters suggests another link with Eisner.

The many parallels between Dickens and Eisner make it all the more poignant that the cartoonist would feel an uncomfortable bond to Fagin, the Jewish villain of *Oliver Twist*. Like Eisner, Fagin is a product of a Jewish ghetto. Fagin's milieu, the London underworld of poverty and crime, is a forerunner to the Depression-era New York that Eisner survived in the 1930s as the child of Eastern European Jewish immigrants. Yet Fagin is also a toxic and potent distillation of profoundly anti-Semitic archetypes. As such, he is not a character with which any self-respecting Jew would identify.

One way to read Eisner's *Fagin the Jew* is to see it as a settling of accounts with Charles Dickens. The graphic novel is an acknowledgment of the novelist as a distinguished precursor to modern cartooning, but also an attempt to challenge and overturn a poisonous element within the Dickensian inheritance.

Fagin the Jew is a natural outgrowth of two longstanding obsessions that Eisner would return to in the many graphic novels and shorter comics stories that he produced in the last quarter-century of his life: a major fascination with Jewish history and a lesser but still important attraction to literary classics. Eisner's concern with the Jewish experience—which pervades everything from his landmark graphic novel, *A Contract with God*, to his last book, *The Plot*—sprang not only from a natural interest in his own upbringing and family but from a desire to redress a major problem in comics: the suppression of ethnic identity. When Eisner started working in the commercial comic book industry in the 1930s, there were many Jewish artists but it was almost unheard of to create Jewish protagonists. Eisner's assistant Jules Feiffer once joked that his boss's noir detective hero, the Spirit, was secretly Jewish. "The Spirit reeked of lower middle-class," Feiffer argued in his 1965 book *The Great Comic Book Heroes*. "His nose may have turned up, but we all knew he was Jewish."

But to have a covert Jewish hero whose ethnicity was recognized only by insiders like Feiffer was hardly satisfying to Eisner, who was steeped in Jewish life and appreciated its rich complexity and piquant texture. In his mature work, Eisner strove not only to capture the saga of Jewish immigrant life in America—the long journey from Ellis Island to assimilation—but also to bear witness to the barriers experienced by his people. He was vexed by the existence of anti-Semitism, a subject to which he returned in works like the 1991 graphic novel *To the Heart of the Storm*, his semi-autobiographical account of encountering prejudice before and during the Second World War, and 2005's *The Plot*, his exposé of a notorious forged document that is the source of many anti-Jewish conspiracy theories.

Along with his exploration of the Jewish past, Eisner also tried his hand, in his later years, at adapting literary classics into comics form. Among the masterpieces he tackled were *Hamlet*, *Moby Dick*, and *Don Quixote*. Eisner's interest in the classics was intertwined with the larger project of showing the expressive range of comics, a form he felt was capable of telling the most complex stories. One characteristic of all these adaptations is that Eisner almost always borrows just the main elements of the plot but otherwise goes out of his way to rework the material into the language of comics. Melville's *Moby Dick* is more than 200,000 words long, most of which disappeared when Eisner gave his own rendering of the whale-hunting story. This freestyle approach to adaptation can be contrasted with more literalist techniques adopted by cartoonists like Robert Crumb, whose version of the Book of Genesis includes *all* the text, with drawings that maintain a painstaking fidelity to Scripture.

A prime example of the liberties Eisner took in his adaptations is his 1981 rendition of Hamlet's "To Be or Not To Be" soliloquy, published in *The Spirit Magazine* #29 as "Hamlet on a Rooftop" and later reprinted in Eisner's *Comics & Sequential Art*. Instead of being set in a Renaissance court, this version of *Hamlet* takes place on a contemporary New York rooftop, with a knife-wielding ghetto-dweller acting out the role Shakespeare assigned to a prince.

Eisner's decision to transform Charles Dickens's *Oliver Twist* into a twenty-first–century graphic novel should be seen as the result of a convergence of the artist's various pursuits. As a classic work of literature with a notorious Jewish villain, *Oliver Twist* presented Eisner with a chance to display his cartooning chops in exactly the subjects that most concerned him: great literature, Jewish history, and the problem of countering anti-Semitic stereotypes.

Oliver Twist is a great work of literature but makes for troubling reading because the anti-Semitism is amplified by literary genius. Nearly two centuries after Dickens penned it, it is still easy to get caught up in the drama of the orphan Oliver, to wonder about the mysteries of his origins, to grow indignant as he's mistreated at the orphanage, to worry about him as he flees into London, where he finds himself ensnared by the gang of thieves led by Fagin. But it's with Fagin that the novel takes a disturbing turn.

Here is the first description we get of Fagin: "There was a deal table before the fire: upon which were a candle, stuck in a ginger-beer bottle, two or three pewter pots, a loaf and butter, and a plate. In a frying-pan, which was on the fire, and which was secured to the mantelshelf by a

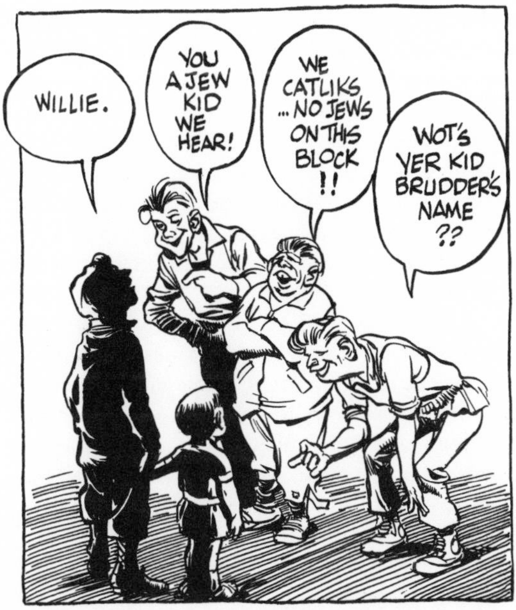
WILLIE.
YOU A JEW KID WE HEAR!
WE CATLIKS ...NO JEWS ON THIS BLOCK !!
WOT'S YER KID BRUDDER'S NAME ??

An early encounter with anti-Semitism in young Will Eisner's life. From the semi-autobiographical *To the Heart of the Storm* (1991).

string, some sausages were cooking; and standing over them, with a toasting-fork in his hand, was a very old shrivelled Jew, whose villainous-looking and repulsive face was obscured by a quantity of matted red hair."

Fagin's "villainous-looking and repulsive face" perfectly matches his character. He is a corrupter of the young and lives off their labor, teaching street urchins how to pick pockets and deliver the stolen goods into his greedy hands. The arch-criminal comes close to instilling into Oliver's soul "the poison which [Fagin] hoped would blacken it." Summing up, Dickens notes that "the wily old Jew had the boy in his toils."

Fagin has no loyalty to his confederates and secretly informs on some of his criminal partners after he no longer needs their services. This is done with the intent that they be executed. As he chortles early on in the novel, "What a fine thing capital punishment is! Dead men never repent; dead men never bring awkward stories to light."

Utterly bereft of decency, Fagin seems scarcely human and, in fact, is frequently linked to either animals or the Devil. Here is Dickens's account of Fagin making the rounds at night: "The mud lay thick upon the stones, and a black mist hung over the streets; the rain fell sluggishly down, and everything felt cold and clammy to the touch. It seemed just the night when it befitted such a being as the Jew to be abroad. As he glided stealthily along, creeping beneath the shelter of the walls and doorways, the hideous old man seemed like some loathsome reptile, engendered in the slime and darkness through which he moved: crawling forth, by night, in search of some rich offal for a meal."

In the above passage, as elsewhere in the novel, Fagin is referred to not by name but by the epithet "the Jew"—as if Jews were a species of which he was a representative example. Fagin's Jewishness is not an incidental feature of his character but rather is the term that is used to sum up what he is.

When not compared to subhuman creatures like reptiles, Fagin is associated with the super-human evil of Satan. Dickens describes Fagin

Fagin in the condemned Cell

Only in one scene at the end of *Oliver Twist*, as Fagin awaits execution, does Dickens portray the character in a more sympathetic light. Original illustration by George Cruikshank for the 1838 novel.

as wearing "an expression of villainy perfectly demoniacal." The prostitute Nancy describes Fagin as a "devil . . . and worse than devil." According to the ruffian Bill Sikes, Fagin looks like "the devil when he's got a great-coat on." These characterizations of Fagin are fully vindicated in the last section of the novel when the criminal mastermind convinces Sikes that Nancy has informed on him. This leads to Nancy's murder by Sikes, who in turn is hounded to death.

If we accept Dickens's description of Fagin as "the Jew," then what conclusions can we draw from reading *Oliver Twist*? The Jew is filthy, the Jew is a criminal, the Jew is a corrupter of children, the Jew values money more than human relations, the Jew is linked with poison, the Jew is a Judas-like betrayer, the Jew is an animal, the Jew is a murderer, the Jew is the Devil. In sum, a large part of what makes Fagin's character so oppressively unforgettable is that he combines in one package centuries of loathsome anti-Semitic stereotypes.

Shakespeare's Shylock was also an anti-Semitic stereotype, but the Elizabethan dramatist humanized his Jewish villain by letting him speak eloquently on his own behalf, asking, "If you prick us, do we not bleed? If you tickle us, do we not laugh? If you poison us, do we not die?" Except for one brief scene at the end of the novel when Fagin faces execution, Dickens doesn't extend to his Jewish malefactor the empathy that Shakespeare tendered to Shylock.

The stark portrait of Fagin as almost completely evil is in part due to the fact that, in his early fiction, Dickens was writing moral allegories showing the combat of decency and corruption. As Dickens explained, "I wished to show, in little Oliver, the principle of Good surviving through every adverse circumstance, and triumphing at last." If Oliver is the principle of Good, then the fiend who tries to corrupt the orphan is a living embodiment of evil.

The anti-Semitism that pervades *Oliver Twist* shouldn't be seen simply as evidence of personal prejudice on the part of Charles Dickens. The novelist created Fagin, but he did so out of raw material provided by centuries of Christian mythmaking, while reflecting ideas that still permeated British society at that time.

Britain was less anti-Semitic than many other European societies, but Jews were still second-class citizens when Dickens started his career as a writer. As the literary historian Harry Stone has noted, when Dickens reached adulthood in 1830, "a Jew could not open a shop within the city of London, be called to the Bar, receive a university degree, or sit in parliament."

The prejudices and legal barriers faced by Victorian British Jews can be compared to the situation of African-Americans in the early decades of the twentieth century, and British Jews also created an active civil rights movement to fight against bigotry. To his credit, when Charles Dickens was challenged by proponents of Jewish civil rights, he overcame his earlier prejudices and championed Jewish equality. This shift in Dickens's thinking parallels Eisner's own evolution on the question of depicting African-Americans, as discussed in his introduction

to *Fagin the Jew*. Just as Eisner came to regret Ebony White, the Spirit's minstrel sidekick, Dickens eventually recognized that in creating Fagin, he had committed an injustice.

Jewish civil rights activists mobilized not just to change anti-Semitic laws but also to shift public opinion, so writers such as Dickens started receiving letters imploring them for a more just representation of Jews. Beginning in the early 1850s, we can see evidence that this campaign was starting to influence Dickens in fits and starts, although he continued to make stray anti-Jewish remarks. In *A Child's History of England*, a book he wrote from 1851 to 1853, Dickens explicitly condemned medieval anti-Semitism. In the same period, he took up the cause of winning legal equality for British Jews. From the 1850s until his death in 1870, Dickens owned and edited two magazines, *Household Words* (1850–59) and *All the Year Round* (1859–70), and there was a noticeable drop in the amount of anti-Jewish content in these magazines, particularly by the 1860s.

One of the key turning points in the evolution of Dickens's thinking about these issues occurred during a correspondence with a Jewish acquaintance, Eliza Davis. In 1863 Davis wrote to Dickens upbraiding him for his portrayal of Fagin. Dickens defensively responded that he bore no malice towards Jews and that "Fagin, in *Oliver Twist*, is a Jew, because it unfortunately was true of the time to which that story refers, that that class of criminal almost invariably was a Jew. But surely no sensible man or woman of your persuasion can fail to observe—firstly, that all the rest of the wicked *dramatis personae* are Christians; and secondly, that he is called a 'Jew,' not because of his religion, but because of his race."

As Davis noted in a spirited counter-thrust, Dickens's arguments were disingenuous on a number of points. None of the Christian villains were identified by their religion. Further, in Judaism, ethnicity and religion are intertwined, so to identify Fagin constantly as a Jew was to conflate him with all Jews.

Dickens took these criticisms seriously and made amends in two ways. In 1867–68, he revised

Oliver Twist and took out many, though not all, of the references to Fagin as "the Jew." More substantially, in his last completed novel, *Our Mutual Friend* (written in 1864–65), Dickens created a character clearly meant to be an anti-Fagin: Mr. Riah, the kind-hearted Jewish manager of a money-lending operation. Benevolent and paternalistic, Mr. Riah serves as a "fairy godfather" to many of the characters in the novel and forcefully speaks out against anti-Jewish prejudice. The major objection that critics have had to Mr. Riah is that the character is almost too good—so benign that he's scarcely believable. Be that as it may, Mr. Riah was Dickens's attempt to make amends for Fagin.

Despite Dickens's remorse, Fagin has continued to have a long afterlife due to the literary genius of his creator. The startling intensity of Dickens's writing has insured that Fagin continues to live on in the popular imagination in much the same manner as Oliver Twist himself, Ebenezer Scrooge, Uriah Heep, Wilkins Micawber, Miss Havisham, and other memorable figures. Indeed, beyond his Dickensian origins, Fagin is now one of those characters whose name is a household word, a fame shared by select creations such as Hamlet, Don Quixote, and Sherlock Holmes.

The enduring popularity of *Oliver Twist* and the large cultural shadow still cast by its Jewish miscreant surely played no small role in Will Eisner's decision to retell the story of Fagin in graphic novel form but in a way that would rebuke and even overturn the anti-Semitism of the original novel. *Fagin the Jew* isn't just a graphic novel; it is also a counter-narrative, an attempt to provide an alternative take on a familiar, well-worn story. As a counter-narrative, *Fagin the Jew* falls into the tradition of such works as Tom Stoppard's *Rosencrantz and Guildenstern Are Dead* (a response to Shakespeare's *Hamlet*), John Updike's *Gertrude and Claudius* (also a response to *Hamlet*), Jean Rhys's *Wide Sargasso Sea* (a response to Charlotte Bronte's *Jane Eyre*), J. M. Coetzee's novel *Foe* (a response to Daniel Defoe's *Robinson Crusoe*), and many other similar works.

Animating the tradition of the counter-narrative is the idea that a classic is a work that deserves not only to be read but also to be responded to and rewritten. Counter-narratives pay tribute to the classics by offering new ways of looking at the old stories, often paying attention to gaps and lacunae that cry out to be filled in.

Eisner's Fagin is much more sympathetic than Dickens's original villain. The fellow-feeling that Eisner is able to conjure up for Fagin has several sources. Visually, Eisner's Fagin looks benign and grandfatherly, almost resembling Santa Claus. This is a sharp contrast to the original drawings of Fagin done by George Cruikshank, who depicted a hook-nosed, sinister Fagin every bit as ugly as the one Dickens described in prose.

In terms of narrative, Eisner's most radical decision is to give Fagin a back story. Because Dickens's Fagin was a devil figure, he's never given more than a hint of a past. As the critic Irving Howe noted, in *Oliver Twist* "[Fagin] barely exists as an individual—barely needs to. We learn nothing about his interior life, we are not invited to see him as 'three-dimensional.'" By contrast, Eisner's Fagin very much has a past, a family, experiences of prejudice and injustice,

Eisner's Fagin is benign and grandfatherly, and benefits from a humanizing back story.

and reasons for becoming a criminal. All the humanizing touches that Dickens denied his Fagin are presented in Eisner's portrait.

When Eisner's account of Fagin's life starts to overlap with the plot of *Oliver Twist*, he is careful to rework the story so that the major narrative arc is the same, but Fagin isn't the instigator of evil. Unlike the fiend of *Oliver Twist*, Eisner's Fagin has no blood on his hands. He doesn't snitch on his accomplices, and he urges no one to murder.

Yet for all of Eisner's reweaving of Dickens's narrative, the cartoonist keeps true to the spirit of the original novel. To a surprising extent, Eisner turns Fagin into a very Dickensian hero. Almost all of Dickens's novels center around an orphan. In Eisner's account we learn that Fagin, too, has lost his parents and had to fend for himself. Fagin's sojourn to one of the colonies recalls the plot of *Great Expectations*, in which a major character is "transported" for a crime and then returns to England. There is a similarly Dickensian feel, to those who can appreciate its meaning, to the story of Fagin's lost love, his stolen inheritance, and the return of a treasured heirloom. Eisner's use of coincidence and his general tone of hearty sentimentality are also tributes to Dickens.

What makes *Fagin the Jew* such a rich work, one that rewards many readings, is that Eisner manages the complex task of arguing with Dickens

while also paying homage to the great novelist. In humanizing Fagin, Eisner strikes a blow against anti-Semitism, but he also does it in a way that the creator of Fagin would surely have understood and admired.

SOURCES CONSULTED AND FURTHER READINGS

Feiffer, Jules. 1965. *The Great Comic Book Heroes*. New York: Bonanza Books.

Heller, Deborah. 1990. "The Outcast as Villain and Victim: Jews in Dickens's *Oliver Twist* and *Our Mutual Friend*." In *Jewish Presences in English Literature*, edited by Derek Cohen and Deborah Heller, 40-60. Montreal: McGill-Queen's University Press.

Howe, Irving. 1990. "Oliver and Fagin." In *Selected Writings, 1950–1990*, 365-373. New York: Harcourt Brace Jovanovich.

Rosenberg, Edgar. 1960. *From Shylock to Svengali: Jewish Stereotypes in English Fiction*. Palo Alto: Stanford University Press.

Stone, Harry. 1959. "Dickens and the Jews." *Victorian Studies* 2 (3): 223-253.

A cultural journalist and academic who divides his time between Toronto and Regina, Jeet Heer has written for many publications, including the *National Post*, Slate.com, the *Boston Globe*, the *Walrus*, *The American Prospect*, *The Literary Review of Canada*, the *Virginia Quarterly Review*, and the *Guardian* of London. He has co-edited eight books and been a contributing editor to another eight. With Kent Worcester, Jeet Heer co-edited *A Cultural Studies Reader* (Jackson: University of Mississippi Press, 2008), which recently won the Peter C. Rollins Book Award, given annually to the best book in American Studies or Cultural Studies. He has also won a Fulbright Scholarship. His essay "Drawn from Life" was featured in the anthology *The Best American Comics Criticism* (Fantagraphics). His essay "Canada Reads . . . at what cost?" was included in *The Best Canadian Essays* collection for 2012. With Chris Ware, Jeet Heer continues to edit the *Walt and Skeezix* series from Drawn and Quarterly, which is now entering its fifth volume.

ACKNOWLEDGMENTS

I am most grateful for the research assistance provided
by Benjamin Herzberg, which went beyond my expectations.

To Dave Schreiner, my thanks for his keen insight and his reliable editing.

And as always, I acknowledge my dependence on the patient, wise,
and enduring encouragement from my dear wife, Ann.

—Will Eisner, 2003

It took a village to make this
tenth-anniversary edition of Will Eisner's *Fagin the Jew*.

In addition to the people credited herein, all of whom
worked directly on the production of this book, thanks are also due to:

Ann Eisner, for trusting us with her husband's work and his original art;
Denis Kitchen, for efforts above and beyond; and Stacey Kitchen, for providing missing scans;
Carl and Nancy Gropper, for overseeing the details;
and Judy Hansen, for the legalities.

Teresa Gresham and Brendan Wright, for their assistance;
and Greg Preston, for the photo.

Bernard Mahé, Peter Janda, and All-Star Auctions provided
several scans made from the original art for use in this graphic novel.

Marilyn Scott facilitated scans of page 30 from the Will Eisner Collection
at The Ohio State University Billy Ireland Cartoon Library & Museum.

Special thanks to Lloyd Greif for surrendering his framed
original art pages 14 and 15 to Dark Horse for scanning.

And last but far from least, thanks to Will Eisner,
whose spirit guided every moment of this book's production.

—Diana Schutz, 2013